Complex Pleasure

COMPLEX PLEASURE

FORMS OF FEELING IN GERMAN LITERATURE

Stanley Corngold

STANFORD UNIVERSITY PRESS

STANFORD, CALIFORNIA

1998

Stanford University Press
Stanford, California
© 1998 by the Board of Trustees of the
Leland Stanford Junior University
Printed in the United States of America

CIP data appear at the end of the book

For Regine

"To note the curious hard logic of passion, and the emotional colored life of the intellect—to observe where they met, and where they separated, at what point they were in unison, and at what point they were at discord—there was a delight in that!"

ACKNOWLEDGMENTS

Portions of Chapters 1, 4, and 5 previously appeared in *Modern Language Notes*, *Studies in Romanticism*, and *Neverending Stories* (Princeton University Press, 1991), respectively; they are reprinted with permission. I am grateful to Anon., Ian Balfour, David Halliburton, Michael Jennings, Henry Staten, and Geoff Waite, who read the manuscript with unstinting care and made me happy by asking hard questions. My editors at Stanford University Press, Pamela MacFarland Holway, Ann Klefstad, and Helen Tartar, contributed their kindness and precision.

All translations, when not otherwise indicated, are my own.

CONTENTS

PREFACE

At Princeton, where I am writing this, a student has just come in to see me in order to switch her major from philosophy to German literature. She wanted to do so, she said, because she found only in literature "the tension of reason and imagination," which produced "new forms of feeling." I am struck to hear restated by an avant-garde sensibility near the year 2000 the thrust of a famous passage written 200 years ago. This source, according to Nietzsche, is "the best German book there is"— Eckermann's *Conversations with Goethe*.[2] Hearing Eckermann comment on the apparent incoherence of the Helena scene in *Faust II*, Goethe replied:

I only wonder what the German critics will make of it. Will they have the free- dom and courage to ignore the inconsistencies? The French will be hampered by their reason [*Verstand*] and fail to recognize that imagination has to abide by laws of its own which reason neither can nor should comprehend. Imagination would hardly be worth bothering about if it did not create things which will re- main eternally problematic to reason. This is the difference between poetry and prose. In prose, reason is and may and should be at home.[3]

Better than Goethe's distinction between the French and the Ger- man—since, as it turns out, there is none, for both are bothered by in- consistencies—better than the distinction between prose and poetry, since both are tautological figures, for reason and for imagination—is the conflict of these faculties and its lodgment in literature.

The conflict is lodged *in* literature and not where Goethe has it, half-in, half-out. The tension of reason and imagination, or, as we had better say today, of logic and rhetoric, belongs inside literature. Then again, it belongs "inside" only in the sense that this tension does not originate from a pure exterior, the "France" of reason, a site, for Goethe, of consternation and waste.[4] The conflict of reason and imagination, of logic and rhetoric, is found wherever literature is, sustaining the difference between the parties. Jacques Derrida alludes to this tension in noting that "in literature, philosophical language is still present in some sense, but it produces and presents itself as alienated from itself, at a remove, at a distance."[5] This distance is a function of the field in which it is situated, of which one pole is imaginative language, or rhetoric.

The immediate experience of the tension between reason and imagination is, I shall be claiming, some manner of literary feeling.[6] The positing of such a thing is necessary even when the literary work is seen as an active play of differences. For then the question must still arise of how such tension can be experienced as an object of theoretical interest. Certainly you can give a name to the conflict, calling it, precisely, *différance*, the self-differing difference, the aporetic, the non–self-identical, but how are such terms to be grasped? Not as concepts: as Derrida points out, *différance* is not a concept and is least of all an image.[7] But before the "notion" of *différance* can be utilized, it must first be experienced—and if as a "play" of signifiers, then presumably with elation at the play, and hence as a type of feeling. It is revealing that Paul de Man's category for such literary uncertainty is "emotive," "an anxiety (or bliss, depending on one's momentary mood or individual temperament) of ignorance,"[8] or again, following Gérard Genette, the *vertigo* of the whirligig.[9]

So we come to "literary feeling" as the term for feeling, in literature, of reason (logic, philosophy) alienated from itself.

How can we know this feeling? Since we cannot speak immediately about feeling, let alone about "literary feeling," the matter might best be put again as one of tension: What are the distinctive forms of literary tension?

Where there is literature, tensions arise from the conflict between what sentences say and what they do, between the propositional meaning and the rhetorical effects of individual sentences taken together[10]—tensions produced by "style, form, idiom, irony."[11] This is the real locus of the conflict of the faculties. What literature says is not what happens; what happens in literature is not even what literature says happens. The tension is conveyed by the "smooth" or "severe conjuncture" of images[12] moving in incisive rhythms through a charged phonic space.[13] But are such tensions found nowhere in writing outside literature?

In literature, I believe, such tensions are concentrated to elicit new forms of feeling, in the sense of Mary Wollstonecraft's aperçu, "We reason deeply when we forcibly feel."[14] The depth of this other reason in forcible feeling is informed by what Goethe calls imagination (hence we deal with imaginative feeling). The word "force" is as important here as "feeling," as the imprint of the tension that springs it. There is, as Gerhard Neumann writes, a "sort of thought that is also feeling. From Pascal and Novalis on, at the latest, the limits of what can still be termed thought are extended further and further into the domain of something indeterminately 'like feeling.' "[15] Such reasoning was to be identified by Kafka as "a special method of thinking. Shot through and through with feeling. Everything that has access to itself as feeling, even what is least definite, becomes thought."[16] It was perhaps because he believed he was made entirely of literature that Kafka could discover this sort of rational sensation.[17] "My thinking is more darkly mixed with sensation," reflects the literary character Christa T., who is assuredly made entirely of literature.[18] In twentieth-century literature, the most direct attribution of an intellectual source to feeling, to which feeling returns, is found in Thomas Mann's *Doctor Faustus*, where it inspires an imaginary masterpiece *The Lamentations of Doctor Faustus*—"a recovery . . . of expressivism, of the highest and profoundest claim of feeling to a stage of intellectuality and formal strictness."[19] This claim draws its authority from Nietzsche, Leverkühn's double, for whom the tensions of the (intellectual) will to power have the basic form of "pathos."[20]

The purpose of such a claim is not to restore to feeling the authority it allegedly lost to reason at the beginning of the social contract. Nor does it mean to rehearse formulaically the "fateful" rise of subjective feeling in mid-eighteenth-century bourgeois Europe.[21] Rather, this claim to the intellectuality of feeling presents artistic feeling as kindred to thought—thought's quick precipitator. Wittgenstein typically objected to Rabindranath Tagore's play *The King of the Dark Chamber* for lacking this authority:

It seems to me as if all that wisdom has come out of the ice box; I should not be surprised to learn that he got it all second-hand by reading and listening . . . rather than from his own genuine feeling. Perhaps I don't understand his tone; to me it does not ring like the tone of a man possessed by the truth.[22]

After reading the poems of Georg Trakl, however, Wittgenstein remarked: "I don't understand them, but I'm delighted by their tone. They have the genuine tone of genius."[23] The key words in this discourse of feeling as wisdom are "tone," "possession," "truth," "delight."

There would seem to be no discernible wisdom in possession until that wisdom is released; but, equally, there is no wisdom to be released from literature except from a state of bodily possession. The passion of meaning hangs on the meaning in passion; the condition of the hermeneutic task is the complex pleasure of possession, a point you find in Emil Staiger's famous injunction to the reader to "grasp" what has "gripped" him.[24] The immediate phenomenal sign of literature's happening is complex pleasure, the felt tension of reason and imagination, logic and rhetoric, argument and performance.[25]

This pleasure, being complex, is motivated. If, for Stendhal and for Nietzsche, beauty is the promise of happiness, then literary pleasure is the promise of intelligibility. The literary mood takes pleasure in the obscurity felt to be dimly breaking; it imputes intelligibility to the aesthetic object on the strength of the obscure pleasure it feels. In this uncertain light literature comes forward as a temporal chiaroscuro charged with feeling; and as we survey the intellectual history of this model, we will see that it has been a breeding space. The field tensed—in a word, pleasure—engenders various entities en route to its solution, entities held to be cognate with literature: for example, "wit," an initial obscurity that breaks as a *pointe*, consistent with Kafka's description of the aesthetic object as one that "hovers between the aesthetic edge and fatigue."[26]

The idea that the truth of literature is the concrete truth of feeling has been the main utopian proposition asserted about literary experience. It is not, however, self-evidently binding on the writers treated in this book, for each needs to speak of a different form of feeling, each renames literary feeling by specifying it. The giving of new names may be understood as inspired by the intent that literary feeling should signify more than mere feeling. Each writer claims a principal distinction for feeling; but the name of this feeling, this form-feeling, has got to be said right. There is always work to be done in discriminating the feeling that binds from the feeling that is only an accident of literary tension.

As a result, a moving historical field encloses both the individual experience of literature and the views about this relation held by these writers. Both Lessing and Kant, for example, oppose the radical contingency implied when literary pleasure is identified with "wit" (pleasure in excess of truth) or with "sensation" (untruth in excess of pleasure). For Kant, therefore, the disclosure of aesthetic judgment is necessarily bound up with the pleasure of the attunement of the faculties.[27] On the other hand, for Nietzsche—to take the decisive modern example—ecstatic moods inspired by Wagner's music-drama are no guarantee of the truth of Wagner's performance: they are contingencies that call for vivisection. But this analysis, which, in *The Genealogy of Morals*, leads Nietzsche to demythify Wagner in the name of Schopenhauer and then to discredit Schopenhauer in the name of Stendhal, on the grounds of the quality of feeling inspired by their work, is a job of critical work well worth doing and crucially assigned by a feeling response to art.

My theses:

(1) I want to make the fact vivid that where there is literature, there is complex pleasure;

(2) that this pleasure is complex because it involves the impression of a disclosure;

(3) that this fact is foremost in the minds of a number of canonical writers;

(4) that important literary works in the German tradition—fiction, poetry, critique—can be illuminated by the way they identify and discuss literary feeling;

(5) and that as a result the forms of feeling continually vary.

The cognitive upshot of this is that the necessary condition of asserting truths from literature is the presence of a distinctive complex of feelings. Since Lessing, at least, the relation of the content of the articulation to the posited content of the feeling has been grasped as changing. This relation moves from a position of absolute congruence to one of irritated fascination that tries to get the feeling under control, an effort impressing a certain rhythmic figure on the history of aesthetics. You can observe the impulse to establish aesthetic pleasure as essential (as essential to literature, and as essential in the sense of making a decisive disclosure), as well as the awareness of the difficulties that stand in the way. How good, for example, is a disclosure that cannot be conceptualized? How good is the truth of a cognition, even if not of the "truth-only" kind, when it emerges as an embodied and hence particular representation? But the response, a de-idealizing gesture, founders on the shoals of a feckless nihilism, a reactive idealization of "modernity."

Writers and thinkers on literature have been writing about the elusive domain of literary feeling even when they have used different names for the hybrid entities spawned in it—"hybrid" in the sense that they are intrinsically heterogenous forms of feeling. In this book, I shall be studying, in a number of key German writers, the various sorts of feeling tensed between reason and imagination that figure in the production of literature (*poiesis*)—and as the things that literature may be "about" (*mimesis*)—and as effects owed entirely to the literary process (*aesthesis/catharsis*).[28] These forms of feeling are types of apprehension and intellectual life associable neither with reason nor imagination alone but produced by and between their conjuncture.[29] They include such items as wit—the startling perception of likeness—and aesthetic judgment that is predicated on pleasure; "disinterested" pleasure and Hölderlin's "swift conceptual grasp [*schneller Begriff*]," stressing "the *tempo* of the process of thought";[30] finally, "artistic imagination" (Hölderlin's "*schöpferische Reflexion*"), mood, sadistic enjoyment, rapturous distraction, homonymic dissonance, and courage, as a suffering of "perceptual-intellectual" totality. All are distinctive forms of Benjamin's "feeling mode of comprehension [*fühlendes Erfassen*]." They belong partly to literary language and partly to the experience of literary language—to "readings" in both objective and subjective senses, as one speaks of readings *in* German writers of the eighteenth through the twentieth century (which introduce books as a collection of real features) and readings *of* German writers of the eighteenth through the twentieth centuries (which stress the energizing difficulties in the way of reading these books).[31]

A word on the methodological bias in this book on the topic of pleasure. Its title is *Complex Pleasure: Forms of Feeling in German Literature*. The "forms of feeling" in the subtitle are not subordinate to the topic of complex pleasure; they mean the same thing as complex pleasure, they are its only definition—an ostensive one.

So, all that you will learn here about complex pleasure is what you will learn about these forms of feeling—that, for example, Lessing's aesthetics, in the words of Rolf Grimminger, concern "the affective possibilities of persons . . . as these possibilities are inscribed in social existence. Aesthetic pleasure consists of a unified relation of sympathy and identification with the work of art."[32] Kant, on the other hand, projects a time of complex pleasure that is at once unified and tense.[33] This pleasure at once precedes and follows a judgment made by the self on its own mood; the redoubled emergence of this pleasure guarantees aesthetic judgment. Despite being spanned between activities of reason and imagination, the self moves "freely" all this time, unlike the subject of the "negative pleasure [*die negative Lust*]" of the sublime, which must first suffer a convulsion, "a momentary check to the vital forces."[34] (The more you accent the relation of understanding and imagination as harmonious, the more you identify an experience of the beautiful. The more you accent their conflict, the more you have to do with a virtual experience of the sublime.[35] These are separate ministries—of beauty and of dread.)

Hölderlin's notion of "swift conceptual grasp" exhibits a productive complexity like the one Nietzsche associates with inspiration, "A rapture . . . , a depth of happiness in which even what is most painful and gloomy does not seem something opposite but rather conditioned, provoked."[36] Even swift conceptual grasp evokes a lofty sort of pleasure: "eternal serenity," "divine joy." Except for "eternal" and "divine," these attributes match perfectly those of Kant's aesthetic judgment of the beautiful, though Hölderlin's account includes a swiftly sublated trace of pain. Nietzsche, too, according to Heidegger, grasps will to power as "joy."[37]

A character in Robert Musil's novel says on behalf of his friends: "You've only got to drop the idea that there's any relationship between us and Basini other than the pleasure we get out of what a rotten swine he is!"[38] By sexualizing mood, Musil conjures the nervous ecstasy of self-loss. At a loss in an urban world, Kafka picks out the flaneur's "harried feeling of pleasure." Trakl's poetry rewards the reader with the weak Dionysian bliss of shattering tropes. And here, finally, on complex pleasure, is the youthful Benjamin, not easy to understand but engaging:

The construction "be rhymed for joy [*Sei zur Freude gereimt*]" [in Hölderlin's ode "Timidity"] presupposes the sensory order of sound. And here too, in rhyme, the identity between that which determines and that which is deter-

mined is given—the way, let us say, the structure of unity appears as half a dou-
bling. Identity is given not substantially but functionally, as law. The rhyme
words themselves are not named. For, of course, "rhymed for joy" hardly means
"rhymed *with* joy". . . . As that which is opportune was recognized as a relation
of the genius (not *to* him), so is rhyme a relation of joy (not *to* it). Rather, that
dissonance of the image, which given the most radical emphasis suggests a tonal
dissonance, has the function of making the inherent intellectual temporal or-
dering of joy in time perceptible, audible, in the chain of an infinitely extended
event corresponding to the infinite possibilities of rhyme.[39]

The joyous possibilities of rhyme are only a small part of the possibilities
of literary pleasure. It is so doubtful that these possibilities reduce to one
thing or principle—let alone a thing or principle that could be demon-
ized as "*the* aesthetic ideology"—that the injunction to forswear such
seduction as "polluting" disinterestedness must be discarded for a time,
perhaps forever.[40] It is the purpose of this book to fill in this time with
suggestions of the indispensable complexity of literary pleasure.

And its higher implication, too. My method is to take such pleasure
further by displacing its aporias, by showing that they belong to systems
having higher features. For example, wit, as a sociable phenomenon, returns to the foundations of cognition as such—the perception of harmony. The circularity of Kant's derivation of the aesthetic judgment returns to the circularity of the hermeneutic encounter of the self with itself as "felt life." Hölderlin's "swift conceptual grasp" has a wider logic:
it means to organize the poetic self vis-à-vis its historical moment.
Mood, for Nietzsche, is transcended in affect, which, "in its primitive
form," is will to power.[41] Musil's moods of lived experience authorize a
cruelty usable in the excavation of new moods; having a mood justifies
going abroad in search of more "subtle and sensitive" counterparts.[42]
Tourism, in Kafka, turns out to be the very condition of allowing violence to happen to the self—a vertigo of atomization, particularization,
the detail come loose from the whole. A specific instance of homonymy
in Trakl leads to an experience of the universal, virtual shattering of
tropes, his wordplay an ecstatic correlative of anxiety and lostness. But
Benjamin's reading of the superiority of one of Hölderlin's odes advances a coherence theory of truth in feeling.

I hope to show in detail how the higher implications of complex
pleasure are produced.

—S. C.

Complex Pleasure

INTRODUCTION

At present, feeling is the only thing I understand.
—Balzac, in *Père Goriot*[1]

This book concerns the forms of feeling that come to light in literature—types of aesthetic experience that have still to be fully acknowledged in their variety. Among them are wit and aesthetic judgment, bliss and swift conceptual grasp, sadistic moods, "preternatural" distraction, sensory confusion, and the felt comprehension of myth as a type of totalizing consciousness. These forms are neither cognitionlike nor feelinglike alone but arise through the tension of the faculties. Here they will be shown in the perspective of Romantic and neo-Romantic high modernist reflection on what Heidegger calls the "disclosure" accomplished by literary feeling.

Literary feeling is a type of aesthetic feeling, by which I mean to highlight the complex pleasure of literary experience. Literary experience may be intricately pleasurable or negatively pleasurable, but, as aesthetic experience, it will have to be pleasurable. In saying this, I am appealing to a scarcely broken tradition since Aristotle's *Poetics* (1448b), and certainly through to Heidegger's *Being and Time*, that holds literary works of art to involve complex, pleasurable feeling, capable, in the alert body, of making a distinctive sort of disclosure in tension with conceptual reason.[2] The aesthetic experience of literature gives a specific sort of cognizing pleasure, a pleasure of its own.[3] The traditional division of subject matter in aesthetics—art as the truth of beauty versus art as the occasion of aesthetic experience—vanishes when one speaks of the disclosure accomplished by aesthetic experience. The disclosure is not the truth of conceptual (theoretical/logical) cognition: it is another kind of "acquist of true experience." The mercury thermometer does not lie; the pleasure thermometer is unreliable as it registers incessantly.[4]

What each type of literary feeling discloses will vary unforeseeably from case to case. Heidegger approaches an identification of the disclosure generally. In "poetical discourse," he writes, "the communication of the existential possibilities of one's state-of-mind can become an aim in itself, and this amounts to a disclosing of existence."[5] But "existence" only throws one back onto a web of indiscrete "possibilities." Or perhaps, with John Passmore, "we can say of literature what Wittgenstein says of philosophy, that it consists in 'assembling reminders for a certain purpose.' "[6] But there is no purpose I know that invariably lends itself to the feeling of purposiveness. The disclosure of literary pleasure is irremediably particular within the type.

There is more variation as a result of the concrete kind of feeling involved. The "kind of feeling" can refer to one of the dozen or so existing empirical emotions with which aesthetic realists have identified literary feeling, like pity and terror, or joy, or *jouissance*. But this is not the main sense of the phrase as it figures in the works of the writers discussed below. Each of them gives a categorical name to literary feeling precisely in order to distinguish it from empirical emotion—even when, in the words of John Dewey, such "theories" may not be "inherent in the subject-matter but arise because of specifiable extraneous conditions."[7] Such theories also tend to arise, however, because of the constitutive extraneousness of the literary work to its own subject matter. This is the sort of thing that Passmore registers in attaching the literary aesthetic to the *formal* qualities of depicted emotion.[8]

The disclosure made by literary feeling will vary, too, according to the position from which it is made. The position can be that of theme, as in works about feeling, like the German "lachrymose comedy," or it can be that of animating impulse, like the one described by Kafka: "I know only this kind of writing . . . : it is vanity and the craving for enjoyment, which is forever whirring around one's own form or even another's."[9] The position from which the feeling disclosure arises can even be grasped as an indwelling rhythmicalness, a passion of the work, leading T. E. Hulme to define "art" as a "passionate desire for accuracy."[10] Or, again, that position may be one of pragmatic imputation: Kant demands that one's aesthetic pleasure be ascribed to others, and I. A. Richards sees poetic attitudes as "imaginal and incipient activities or tendencies to action."[11] Or, finally, the position can be that of a receptive state of mind, the reader's intellectual emotion, or what has been called the "feeling intellect."[12] This part of the field crops up most often in the accounts I give below of the way that feeling is implicated in literary works.

Aesthetic feeling varies, finally, according to its authenticity, the degree to which the disclosure is essentially constituted by feeling. In other words, the disclosure can occur principally *as* feeling or in an only looser sense *through* feeling, in a field merely attuned by tension. When, for example, the eighteenth-century aesthetician Johann Jakob Breitinger refers the judgment on the verisimilitude of "the marvelous" to subjective states, he locates the poetic disclosure in illusion, affect, passion, madness.[13] The disclosure occurs *as* some manner of constellated feelings. But when, on the other hand, Breitinger's polemical target Johann Christoph Gottsched makes verisimilitude a rational affair of comparing the poetic image with an empirical source-image, he conceives of aesthetic pleasure as only a corollary of judgment. What is at stake in this discussion is the truth-content of the feeling involved, or what can also be called its value.[14] Staiger's injunction "Grasp what has gripped you," to which I alluded in the Preface, might be more aptly translated, for the wider case, as "Grasp *why* you have been so gripped." This reading allows for feelings that are wrong but whose strength gives away something interestingly factitious about their production, like, let us say, being swept away by Klopstock, *Werther*, Wagner, or worse.

It is evidently not the intensity of the feeling that is all-deciding. Heidegger's distinction between "genuine [*echt*]" and "not genuine [*unecht*]" authenticity—a distinction that turns on the more nearly essential relation of the feeling to the disclosure—is pertinent:[15] "The issue is one of existential modes, not of degrees of 'feeling-tones.'"[16] Something does not become genuine on account of the intensity with which it is immediately felt. Only in the dimmer case could something genuinely allusive come to light. Attention to the conceptual pairs "authentic" versus "inauthentic" and "genuine" versus "not genuine" helps to distinguish a redemptive view on the aesthetic from one that holds "higher" feeling to be in bad faith on grounds of its blatancy. This sort of concern inspires Benjamin's valorization of aesthetic *Erfahrung* (experience) over *Erlebnis* (the thrill of the hour).

Meanwhile, the very fact of this variety unsettles the prevalent view on aesthetics as *the* aesthetic ideology complicit with fascist politics.[17] It is by means of a claim of the validating type—no mere aberration in the history of aesthetics—that Kant links the "disinterested pleasure" in the beautiful of art to the imputation of free judgment to like-minded men and women. As a consequence there is an emancipatory moment simply in insisting on the variety and complexity of aesthetic feeling. Because aesthetic feeling, in a Kantian sense—feeling constitutive of its disclosure—has a socially communicative thrust, simply the having of aesthetic experience imputes complexity to one's fellows. The alleged purity, homogeneity, and closure attached to the art object by a German Idealist tradition of aesthetics is never a feature of aesthetic *experience.*

·ᴖ·

I shall begin by introducing some of the ways in which aesthetic feeling has been stressed and some of the issues that arise in light of its variety.

Kant's situating the aesthetic between critiques of pure and practical reason in his *Critique of Judgment* (1790) is crucial. Alexander Baumgarten's *Aesthetica*, composed forty years earlier, deserves pride of place for originating the conceptual structure in which aesthetic feeling acts as a third term, an in-between term, mediating between reason and sensibility. But it is only in the Third Critique that Baumgarten's three-tier mapping of the faculties acquires its main impressive ordonnance and charge.[18] Here Kant grants a special power of disclosure to a type of judgment—the aesthetic judgment of the beautiful—which discloses, as a mood, the attunement of faculties of conceptuality and imagination required for cognition in concepts. This mood has an implicitly moral and intersubjective bearing, since the individual percipient must impute agreement to all others as the condition of his pleasure.[19] Yet, even if Kant innovates a universalist dimension of the aesthetic moment, he remains a great articulator of a late eighteenth-century science of the counter-faculties of reason.[20] In his earlier *Anthropology* Kant acknowledged the weightiness of his debt to Rousseau on questions of moral philosophy, noting, "Rousseau set me right."[21] It is reasonable to conclude, therefore, that Kant's conception of aesthetic judgment is prefigured by Rousseau's celebrated "*sentiment de l'existence*."[22]

Within the world of German letters in the eighteenth century, it is Lessing—however short the shrift given him by Kant in the Third Critique—who establishes the primacy of feeling in art by making a wide claim for the feeling character of moral judgments. (Just how Lessing nuances artistic feeling is discussed in Chapter 1.) In the *Hamburg Dramaturgy*, Lessing turns Mary Wollstonecraft's point—"We reason deeply when we forcibly feel"—to a genetic account. In his advice to actors, he writes:

Every moral [judgment] is a general proposition. . . . But it is also the result of impressions made by individual circumstances on the acting persons. It is not a mere symbolic conclusion; it is a generalized feeling [*generalisierte Empfindung*] and as such needs to be spoken with a certain fire and enthusiasm.[23]

Here Lessing proleptically reverses Nietzsche's point: "Moralities are a sign-language of the affects."[24] For Lessing, affects—fiery ones—are the visible sign-language of moralities. This means that the judgment of value in tragic art, an affair of affect, of pity and of terror, is rooted in moral judgment. Morality is responsive to human "nature," just as aesthetic judgment is responsive to the work of the "genius" whose rule is nature. The genius of art is the same that speaks with fire from out of every moral mood.[25]

Kant shares with Lessing a readiness to assimilate aesthetic to moral forms of judgment in the (self)same person on the strength of a capacity for affection. In Lessing, moral sensibility is the grounding principle of aesthetic thought; in Kant's critique of aesthetic judgment, morality is a ground to which he returns only circuitously (see Chapter 2), having first departed from it in order to define an autonomous aesthetic judgment.[26] But the potential conflict, over which Kant readily enough passes, is only theoretical: there is nothing here like the massive acquist of lived experience which in Schiller, his disciple, causes dimensions of the aesthetic and the ethical to cleave apart.

What distinguishes the poetics of Lessing and Kant from that of Schiller is most fundamentally Schiller's experience of the Reign of

Terror. For him the harrowing result is that art acquires not so much the weak Messianic power of enlightenment as the task of subduing strong, archaic Messianic anticipations, like those that led to the carnage of the revolution. Schiller dreams of overcoming through cultivated literary sensuality the harsh disparity of the two reasons, which has meant the denaturing of the first:

Only literature [*Dichtung*] brings the separated powers of the soul together in unity, occupies head and heart, insight and wit, reason and imagination in a harmonious bond. Only literature can avert the saddest fate confronting the philosophical understanding: . . . to die to the joys of the real world in an abstract world of reason.[27]

The "abstraction" of reason is not harmless: in dying to the joys of the world, it will revenge itself on what it renounces, turning its own death into the death it means to inflict. This conclusion can be drawn from Schiller's critique of "form" as it has been politicized in the *Aesthetic Letters*.

Schiller's hope of a unifying aesthetic experience recurs in the history of aesthetic thought in the two centuries following. As a result he has been singled out as a source, and his misread position has been coalesced into *the* coercive aesthetic ideology. But in this tradition of recurrences, there are as many forms and nuances of "unity" as there are of disparity; and it would be just as wrong, as Adorno says, to hypostatize separation as to hypostatize unity.[28] Meanwhile, the value of the effort to unify in aesthetic experience "reason and passion, self-division['s] cause"[29] should not be disparaged on grounds of its alleged ignorance of inexpungable universal "de-facement."[30] This Platonic, neo-Platonic, and thereafter Kantian problematic generated immensely productive intellectual work among German Idealist writers—Schelling especially, to whom, in fact, we owe the keenest consciousness of *différance*.[31] It is this awareness in Schiller that produces, against the grain of his poetics, his failure to transcend Kantian divisions by thinking on Kantian lines.[32]

In Schiller's follower Hölderlin, Schiller's view of "the joys of the real world" is more shaded, his view of the "harmonious bond" of the faculties more differentiated; and hence the envisaged working of poetry is less meliorist. Hölderlin conjures a heightened naivety that can feel emotions "unknown to thought [*die der Gedanke /nicht kennt*]," like the pain, wrath, and joy of the gods.[33] And then it can seem that these are exactly the (composed) emotions that sound throughout his elegies, odes, and hymns. But the naive is only one such tone, and it must be complicated by tonalities of striving and reflection.

In Hölderlin a certain phase in the thinking of feeling comes to its end. His project of rendering in tragedy a "feeling of totality [*Totalempfindung*]"[34]—tragedy being the "metaphor of an intellectual intuition"[35]—breaks off grievously with his failure to complete the drama *Empedocles.* What survives from this fragment as the distinctive poetic possibility of modernity is the more subjectively immediate "tragic ode," borne by "the immediate language of feeling."[36] This possibility, in a story often told, devolves in nineteenth-century bourgeois culture into the pseudo-private, pseudo-individualizing, commodifiable product of "genius," in which all that appears to survive of the Kantian notion of genius is the commodity's own bleak parody of autonomy.[37]

What I want to do now is collect evidence of some of the live "principles of feeling" (Lessing) among writers writing in the decades following Hölderlin, even if it means crossing German borders to do so. These principles inform their own defense and illustration in literature.

Stendhal, who has an honorary place in the German tradition spelled out by Nietzsche, defines, like Goethe, a "logic of passion" homologous with that of the imagination. Unlike in Hölderlin, however, this logic is already informed by a heroic dimension. The logic of passion is something to die for, "insistent" because of "the profound interest it feels in knowing the truth."[38] The death that the passionate few die is a good death because they have lived the knowledge of its principle. The discovery of power in feeling strikes the Romantic mind as by and large a great promise. You can pick up the tonality even in Byron's rendering of it as a loss:

> No more—no more—Oh! never more on me
> The freshness of the heart can fall like dew,
> Which out of all the lovely things we see
> Extracts emotions beautiful and new,
> Hived in our bosoms like the bag o' the bee.
> Think'st thou the honey with those objects grew?
> Alas! 'twas not in them, but in thy power
>
> To double even the sweetness of a flower.[39]

"The poet knows that he speaks adequately then," wrote Emerson, "only when he speaks somewhat wildly, or 'with the flower of the mind.'"[40]

The involvement of the intellectual in the feeling life can also include a paradoxical claim to their separation. Observing in *Billy Budd* how "envy and antipathy, passions irreconcilable in reason, nevertheless in fact may spring conjoined like Chang and Eng in one birth," Melville evokes the strength that thought may finally take from what it first excludes. In a gentler time, he writes, "the better sort are inclined to incredulity when [envy] is imputed to an intelligent man. But since its lodgment is in the heart not the brain, no degree of intellect supplies a guarantee against it." Even Claggart's high degree of intellect is no guarantee of protection; but in a paradoxical way, reason may be distinctively heightened by its own impotence. "The master-at-arms was perhaps the only man in the ship intellectually capable of adequately appreciating the moral phenomenon presented by Billy Budd."[41]

The paradox of the separation and interinvolvement of types of mental life—which cannot be conceived in visible terms—has been imbedded in the trope of the vanishing circle. In *Young Törless*, another novella of agonized adolescence,[42] Musil offers the flowery insight: "Any great flash of understanding is only half completed in the illumined circle of the conscious mind; the other half takes place in the dark loam of our innermost being. It is primarily a state of soul, and uppermost, as it were at the extreme tip of it, there the thought is—poised like a flower."[43] It is like a certain "naive" love of appearances, which, for Nietzsche, "must be conceived as the blossom of the Apollinian culture springing from a dark abyss."[44]

Nietzsche—Musil's source, as Emerson was his—continually developed the challenging moral implications of so much dark loam in the soul. "Considering that the multiplicity of inward states is exceptionally large in my case," he wrote, "I have many stylistic possibilities—the most multifarious art of style that has ever been at the disposal of one man."[45] If *le style c'est l'homme même*, how is one to "appreciate" the man of "multifarious" styles? With each of these styles there correlates a state of soul. So the act of morally imagining others (including their loam-strewn prose) correlates intellectually with affects—or half-understood states of soul.

Now, the point of these remarks is not to stress the "otherness" of literature as a concentration of hidden affects. The category of otherness belongs more nearly to theology than to literary criticism: "You are like the spirit whom you comprehend / Not me" is spoken to Faust by a demigod—the Earth Spirit. The critic enlisted in the agenda of otherness is the institutional equivalent of the Idealist ego that merely posits the non-ego, for there is no access to the unposited Other. Over-reachers of the Other had better beware: We reason deeply and feel forcibly when our reason is excited by the imagination of our kind. Barthes comments that "All criticism is affectionate. . . . This should be carried even further, almost to the postulation of a theory of affect as the motive force of criticism."[46] For J. M. Bernstein, who is the least solipsistic of critics, "Aesthetic judgment intends a cognition of what is significant or worthy in itself through the way it resonates *for us*" (emphasis added).[47] Recall that Claggart's "intellectual appreciation" of Billy Budd is made possible by the "lodgment in the heart" of that same affect. So, being intellectually capable of adequately appreciating a moral phenomenon means being able to produce affectively an inter-pretation of one's kind. What I want to stress is the fecklessness of postu-lating any such thing as the "inhuman" of literary language—we have no access to it!—and on the other hand, the necessity of conceiving interpretation as an imaginative correlation of affects. Walter Benjamin, as a sort of proof, wrote of the difficulty of gaining any kind of access to the "perceptual-intellectual order" of a poem by Hölderlin ("Timidity [Blödigkeit]"), since "the impenetrability of its relations resists every mode of comprehension other than that of feeling [*jedem anderen als fühlenden Erfassen*]."[48]

I have emphasized that the constitutive tension of reason and imagi-nation (or of logic and rhetoric) in literature produces at the order of aesthetic theory a host of new names for the kinds of feeling entities this tension spawns. This continuing variety is not just a natural or categori-cal fact but the outcome of a drive to conceive the tension anew and aright. It is typical of how names fray paths that from Kant's earliest aes-thetics on, "form" can become a way of specifying the "reasonable" product of aesthetic activity and hence a way of furthering the claim of an aesthetically autonomous truth-bearing agency. But we will have to note the slippage, the fact that the term is liable to throw off the traces of its origin. Form arises in the vicinity of the object of rational perception, but it must become something different too. Form is the very own name of the object of aesthetic judgment, distinguishing it from the proper object of conceptualization. As a result, the wavering difference between them will be hard to specify.[49]

One transformation of the terms of this discussion, however, is noteworthy. Writers on literature, from the mid-eighteenth century on, have tended to oppose literary form to a feature of literary feeling. Max Brod, for example, distinguishes the chief elements of the "literary work of genius" as "mood" (*Stimmung*) and "economy" (*Ökonomie*). In the term "economy" we recognize a congener of "form."[50] This thought model extends deep into our century, far beyond Walter Benjamin's seminal essay (in 1915, on two odes of Hölderlin) with which this book concludes.

The opposition between form and feeling is not the same as that between a cognitive and a feeling feature. This point follows from Guido Morpurgo-Tagliabue's description of the main lines of aesthetic thought. On the one hand, he writes, there is "an aesthetics of measure and symmetry, *consonantia* and *proportio*, the *unum-multum*, the aesthetics of knowledge, the play of the faculties, totality, form"; on the other, "emotions of pity and fear and their catharsis, enthusiasm, the sublime . . . empathy, expressiveness."[51] The formal dimension may be an "aesthetics of knowledge," a place where the knowledge of something true in the sense of being conceptually verifiable is displayed or produced in a reader; but of course—as we think of "formalisms" of all kinds—this is not always the case. I am referring to the tendency of Romantic and neo-Romantic poetics to subdue the truth-only cognitive factor in literature and to recast all reason as "form-giving" and hence as irreducibly "poetic" (see Nietzsche's "poetizing reason [*dichtende Vernunft*]"[52] and Heidegger's trumping reason with "poetic thinking").[53]

Recall, too, that we saw Kant constitute the aesthetic moment chiefly from the terms "form" and "feeling": a form is given to the faculty of judgment, whose task is to gauge its ability to produce disinterested pleasure. The outcome, unlike that of Schopenhauer's interpretation of Kant, is not a deep *cognition* of the form.[54] Nietzsche dramatically accentuates this shift, contrasting, in *The Birth of Tragedy*, the Apollinian art moment in which "all forms speak to us" to the "blissful ecstasy" of Dionysus on the collapse of the illusion of form.[55] A certain kind of lower-order cognition continues to belong to the Apollinian pole—a leftover from Schopenhauer's world of individuation and the fourfold root of the principle of sufficient reason. But the vastly more important disclosure of knowledge now belongs to the Dionysian, the feeling pole. If form is a guarantee of lower-order cognition, passion is the promise of "Dionysian knowledge."[56]

In the years following, a critic like Friedrich Gundolf, smartly punished by Benjamin after 1915 but still a creditable influence on his early work, considers the formal feature a product of "force" (this is his legacy from Dilthey). For Benjamin, in his essay on Goethe's *Elective Affinities* (1924), in which the savaging of Gundolf is done, "Form enchants chaos momentarily into world."[57] At another level Johannes Pfeiffer, writing in 1936, conceives of form as a modality of mood (this is his legacy from Heidegger in *Being and Time*),[58] and Santayana—an honorary German aesthetician—remarks that "some forms give pain by causing a shock of surprise."[59] Indeed, an idea of force or shock is already inscribed even in the opposite pole, in the German notion of imagination—*Einbildungskraft*—which combines ideas of inscription, imaging, forming, and force. At this point, "form" and "feeling" can no longer be regarded as opposite poles.

When a transposition of such terms occurs, and form is stripped of a cognitive dimension in exchange for something else that is itself like feeling, then poetry becomes form entirely. Thus, in the line of Benedetto Croce, form becomes the vehicle of a type of poetic expression.[60] In later versions, form comes to express only one thing: the death of "natural" expression, "the pure lament," as it is associated with Kafka, in his *Diaries*, and with Thomas Mann's Nietzsche-figure, Adrian Leverkühn, in *Doctor Faustus*. For Adorno, a student of Benjamin's work on Hölderlin, "form itself [in Hölderlin] becomes a reflection [*Reflex*] of content, and the meaning is no longer marked by a center but dwells in the gaps of the paratactic structure."[61] One can add that these gaps in Hölderlin are illustrated by solitary images in paratactic isolation from argument.[62] As "myth" would be the asserted identity of image, argument, form, and feeling, parataxis becomes a demythologizing strategy or residue.

The fortunes of a hegemonic "form" begin to reveal, among other things, the loss of aesthetic value: form, not being "reasonable," may lack truth content; form having absorbed feeling may have etiolated pleasure to the vanishing point. Form becomes play, as in high post-structuralism, but its play is not notably playful—not really play at all but attenuated chaos.

It would have been a truism for the eighteenth century that the play of understanding and imagination is a source of pleasure. In the more exasperated mood of recent modernity, aesthetic speculation has aimed to name the faculties better—in passing from faculties to agencies to structures to neologisms. So we have seen reason complexly, deviously, become form become logic become grammar—and imagination become expressiveness become rhetoric; but in the process of renaming, the topic of pleasure has been isolated except for being tacitly expunged in the chiefly ascetic mood of deconstruction. One of my concerns is to reinsert into the forms of literary perception this neglected component—pleasure—in claiming that pleasure is the spur to interpretation. Literary pleasure is dependent on intelligibility dawning. Its pleasure is in an objective sense intentional: it aims at understanding all the time it suspends the possibility of final satisfaction. It is in this field of expectation, as a function of the intensity of longing, that something like a disclosure, a knowledge of one's own, could come to light.

A word or two now about the way I shall be proceeding and how I want these remarks to be oriented. Certainly it is the historian's ideal to describe consecutive modifications of such tension in the aesthetic—to reproduce, as Nietzsche famously says, "the entire process semiotically concentrated" in these concepts, the "continuous sign-chain of ever new interpretations and adaptations."[63] He must do this while somehow acknowledging, every step of the way, that, as he surveys his object, his discourse is also implicated within it, helpless to resist "the recoil upon thought of that which it is attempting to overcome."[64] Such a history, if it could be written, would be an ultimate resource for the articulation of the aesthetic ideology—a matter of the greatest importance, for, on this view, aesthetics supplied a coercive element of fascist politics, so the stakes in this debate are enormous. But this view on the aesthetic also circulates with a crudity that discourages interest in its applications. I want to mention right away one reason for this terrible simplification, since it bears critically on the usefulness of the idea.

The single major source of the formulation of the aesthetic ideology is a sentence found at the end of Walter Benjamin's essay, "The Work of Art in the Age of Its Mechanical Reproduction," where Benjamin identifies "the situation of politics which fascism is rendering aesthetic." For many, the sentence asserts the complicity of an entire tradition of aesthetics in the making-fascist of politics. But this conclusion is wrong because of what Benjamin's preceding sentence says: "[The] self-alienation [of mankind] has reached such a degree that it can experience its own destruction as an aesthetic pleasure of the first order."[65] The aesthetic pleasure offered by the Nazis is the "pleasure" of self-destruction; only an aesthetics of self-destruction will do. What, then, have contributors to a holistic, vitalistic aesthetics that has been held to be vicious—thinkers such as Schiller, Stendhal, and Nietzsche—to do with an aesthetics of self-destruction?

Beyond this Benjaminian gesture, reflection on the aesthetic ideology has tended to reduce itself to displacing and otherwise moving about two allegedly distinct types of literary rhetoric as the source of aesthetic effects: one, the diction of organic symbolism, with connotations of unity and harmony and the coincidence of sign and meaning; the other, the rhetoric of allegory, with its higher-tone connotations of temporality, decalage, noncoincidence, nonautonomy, death—the former mode being declared blindly ideological, the second anti- or non-ideological.

The point of my chapters is to emphasize the variety of responses to the aesthetic, which is never an affair of either organic beauty or the allegorical disjunctive sublime alone: these two rhetorical modes are not what literary language is made up of and not alone the kinds of thought, disposition, and feeling it produces. It might be assumed that the fact of their irreducible variety and constitutive intertwinedness were better known: it was shown with eminent clarity in Gadamer's *Truth and Method*, as part of a discussion of the *many* types of faculties that ground humanistic learning even when the humanities do not know that this is the case and whore after strange gods of scientificity—and when feeling masquerades as rigor.[66] Gadamer dwells on the mid-eighteenth-century development of aesthetic judgment—of taste and empathetic interpretation—its grounding in a postulated common sense and its relation to an older ideal of rhetorical *Bildung*, chiefly in order to point up the fateful separation of art interests from cognitive interests. But this conclusion does not have to follow from Gadamer's account of the intellectual historical state of affairs in which the aesthetic emerges—and continues to emerge; his account does not point inexorably to this alienation. For one strain in Kant's Third Critique is of the type of aesthetic modernism that actually regrets the enlightened modernity founded on the tacitly accepted cleavage of art and truth.[67] I shall be dealing with the survival of Gadamer's historical categories into modern times.

The worry about the pernicious effects of the alleged aesthetic ideology reinforces the urgency of a systematic historical articulation of literary aesthetics. The goal of this book, however, is more nearly preparatory. It wants to make an opening—a series of openings—of the kind that precede a knowing organization for the sake of performative, practical results in advance. I want to provide new directions for the historian's task by illustrating in detail a number of major variants of the term of feeling. I identify, once more, such terms as wit, disinterested pleasure, mood, and rapture in writers who wrote successively in German literary tradition, so there is a diachronic bearing in this account. For example, I describe the *supersession* of wit by judgment as a privileged organ of literary reception in the time of Lessing and Kant; Nietzsche's *abandonment* of the category of mood at a precise stage in his writing career; Musil's *taking up* of mood in a posthumous Nietzschean manner; and Benjamin's *anticipation* of the Heideggerean modulation of the mood of courage. But such temporal connections are intermittent and unpredictable; I do not offer a certifiable genealogy of *mi*-formal / *mi*-feeling hybrids through a century and a half of literary composition from Lessing to Benjamin—partly because I do not believe that as one category lay dying, it gave birth to a different one. The period of 150 years is too brief to allow for the firmest stipulations of social and cultural differences as productive of aesthetic positions, and certainly there are no good enough categorical period terms to specify their sites.[68] *Pace* Adorno, there is too much likeness, for example, between Johannes Pfeiffer's view in 1936 of the absolute primacy of mood over generic structure and Goethe's assertions around 1770 of the primacy of the one true feeling ensuring aesthetic wholeness. Goethe declared, "And even if such creation consists of the most arbitrary forms, they will be in harmony [*zusammenstimmen*] even without structural relation [*Gestaltsver-hältniß*], for One feeling made it into a characteristic whole."[69] A history of aesthetics from Goethe to Heidegger would be abstruse if it meant to fit "the pattern of procreation and generation found in the genealogically imagined plot" of whatever stripe.[70] There are too many complications at work of the sort that Sartre called *hysteresis*, or laggardly overlap; too many synchronic intertwinings of the residual, the dominant, and the emergent that must be overlooked if there is to be a chronology of causes.[71]

At times, then, I do propose models about how to view the career of these hybrids of formal feeling in intellectual history. But mostly I want to exhibit and define the many kinds of offspring that arise from or about the tense union of form and expression, of reason and imaginative feeling, in some major German literary works—offspring that are not certifiably legitimate and are more nearly like Plato's "bastards of script."[72] Each of these hybrids occupies a distinctive place between its framing ideas, a space determined and attuned by specific kinds of form and feeling. Thus, each of these German books has its own historical character, which shapes, enlarges, and burdens that of other books and readers. Gerald Bruns develops this thought so interestingly, I would like to cite him at length. The words of which he speaks are the words in books one reads:

Words do not just echo or resonate with their historicality, that is, they are not just expressive or reflective of their contexts in the forms laid out by the various historicisms old and new. Rather it is that words situate you in their historicality in the sense of exposing you to it, placing you under its claims and also under the claims against it. Imagine being inserted into another's history.[73]

Then you would have to feel some of the things with some of the faculties that this book talks about.

·～·

A final word about the bodilyness, bodilessness, and the something in-between of imaginative feeling.

There is a powerful Romantic view that identifies the danger in the involvement of imagination in feeling. In Goethe's *Elective Affinities* (1809), the wrong lovers embrace, but imagination generates for the somatic feeling life just enough charm to facilitate their coupling:

In the dim lamplight secret affections began to hold sway, and imagination took over from reality. Eduard clasped none other than Ottilie in his arms; Charlotte saw the Captain more or less distinctly before her mind's eye, and so things present and absent mingled, curiously enough, in the most charming and delightful manner.

The outcome, however, will not be "charming and delightful": it is the birth of a child having the features not of the parents but of the parents' ghostly lovers—and who dies young by drowning. Something of his sad end is forecast in the violence of the following sentence: "Yet the present will not be deprived of its monstrous rights." Imagination feeds this monstrosity, and the bodies blindly couple.[74]

The harm is worse in *Notes from Underground* (1864), where the self-analysis of the Underground Man follows a coupling, according to the "logic of vice, which, without love, grossly and shamelessly begins with that in which true love finds its consummation" (metalepsis is the figure of perversity).[75] Needing to turn into a prostitute the woman who understands him, the Underground Man can now

say for certain: though I did that cruel thing purposely, it was not an impulse from the heart, but came from my evil brain. This cruelty was so affected, so purposely made up, so completely a product of the brain, of books, that I could not even keep it up a minute—[76]

Here the truth of feeling must still assert itself from below its own factitious borrowings. In *The Sentimental Education* (1869) the truth of feeling is absconded: the harm of the confusion of imagination and feeling courses everywhere in a universe in which no language, not even that of the narration, is free of contamination. "She looked like the women in romantic novels,"[77] notes Flaubert or the narrator or Frederic Moreau as they score with the fetish of a protruding boot the origin of Frederic's debile passion. This same confusion becomes more complex and interesting in Gide's account, in 1926, of the double counterfeit when imagination gets involved in feeling. Gide puts the argument into the mouth of his intellectual hero Edouard:

In the domain of feeling, what is real is indistinguishable from what is imaginary. Psychological analysis lost all interest for me from the moment that I became aware that men feel what they imagine they feel. From that to thinking that they imagine they feel what they feel was a very short step. . . . And if it is sufficient to imagine one loves, in order to love, so it is sufficient to say to oneself that when one loves one imagines one loves, in order to love a little less and even in order to detach oneself a little from one's love, or at any rate to detach some of the crystals from one's love.[78]

The figure of the crystal marks this text as a *Contre-Stendhal*. It is now seventy years since Gide's *Counterfeiters*, and there is less talk of imagination. In our leaden (better, wired) age of violence and abstraction, imagination does well to stay deep down as the source of thought that can be felt. In this crisis, which Baudrillard calls the "cybernetic peripeteia of the body," it is not so much that "passions have disappeared" as that they have materialized.[79] And so our body has grown most imaginative in its symptoms.[80]

But the somatization of rhetoric, despite the messianic aura of a materialist pantextualism, has not dissolved the conflict of reason and feeling. In 1902 Hugo von Hofmannsthal wrote of a certain Lord Chandos, whose body, at elevated moments, "consists sheerly of ciphers [*Chiffren*]": these stigmata can be read only by a reason that begins "thinking with the heart."[81] "Postmodernism" has not furthered this mode of thought—it figures instead, in the words of Gillian Rose, as "the new baroque protestantism of the body and denigration of the mind."[82] The tension of reason and imaginative feeling cannot be easily subdued, least of all in thought; and we know how rapidly their relation can shift from beautiful play to the consternation, the "negative pleasure [*die negative Lust*]," of the mythical sublime,[83] let alone the unredemptive ugliness of a body in excess of its signs.[84] Deleuze, for one, stresses a coercive moment even in the recuperated ugly of the sublime; it is the moment when the imagination (in Kant's phrase) is forced to "recoil upon itself" and thus to learn that "it is reason which pushes [imagination] to the limit of its power, forcing it to admit that all its power is nothing in comparison to an Idea."[85] That Idea today would have to be the absence of all Ideas.

Addressing the "debasement of the Romantic quest," Brian Tayan identifies another moment of blocked expressiveness. "The failure of feeling in Thomas Mann's *Doctor Faustus* indicates a rupture in Stendhal's 'logic of passion.' And yet Faustus does not represent a resurgence of Enlightenment ideals of abstract thought and knowledge through reason but instead a quest for knowledge 'on the other side of sense and sentiment.'"[86] The cited phrase returns to a passage in the novel where the Nietzsche-figure Kretzschmar broods: "Perhaps it was music's deepest wish not to be heard at all, nor even seen, nor yet felt; but only—

if that were possible—in some Beyond, *the other side of sense and senti-ment*, to be perceived and contemplated as pure mind, pure spirit" (em-phasis added). I want to inflect this formula toward my subject now: it helps me to see that literature means to be "heard" and "seen" and "felt," but here I drop the hypostatic "in the Beyond" for the adverb "beyond" (as I drop "pure mind, pure spirit"). Literature is a special concentration of hearing and seeing and, above all, of feeling whose "deepest wish" is to get "beyond" daily obsession, wanting to be perceived and contem-plated by a mind not "pure" at all but dyed in the color of circumstance yet wanting to get clear of it, to the "other side of sense and senti-ment."[87] This wish is expressed in each of the works treated in this book, yet in Lessing, Kant, Hölderlin, Nietzsche, Musil, Kafka, Trakl, and Benjamin, the sense of where this other side is varies, especially in the degree of its physicalness, since "further from the ordinary" can also mean closer to the body, to a hidden subject, a bodily ego, without im-mediate speech.

In Kafka's *The Boy Who Sank Out of Sight* the extremity of exile pro-duces a hero alienated from even a consciousness of bodily states. The accompanying proliferation of gesture points to an aporia, to a sign that means the very absence of signification for him who presents the sign. The maximum of this condition is the dead hero. In his commentary on Goethe's novel *Elective Affinities* Benjamin discovers a redemptive possi-bility in this muteness:

When therefore [Goethe's] *Maxims and Reflections* characterize the most ex-treme degree of such incapacity to unveil in the profound words: "Beauty can never become lucid about itself," God remains, in whose presence there is no se-cret and everything is life. The human being appears to us as a corpse and his life as love, when they are in the presence of God. Thus death has the power to lay bare like love. Only nature cannot be unveiled, for it preserves a mystery as long as God lets it exist. Truth is discovered in the essence of language. The human body lays itself bare, a sign that the human being as such enters into God's presence.[88]

This aperçu bears immediately on the theory of literary embodiedness if in Benjamin's structure we replace "corpse" with "literature"; "love," with a "high degree of presence"; and "God," with the Superreader. The same structured constellation of figures is projected by Benjamin in a youthful essay, where, addressing the poet-hero of Hölderlin's ode "Timidity [Blödigkeit]" he writes: "Transposed into the middle of life, nothing remains for [the poet-hero] except the motionless life, complete passivity, which is the essence of him who is courageous—except to surrender himself wholly to relationship."[89] Emptied of the consciousness of feeling, the poet *is* pure feeling, is wise passiveness.[90]

Yet no matter how passively conceived, "feeling" identifies an originary understanding occurring closer to the body; its locus is the body.[91] Even Hölderlin's title, "Blödigkeit," is a word saturated with physical connotation. This embodiedness of consciousness is the insight that propels much of Nietzsche: "Can it be," he writes in *Dawn*, "that all our so-called consciousness is a more or less fantastic commentary on an unknown, perhaps unknowable, but felt text?"[92] The "text" is a network of "nerve stimuli." We find this stress in Nietzsche's teacher Emerson, too, who taught Peirce: "The synechist will not believe that some things are conscious and some unconscious, unless by consciousness be meant a certain grade of feeling."[93] These grades of feeling are physical.

And so it becomes obvious to think of literature itself as a kind of body, and beautiful literature as the "transfigured *physis*"[94] of which Nietzsche—and Nietzscheans—dreamt. In writing things seen, Kafka would sublimate his body to a nakedness of breath and light, meaning to uncover the lost luminousness of the higher body, Hebrew to Nietzsche's Greek.[95] This work of clearing has an immediate reward for him in the word as a beautiful body—the sign, the letter, the printed text.[96]

In this book I shall not say much about the beautiful sign. Coming from the dissolution of personality implied in Kafka's wish above, I think of literature sooner as the "sublime" body, which brings to light in tolerable form the corpse beneath the skin. The notion of such a sublime is consistent with the kind of rigorous materialism that holds all matter to be mortified. Literature is the conscious body that must always stage its mortification anew. In this sense it is unreasonable, standing beyond economic reason and aimed practical feeling;[97] and yet in matters of detail and exposition, it continues to be a material display of their tension. This other sort of feeling is reason's recoil from the flow of body images it takes to be of only practical use.

·ᴗ·

Why, finally, stress today something nonconceptually cognitive in literature and literary study? Isn't this just to belabor a giant Kantian cliché, fine in 1790 and dull today? But until recently, with the heyday of a hermeneutics of suspicion and a suspicion of hermeneutics, in types of ideological and deconstructive criticism, disclosive feeling was anything but a factor to be taken for granted. Under the spell of Paul de Man, in whom a hyperawareness of recursiveness was projected into literature as its basic character, writing became an easily penetrable allegory of its own unintelligibility, one that yielded in every case one good master cognition. This is the knowledge of literature's principal opacity and violence. Certainly, one would be hard-pressed to tell what place, let's say, shadings of mood or rapture could have in its system. Such terms might figure there as tokens of a naive, a "preliterary," manner of reading, which, eager to the point of obsession to existentialize what are in reality problems of literary rhetoric, forecasts, under the head of "psychologism," continual inroads of banality, triviality, and bad faith. It is just at this point, however, that de Man opens himself up to the same critique that Adorno leveled against himself—and which Jauss was quick to exploit. If literature does not give pleasure (however complex), a pleasure rooted in empathetic identification with an imaginatively embodied world, how and why should there be such a thing as literature?[98]

De Man's view is negative theology entirely consistent with suburban reclusiveness. But reading involves a messy complex of faculties that cannot be held to the truth-only cognitive work they do—or don't do—in privacy. The logic of deconstruction is based on a late Hegelianism in which the function of art (according to Hegel) is replaced by the function of philosophy (according to Hegel). But there is too much instruction coming from Hegel's real incarnation of the concept in art for it to be abandoned too lightly, and for that matter too much instruction from Hegel's conception of a tension which, more than Kant, but *not* in radical opposition to Kant, conducts the transformative power of the Idea into the depths and surfaces of bodily life.[99] Mark Roche spells this out:

Several moments follow from art's rendering truth sensuous: thinking guided by imagination leads to an abundance of philosophical prolepses—art anticipates the problems of philosophy; artistic truth is more readily visible and accessible than philosophical truth; artistic masterpieces are possible of various kinds and from various traditions—where one philosophical truth excludes competing truths, one sensuous representation does not exclude another; art addresses the imaginative, emotional, and subliminal parts of the self that motivate the soul more than mere argument does; and though accessible to conceptual analysis, the sensuous dimension gives art a complexity that, much like the human subject, is not exhausted by conceptual analysis.[100]

J. M. Bernstein enlarges this account:

> Because art authorizes unique, individual items, it tendentially works against the hierarchy of universal and particular; because art is bound to the life of particulars, it tendentially celebrates the claims of sensuousness and embodiment; because its practices are tendentially governed by the claims of sensuousness and particularity, it instigates an alternative conception of acting, one which binds doing and making, *praxis* and *poiesis* together.[101]

This is to identify analytically a junction and also to imply the makings of a strife of the faculties. The culture wars of the moment point to its empirical realization. And while the great goal of these wars is being fought over—David Bromwich's *Politics by Other Means* has contributed to the victory of "the individual mind"[102]—I should like to have my piece ready when peace comes. These essays are conceived as a contribution to the culture of the human subject by illustrating anew some fundamental features of individuality.

Complex Pleasure is the fourth part of a general project intending to show effects of literature over and above the cognitive results of achieved interpretation. In *The Fate of the Self* I described how works of literature and philosophy, according to canonical German writers, might constitute authorial identity. In *Franz Kafka: The Necessity of Form*, I showed how Kafka's work bears witness to his "being-a-writer [*Schriftstellersein*]." In *Borrowed Lives*, Irene Giersing and I tried to evoke the playful effects of the awareness of literary tradition on the writing of fiction. Now, in *Complex Pleasure*, I examine eight offspring of literary tension—this "crowd of themes, events, and thoughts" and, I now add, exemplarily, *feelings*, "all demanding to be written down."[103]

PROEM

You govern in broad daylight, and your law
Blooms; you hold the scales, Son of Saturn!
And distribute the lots and abide joyous in
The fame of immortal arts of rule.

Yet into the abyss, the bards tell themselves,
You once expelled the holy father, your own,
And down under, there moans,
Where the savage ones before you are by rights,

Innocently the God of the golden age for a long time now:
Once easy, and greater than you, even if
He did not utter any commandment, and no
Mortal named him by name.

So down with you! or do not be ashamed of gratitude!
And if you want to stay, serve the older one,
And grant him that before all others,
Gods and men, the bard name him!

For, as from clouds your lightning there comes
From him that which is yours, look! what you command
Bears witness to him, and from Saturn's
Peace arises every kind of might.

And once I have first felt at the heart
What is living and what you give shape grows dim,
And in its cradle in
Bliss changing time slumbered away from me:

Then I shall know you, Kronion! then I shall hear you,
The wise master, who, like us, a son
Of Time, gives laws and proclaims
What the holy dawn conceals.

—Friedrich Hölderlin[1]

Hölderlin's proud ode (1801) addresses the tension between "nature" and "art" and the kinds of perception they induce. From nature comes the capacity to feel a wholeness of life and to experience "what is living [*Lebendiges*]" as a dawning to the senses, an intuition by glimmers. Art provokes the rational activities of "legislating," "ruling," and "weighing distinctions." The poem develops as the speaker—a bard or poet (*Sänger*)—demands that art, in the figure of the lawgiver Jupiter, acknowledge its origin in Saturn, the earlier god of nature, sunk in a pre-world before time and language.[2]

The mythic matter of Saturn and Jupiter tells about a son who, having castrated and banished his father, now rules. A full restoration would require that the son give back to the father the authority he once took from him. But, except in passing, Hölderlin does not conjure this myth of the return of a golden age. He creates another myth. The son does not have to be supplanted by the father whom he supplanted; the son may rule, but for the first time with legitimate authority, by means of an act—indeed, two acts—of acknowledgment. He must admit, in a sense to be defined, that the father comes "before" him, has precedence; and he must "grant that before all others, / Gods and men, the bard name him!" These acknowledgments link the new figure with the older one by creating a space that they might share, a space between the "might" of feeling and the "might" of reason—one rife with the possibility of acts of gratitude and commemoration—for example, building monuments, holding dialogues, and writing poems.

What is ghostly about this transcription of the myth is the kind of authority that the son will now give away (not back) to his father. It is not the authority defined in the first stanza as an affair of worldliness in its most concrete sense as the power to rule. It is different from the strongest definitions of authority we know, the powers of government: executive, legislative, and judicial. It is a verbal authority, an authority to decide who names whom, and one granted as a verbal concession; and so it implies a world in which acts of speaking have the performative character of worldly acts.

The poet's act of naming will be performed in a world constituted by other poets, which, with this act of naming, enters and indeed masters the world of rule. What poets have been saying now goes; and they have been saying for years that the authority with which Jupiter rules is Saturn's, that Jupiter is illegitimate because he has failed to acknowledge his paternity, and that Jupiter must now admit their right to tell this story starting with Saturn. The bards have been telling themselves the story that Jupiter must grant them the authority to tell themselves the story, and now this story might become true. This event is intelligible only as Jupiter himself becomes poetry, or poetry acquires the cosmic authority of Jupiter, who visibly governs. The poem has a sort of motto: From now on real acts will take place in poetry, and poetry will take place in the sphere of rule. The injustice of worldly things will be rectified to the degree that acts will be like acts of poetic speaking—to the extent that, in the strongest possible sense, the arts of *rule* will become the *arts* of rule: poetry.

Let us for the moment call psychoanalytic the proposition that to know negativity is to be freed from its angriest and most obscure workings: to articulate the curse for the sake of the accursed is to mitigate his pain. Let us call psychoanalytic that authority which arises from an intelligible speech of pain—from poetry par excellence. Hölderlin's vision in this poem, of Jupiter's address to the sufferings of Saturn, might be the triumph of the psychoanalytic.

Might be: to speak of triumph is premature. The most striking feature of the space these gods create and which they might share is its merely virtual, as yet unpopulated character. It is charged with connections in an only metaphorical sense as a space of "giving thanks." This space of gratitude, of service and praise, is only open, possible space. It has yet to be and be organized; it has the sole status of the intentional uptake of a command. More: even if it were realized—supposing Jupiter had agreed to serve Saturn and allowed him to be the first-praised of poets—what form would such service take and what would such original poems in honor of Saturn sound like and look like? This extended metaphor of connection between art and life displaces the poem one order forward into a space in which connections are only imagined. Hence it is a contested place, tensed between extremes of at once realized and unrealized constitution.[3] For there is, first of all, the practical fact of the poem itself, the poet's world in the actual complexity of its thematic, grammatical, and metrical accomplishment, stressed by the sprung intricacy of the Alcaic stanza.[4] But the poem also drives toward an emptying-out of any connection except the formal. At the center of the ode—the fourth stanza—where we might look for a maximally dense concretion of poetic experience, we have only an open space produced by the posited metaphorical command to give thanks.

The mediating term between art (and reason) and nature (and feeling) is gratitude. In being linked to the terms "doing service [*Dienen*]" and "poetic naming [*Nennen*]," it evokes an attitude of faithful articulation, an ethically charged thinking—*Denken*. The celebrated triplet *Danken, Dichten, Denken* worked up in Heidegger's readings of Hölderlin, which now sounds rebarbative, might still be cogent here.[5] The more striking feature of this compressed meditation at mid-poem, however, is the way it returns to nothing more (nor less) solid as an illustration than this very poem as an example of thanking, poetizing, thinking poetically. This peculiar failure of wider realization, its confinement within the metaphor, points to a factor identified by Walter Benjamin in Hölderlin's ode "The Poet's Courage [*Dichtermut*]" which he reads against a later version, "Timidity [*Blödigkeit*]."[6] From the ur-version, radically unfulfilled, Benjamin cites the line: "Does not the Parca[7] herself nourish you for service? [*Nährt zum Dienste denn nicht selber die Parze dich?*]." Here, too, part of the impression of hollowness comes from an unfathomed idea of service. In the second version, "Timidity," this turns auspiciously, according to Benjamin, into a bold "positing": "Does not your foot stride upon what is true? [*Geht auf Wahrem dein Fuß nicht?*]."[8] But in the case of the poem we are reading, "Nature and Art or Saturn and Jupiter," there is no second version to fill in an unrealized figure of service.

The poem creates no unity of reason (Jupiter) and feeling (Saturn) by this tour of self-reflection. It redoubles their difference with heightened force in the tension between the established work of the poem and the open possibility at its center, so that what arises finally is an instance not of mediation but of literature, of poetry conjuring service as mediation, allowed to do so on the strength of the gratitude exacted from reason to pay feeling in whatever form that gratitude might suitably take. The poem stands before us, but as nothing imaginably other than its own unrealized self (because it is *not* myth, and it is *not* already transparently clear to a community of readers what debt of service reason owes feeling, what Jupiter owes Saturn). Short of the living myth—not mythology—a metaphysical decalage cleaves the object whose explicit aim was to mediate oppositions.

Goethe wrote that every new object rightly perceived opens up a new organ of apprehension. Likewise in this zone projected by the metaphor of grateful naming: things there—literary words—produce new ways of taking them in.

"The name," adds Michel de Certeau, "is not authorized by any meaning; on the contrary, it authorizes signification, like a poem that is preceded by nothing and creates unlimited possibilities for meaning."[9] More than this, "literary signification"—that is, literature—awakens new faculties of apprehension, neither reason nor feeling alone, which writers and thinkers in the modern period, certainly "no later than Pascal," know about. They in turn have given new names to the forms of feeling evoked by the ghostly issue of Hölderlin's gratitude. In their light I am inclined to view each of the mediating agencies discussed in this book—wit, judgment, Hölderlin's "swift comprehension," mood, and others—as born of a productive literary negativity, an endlessly self-mediating, self-critical literary generosity: hence, this book of literary tensions.

1

WIT AND JUDGMENT; OR, LESSING AND KANT

Does like not ever summon like?
—Plato, *Republic*, Book IV

It is lovely to compare things.
—Friedrich Hölderlin

A passion for setting up equivalences can easily
bring a person to the point where he forgets the
unlike—a point proved by the Revolution.
—Jean Paul

In the second half of the eighteenth century, in the work of Lessing (1729–81) and Kant (1724–1804), the fortunes of wit and judgment divide.[1] The opposition between these faculties grows ever more marked: in Lessing's *Hamburg Dramaturgy* (1767–68), judgment scourges wit, drastically.[2] And when the faculty of judgment reappears, in central position, in Kant's *Critique of Judgment* (1790), it is no longer as the scourge of wit but as its supercessor. Wit has no place in aesthetic judgment, and Kant substitutes "judgment [*Urteilskraft*]" for what is specific to the faculty popularly called "*Mutterwitz* [mother wit, salt of common sense]."[3] In Lessing and Kant, wit cedes primacy to judgment. But the character of that superior judgment diverges so significantly from Lessing to Kant that, in tracing this change to the root, we can discover fundamental changes in aesthetic and epistemological consciousness.

The short name for the key moment in Lessing's aesthetics is his "*Absage an den Witz* [abjuration of wit]."[4] This farewell, as we shall see, had better be written "Auf Wiedersehen." Lessing means to abandon a form of representation dominated by a logic of resemblance and simultaneity.

In 1771, writing *Emilia Galotti* as a work illustrating the principles of the *Hamburg Dramaturgy*, Lessing aims to replace or curtail a logic of wit in the representation of life in drama. He favors instead an aesthetic judgment responsive to real purposiveness, to natural causality. Judgment functions as a logic of the enchainment of causes and effects between persons.

When, however, in Kant's *Critique of Judgment*, aesthetic judgment reappears, its character has changed fundamentally. The change involves its reorientation toward the aesthetic object as a fiction, which has an only virtual existence, the judgment being "indifferent to the real existence of the object of this representation (§2.43, *41*).[5] To articulate such an object—a form—no concept can or ought to be produced. Kant's aesthetic judgment proceeds off to one side of real purposes, apart from a logic of motivation between agents and acts verifiable by empirical judgment. Experience, as the standard of aesthetic judgment, gives way to a sense of fictive, aesthetic purposiveness, "subjective-formal purposiveness without purpose."[6]

This reflective judgment advances "freely" from the particular form to the sentiment of what subsumes it. Its career is confirmed by the discovery of a privileged mood, or *Stimmung*—beautiful and sublime forms, for Kant, fundamentally giving rise to moods of complex pleasure. The mood of beautiful and sublime art, a type of feeling without purpose, diverges widely from the goal-directed affects of fear and pity of Lessing's tragic norm. If, in Lessing's aesthetic, feeling confirms a representation of experience en route to its own purging, the mood of the beautiful in Kant aims to be, and to endure as, itself—an attunement of the cognitive faculties in the rhythm of conceptual play. Kant's subordination of wit, as an agency of knowledge in art, to aesthetic judgment, as the judgment of a mood, strips cognitive power from the *Mutterwitz* of genius and brings to an end the eighteenth-century trial of wit. With the *Critique of Judgment*, wit is for a time decisively driven off the German stage although, as an *ars combinatoria*, it makes a brilliant comeback in the art and thought of the Jena Romantics at the turn of the nineteenth century.[7]

How can we begin to understand the Enlightenment critique of the cognitive value of wit? Hans Blumenberg's *Process of Theoretical Curiosity* offers a road in by stressing Lessing's and Kant's sense of the specific individuality of acts of knowledge. Human singularity comes to light and sustains itself in the variable labor each human being expends in the acquisition of knowledge. Lessing's famous apothegm beginning, "If God had locked up all truth in his right hand,"[8] lays emphasis, Blumenberg notes, not on "truth" but rather on the "value of man":

The quantity of truth that ought to be given to mankind is measured not by the inner value of this truth but rather by its effect—of moving and heightening powers of human self-development and self-realization. Here, the "work"-character of truth—the "honest effort" that needs to be expended on it—is fully grasped and appropriated.[9]

Why, according to this sense of knowledge, does wit fall short? Consider a current—and adequate—definition by Bernd Schoeller of one "phenomenon of wit": "An attractive meaning suddenly comes to light, having effortlessly travelled the linguistically briefest 'nonsensical' route."[10] What is the value of a truth thus "effortlesly" revealed if the value of truth is measured precisely by the work put into its acquisition? The speech of the stubborn Patriarch in Lessing's *Nathan der Weise* on the case of an adopted Christian child testifies to this insight: "Let Sir Knight Templar be clear on this point / . . . If the gentleman is / Just making it up, / Then the case recounted / Is a play of wit: and so it does not deserve / The effort of being thought through seriously."[11]

The same distinction between "seriousness [*Ernst*]" and "play [*Spiel*]" emerges in the First Version of Hölderlin's verse drama *The Death of Empedocles* with the aim of reversing their relation in a divine perspective:

They said to me: gods think differently
From mortals. What the one takes to be seriousness
The other takes to be jesting. Divine seriousness
Is spirit and virtue, but for them play is
The tedious time of laboring men.[12]

Human play in the minds of the gods is the very tedium and labor—the unpleasure—that human beings oppose to it.

There develops, then, in the middle of the eighteenth century and afterwards, a concept of the labor that alone produces aesthetic value—an "achievement ethic [*Leistungsethik*]" even in the aesthetic field—whose varieties could perhaps be explained sociologically. But here I shall only be glancing at this connection: I am chiefly interested in analyzing a set of changes in the superstructure. A key change is indicated

in a major text from the *Hamburg Dramaturgy*—the "Thirtieth Piece"—
composed by Lessing on August 11, 1767.

Discussing Corneille's *Rodogune*, Lessing distinguishes the power of
genius that could have fashioned this play from the wit that has merely
botched it. Corneille's historical source material includes the Emperor
Ptolemy, Rodogune, and Cleopatra. Of her crimes, Lessing writes:

> This triple murder should constitute only one action, that has its beginning, its
> middle, and its end in the one passion of the one person. What, therefore, does
> it lack as the subject [or stuff] of a tragedy? For the genius, nothing; for the bun-
> gler [*Stümper*], everything. Here, there is no love, no entanglement, no recogni-
> tion, no unexpected marvelous incident; everything takes its natural course.
> This natural course stimulates the genius and repels the bungler. Only those
> events can occupy the genius that are grounded in one another, that form a
> chain of causes and effects. To refer the former to the latter, to weigh the latter
> against the former, everywhere to exclude chance, to cause everything to occur
> that does occur so that it could not have happened otherwise: this is the thing
> for genius when it works in the field of history and converts the useless treasures
> of memory into nourishment for the soul. Wit, on the contrary, which attends
> not to things that are grounded in one another but to the similar or dissimilar if
> it ventures on a work that should be reserved to genius alone, dwells on events
> that have nothing in common with one another except that they have occurred
> simultaneously. To connect these, to interweave their threads so that we lose the
> one at every moment in following out the other and are toppled from one con-
> sternation into another: this wit can do, and this only.[13]

It is intriguing to reflect that the term "bungler" will have a precisely
antithetical sense in the work studied at the close of this book, Walter
Benjamin's essay on two odes of Hölderlin, although the negative outcome is predictably the same. For Benjamin, the bungler is the poet who
attempts to carry over an experience of life directly into art: "The more
the poet tries to convert without transformation the unity of life into a
unity of art, the plainer it is that he is a bungler. We are used to finding
such shoddy work defended, even demanded, as 'the immediate feeling
of life,' 'warmth of heart,' 'sensibility [*Gemüt*].' "[14]

This crucial passage in Lessing's *Hamburg Dramaturgy* was pointed up
some fifty years ago by Paul Böckmann in a work discussing Lessing's repudiation of the "formal principle of wit."[15] According to Böckmann
the *Hamburg Dramaturgy* contributes importantly to the articulation and
resolution of a crisis in the fate of wit. The language of wit will be replaced—by what other language? By a fuller, deeper symbolic discourse

expressive of genuine convictions and feelings—"true artistic form," "the language of the heart," "the authentic expression of the passions." At a place not far from the "Thirtieth Piece," Böckmann concludes, "the poetic ideal of wit dissolves from within. . . . The world of feeling, of sentiment, of experience breaks into literature."[16] (This was precisely what Benjamin detected in "the feeblest artistic achievement.")[17]

Böckmann's univocally valorizing thesis lives on tenaciously in a certain ideological critique of eighteenth-century ideology,[18] according to which a cultural ideal of "the witty sign [*des witzigen Zeichens*]," founded on "a mathematical form of language"—thus Böckmann— gives way to the authenticity, that is, the nonclarity, of lived experience. The abusive style of such an argument, here attributed to Lessing, was arraigned by Georg Lukács in a related context: "The problem is stylized as an answer, and the alleged fundamental insolubility of the problem [of whether man and his language are intelligible to reason] is construed as a higher form of understanding."[19] But Böckmann's stress on, and privileging of, inwardness and "inner form"[20] is actually very little justified by a text that speaks of "chains of causes and effects" and envisages the poet more readily as natural scientist than as Pietist; see his essential activity of "referring the former to the latter," "weighing off the latter against the former," and so on.[21] Lessing's distinction between wit and genius cannot be inscribed into the binaries of head-vs.-heart or transparency-vs.-symbolization.[22]

The *Hamburg Dramaturgy* asserts, instead, the superiority of one type of understanding to another. I believe it would be correct, anticipating Foucault in *The Order of Things*, to speak of the collision in it of two different epistemes. Lessing's text devalues a *witty* perception of similitude in favor of acts of *judgment* constituting a successive order. This is precisely the order that, according to Foucault, defines the Classical episteme, namely, "the order laid down by thought, progressing naturally from the simple to the complex."[23] Foucault continues:

The activity of the mind will [henceforth] consist in establishing the identities . . . [of things], then the inevitability of the connections with all the successive degrees of a series. Discrimination imposes upon comparison the primary and fundamental investigation of difference: providing oneself by intuition with a distinct representation of things, and apprehending clearly the inevitable connection between one element in a series and that which immediately follows it. (55)

Pace Böckmann, the opposition that Lessing sets up has to do with types
of constructive perception: this emerges most plainly in Lessing's formulation of the same matter in the same imagery in the "Thirty-
Second Piece." The task of the genuine poet is "to discover the hidden
organization of his material and develop/unravel [*entwickeln*] it," so that
"we are everywhere aware of only the most natural, most orderly course
of events" (90–91, *128*). Wit is devalued not vis-à-vis the "heart" but
vis-à-vis a flair for organization.

I stress, then, Lessing's rejection of wit on the grounds of its logic of
simultaneity in time and resemblance in space. We catch in Lessing a distinctive predication of what Foucault calls "this moment in time when
resemblance was about to relinquish its relation with knowledge and
disappear, in part at least, from the sphere of cognition" (17).

For Lessing the logic of wit is a relation of resemblance in excess of,
or to one side of, the power of resemblance to produce knowledge. The
same suspicion attends relations said to be strictly dissimilar, that is,
made of antithetical elements. At the outset of his *Axiomata*, for example, Lessing remarks:

> Every clever distinction can be stated in the form of an antithesis by anyone
> with the least competence in his own language. Because, however, not every an-
> tithesis is founded on a clever distinction—because what is supposed to be a
> devastating bolt of brilliance often turns out to be a mere summer lightning of
> wit—especially among our poets, the term "antithesis" has begun to inspire
> suspicion.[24]

The poetic uses of wit that Lessing discusses in various places always
provoke mistrust. Invariably he opposes wit to one of its betters—"true
genius,"[25] "truth" (a work might have "no wit but much truth"),[26]
"spirit,"[27] "sensibility [*Gemüt*],"[28] lastly, "Nature"[29] (the poems of the
Abbé de Charlieu constitute an exception, for "his wit was Nature").[30]
Wit can be grasped as culture (as in the phrase "the realm of the German
mind [*Witz*]"[31] and, as in the case of Marivaux, "cleverness";[32] but normally it is "light,"[33] "false,"[34] "makes reasons unwelcome,"[35] and is
found only exceptionally in conjunction with "a poetic spirit."[36] Even
"the beauties of Horace's laconic wit" are "barbed."[37] Wit is sooner "li-
centious . . . , derides heaven and morals, and sins against the Muse."[38]
Hence the most that can be hoped for from it is that it become critical of
its own facility. In Lessing's "Scattered Observations on the Epigram"
("Zerstreute Bemerkungen über das Epigramm"), Martial is praised for

that reason: "But how many have the knowledge that alone makes false wit tolerable—which Martial possesses in so high a degree? Martial knows that it is false wit, and does not pretend that it is anything else."[39]

The eighteenth-century definitions of wit in which Lessing's critique participates are various—but almost invariably suspicious. Wit appears as an ambiguous sign, at once a reminiscence of the authoritative cognitive power of similitude and a mark of its supersession and probationary removal to poetry and art. As a result of the increasing prestige of judgment, wit will not linger long there either. In 1690, for example, the point that witty combinations transgress the bounds of truth is marked out as an epistemological concern in Locke's *An Essay Concerning Human Understanding*, "*wit* lying most in the assemblage of *ideas*, and putting those together with quickness and variety, wherein can be found any resemblance or congruity, thereby to make up pleasant pictures and agreeable visions in the fancy."[40] Locke's argument confirms the general picture described by Foucault as follows: "From the seventeenth century, resemblance was pushed out to the boundaries of knowledge, toward the humblest and basest of its frontiers. There, it links up with imagination, with doubtful repetitions, with misty analogies" (71).[41]

Locke's denigration of wit reenters Germany through Sterne's witty inversion of this hierarchy in *Tristram Shandy* (1759–67). Sterne trifles with Locke's authority. In Book 3:20 Sterne mentions Locke as having asserted the difference between wit and judgment and the priority of judgment. Citing fictitious authority, Sterne declares:

> Now, Agelastes (speaking dispraisingly) sayeth, That there may be some wit in it, for aught he knows—but no judgment at all. And Triptolemus and Phutatorius agreeing thereto, ask, How is it possible there should? for that wit and judgment in this world never go together; inasmuch as they are two operations differing from each other as wide as east from west—So, says Locke—so are farting and hiccuping, say I.[42]

The first effect of the rude analogy is to give a powerful emphasis to Sterne's rebuttal. If the royal road to the distinction between wit and judgment leads through the distinction between farting and hiccuping, it is not a road that readers will be eager to take. In this way the alleged opposition of wit and judgment—and the standard primacy of judgment—is deflated for want of unsqueamish defenders. It is impossible, however, to resist Sterne's concern that the famous difference be thought precisely along bodily lines, that is, in light of the different tempos of these faculties. The essence of wit is the explosiveness of its outburst, the abruptness of its impropriety. Something of its swiftness and unpredictability is at hand in the description of Yorick's character as of "mercurial and . . . sublimated composition" (I:11).[43] Wit bursts out with a force that makes reason gasp for breath. To this extent, of course, Sterne continues to hold to the opposition between wit and judgment. "Brisk trotting," he writes, "and slow argumentation, like wit and judgment, are two incompatible movements" (I:10).[44] But if "their rhythms and their pace are different, they are not," notes Henri Fluchère, "incompatible in their function."[45] In "The Author's Preface" to Book III:20, Sterne records his "most zealous wish and fervent prayer . . . that the great gifts and endowments both of wit and judgment may . . . be poured down warm as each of us could bear it . . . into our brains."[46] If Sterne finally emerges as a defender of the indistinction between wit and judgment, we have also seen him turn Locke backside up. Within the terms of the hierarchy, he restores dominance to wit: Sterne's manner of doing it, however, forecasts his futurity in the resurgence of the body in Nietzsche's romantic precursors, for example, as the elusive locus of the faculties.[47] But even as Sterne valorizes wit wittily, the exercise is not itself based on firmly specified distinctions. We can't really be certain, for example, that in his line-up, wit goes with farting and judgment with hiccuping; and the link between wit and the east and judgment and the west can be disrupted by a single bodily about-face.

Sterne's point is to stress the uncertainty of the difference within the alleged opposition, and to this extent he does not appeal to the vanished authority of the *similitudo* but instead anticipates the German Romantics' wit of irony. That link can be further strengthened at the order of Sterne's biologism. His seeming valorization of the fart over the hiccup occurs in a unified field of symptoms in which both terms function as sublimated metonymies of a sort of *Wetterleuchten* (summer lightning) of the body; to this extent they resemble the "*Blitz* [flash]" worshipped by Schlegel. In Novalis, too, wit appears as an "intellectual electricity," for which, however, "solid bodies are necessary."[48]

Paul Mog affirms this biological moment in noting the tumescence of Leibniz's "petites perceptions," the tiny undercurrents of the unconscious famously elaborated around 1670 by le Père Bouhours into an aesthetics of the witlessness of the Germans and the *je ne sais quoi*. For

Mog, "by the time Leibniz's *Nouveau Essais* had posthumously appeared in 1765, the 'petites perceptions' had long since grown big: the theory of the *natural* determination of genius was simply an official confirmation of the bond between aesthetics and insentient nature."[49] This way of putting the bond profiles a constitutive feature of the modern subject,[50] inviting, too, an always politically charged exchange of the terms of natural authority and "the creation and imposition of forms."[51]

If we thus frame and situate a culture of wit by a logic of correspondence and similitude, we will find the topos of its critique at least as far back as Aquinas (if not Heraclitus) and as recently as de Man and Derrida. But it will always be interesting to examine closely the rhetoric with which one or the other of its adversary ideals is put forward for signs of entanglement in its rejected opposite and hence evidence of the persistence of an incompletely suppressed wit. The "Thirtieth Piece" of Lessing's *Hamburg Dramaturgy*—the text I introduced as a prime example of the subordination of wit to genius—itself invites such a reading. I shall restrict myself to the witty similitude that closes its argument.

Lessing's attack on false wit makes use of an extended comparison; like the wit whose artifice he decries, Lessing himself makes use of relations that are "similar or dissimilar." In this manner a paradigmatic textual structure arises that can also be found in Lessing's early comedies *The Young Scholar* (*Der junge Gelehrte*) and *The Freethinker* (*Der Freigeist*).[52] Lessing's attack on false wit is carried out by means of a witty similitude (or in the plays, an extended witty similitude) that disrupts the discursive argument.

The relevant part of the passage from the *Hamburg Dramaturgy* reads: "From the incessant crossing [or "criss-crossing," also "thwarting"] of such threads of opposed colors"—Lessing is referring to the plot-threads in a dramatic material that attract the witty bungler—

there arises a texture [*Kontextur*], which to art is what weavers call *changeant*: a material [or stuff] about which one cannot say whether it is blue or red, green or gold; it is both, it seems this from one side, that from another, a plaything of fashion, an illusionistic toy for children.

Now judge whether the great Corneille has used his material [or stuff] like a genius or like a wit. For this judgment nothing else is required but the application of the axiom disputed by none: genius loves simplicity, and wit complication. (83, *121*)[53]

Lessing's explicit intent is to "destroy" mere wit; to this end he employs a controlled simile secondary to and illustrative of the discursive argument. This figure likens the wit's treatment [*Bearbeitung*] of the "threads" of dramatic material to the weaver's treatment of particolored threads. The authority of this analogy is based on its perspicuousness and on its limited function as an example. It is meant to be clear, and it is not supposed to have an effect after it has made its point—namely, after Lessing has condemned the work of wit as "a plaything of fashion, an illusionistic toy for children."

But the simplicity (*Einfalt*) of Lessing's witty figure is captious: its use will therefore be difficult to control. Consider, first: the weaver treats his raw material, threads, by weaving them into cloth (*Stoff*), in this case, *changeant*. He *begins* with threads and *ends* with cloth. It would seem that so too does the witty dramatist: he begins with "threads" (of action) and then treats them by weaving them into a "tragic stuff [*Stoff*]." But in one sense this analogy is tangled. The wit *began* with a real *Stoff*, with the historical story of Rodogune and Cleopatra. Even if this material struck him as utterly threadbare, still it was for him the stuff of his play. This is a first complication: the witty parallel reverses the relation of raw material to product found in the literal part of the parallel. The weaver's material is the elaborated product of his work, unlike the wit's, which, as the "stuff of tragedy [*Stoff einer Tragödie*]," is something given to him. This is the analogy's point of reversal, which I stress, because it cannot be limited to the similitude proper: it produces knots throughout the rest of the text. For when, in the next paragraph, we are asked to say whether the great Corneille treated his material more like a genius or a wit, we are at a loss to decide what the thing is which is here called "material [*Stoff*]": the word has itself turned into a sort of *changeant*.

This moment of indetermination also has a retroactive effect. Consider: the wit, like the weaver, weaves threads together to produce a sort of material, "an artistic texture [*eine künstliche Kontextur*]." The point is plain why this second sort of material is inferior: it is an artificial supplement—inauthentic, a makeshift—created out of the wit's blindness to the fact that what he has before him from the outset is the genuine stuff of tragedy, authentic by virtue of its "natural course." The distinction between the genius and the wit is the important distinction between a tragic material that is natural and primordial and one that is artificial and derivative. Well and good, but the material that occupies the genius is also neither natural nor primordial. It consists of "chains of causes and effects." By what queer metabolism (*Stoffwechsel*) do "chains" come to be part of a natural substance? They have had to be hammered out of the "useless treasures of memory [*unnütze Schätze des Gedächtnisses*]." This then is the scene of genuine origins—namely, the useless, *das Unnütze*. The material worked by the genius—its "chains of causes and effects"—had to be manufactured by him. So like the material that was and was not material for the wit, being even in its raw state a kind of *changeant*, so too the genius's material is and is not authentic nature, being also in its raw state, with respect to its natural status, a sort of *changeant*. Much of this difficulty is brought about by the analogy that substitutes the sense of material as product for the sense of material as origin and which dominates the discursive argument.

From now on the argument never stops spinning. Wit is guilty of unsettling things: it entangles theses, partly by inducing a reversal in the positions of the terms whose sequence constitutes the argument, partly by bringing to light and focusing an already existing uncertainty in the distinction between the terms that make up this sequence. In order henceforth to produce secure results, the determination of truth must be on guard against the seductions of a witty logic. For wit does not easily lend itself to the discourse of enlightenment. The intent of subordinating wit runs the risk of releasing an unsettling rhetorical force throughout the entire text.

· ᜶ ·

In his *Anthropology from a Pragmatic Point of View,* Kant defines wit by translating into pure Kantianese a view current throughout most of the eighteenth century: "Wit pairs off (assimilates) dissimilar ideas [*Vorstellungen*] that are often far removed from one another according to the law of imagination (of association) and is a peculiar ability to find similarities [*Verähnlichungsvermögen*], which belongs to understanding (as the power of knowing the universal), insofar as it brings objects under genera."[54] Of course, this definition applies only to pair-bonding wit—"the disguised priest," according to Jean Paul, "who unites every couple [*der verkleidete Priester, der jedes Paar traut*]" and, to be sure, especially those couples—as Friedrich Theodor Fischer adds—"whose marriage the relatives (the true methodical context) refuse to sanction [*deren Verbindung die Verwandten (der methodische wahre Zusammenhang) nicht dulden wollen*]."[55] In Kant, however, something more is meant by "*Mutter*witz" than a faculty that does not gladly tolerate unpromising unions. It is more than a faculty for producing affinities and more than a faculty for subsuming things present-at-hand. It refers to the entire stock of general and inborn rules of understanding.[56] Its specific character is nothing less than the faculty of judgment. Thereafter Kant undertakes in the *Critique of Judgment* to establish the principle of the specific character of *Mutterwitz* itself—namely, objective purposiveness in nature and subjective purposiveness in beautiful art.

There is something national and territorial about Kant's *Critique*, about his fundamental and organized project of giving native grounds to that subjectivity of aesthetic feeling which French aestheticians like Batteux treated rationally and prescriptively and English aestheticians like Burke treated physiologically and empirically. Kant founds aesthetics on the *Gemüt* which prescribes the law unto itself—that law of self-reflection engendering a play of forms. Aesthetics according to such a rule, which Kant was the first to codify and legitimize, was called by Dilthey "the German aesthetic,"[57] with the result that we may say of the *Critique of Judgment* that in subordinating the category of wit to *Mutter*witz, it brings about in aesthetics a *mutterländische Kehre*, a turning to the motherland.

The Kantian "turn" also constitutes a turn within the aesthetics dominant in eighteenth-century Germany in the period between Lessing and Kant. This development, which defines the root circuit of the changes in the contest between the faculties of wit and judgment, has been construed intellectualistically by Rolf Grimminger. Grimminger begins by recalling that Lessing's aesthetics concern "the affective possibilities of individuals . . . as these possibilities are inscribed in social existence. Aesthetic pleasure consists of a unified relation of sympathy and identification with the work of art." In this way art acquires, by means of catharsis, a socially constructive function. Now, addressing the dialectic of the reversal, Grimminger writes:

At the time of German classicism [*Klassik*], [pleasure] had become the market principle of an entertainment literature grown over some twenty years to monstrous proportions. Contemporaries attacked its "barbarously" moving "sentimentality" [*Empfindelei*, Kant] precisely because of its possibly abusive effects on practical life. The classical intellectual elite then sets itself off against it: they re-aristocratize aesthetic form to a new ideal of dignified reflective pleasure in the work of art and those portions of existence that befit it.[58]

However one understands this thesis—whether the transition from Lessing to Kant is to be grasped as the passage from a more nearly democratic aesthetics to an elitist one, or from an affective aesthetics to an intellectualist one—its persuasiveness finally depends on the sociological similitude that informs the category of re-aristocratization. Hence I find Grimminger's thesis too witty.[59] I see the specific achievement of Kant's aesthetics otherwise: Kant secures, foregrounds, and heightens an aspect of Lessing's *Hamburg Dramaturgy* that still lay half-hidden in the texts with which we have been concerned. The project of the *Critique of Judgment* is to found aesthetics. Kant's ultimate horizon is the ontological status of the beautiful artwork in its distinction from nature, even when, in the course of stressing its constitutive lack of intelligible being, he raises the possibility that such questioning cannot produce conceptually satisfying results.[60] Because this claim is a contentious one, I would prefer to put it more tactfully: the net effect of Kant's aesthetics is to detach beauty from any possible object as its attribute—and to layer it instead, as the analogue of a securely grounded cognitive function, into the mind at a deep, constitutive place. Even when the charge on this point is reduced, Kant's concern with the being or nonbeing of the beautiful work of art shows through.

What's significant in this is the radically formal, fictive character of the beautiful work of art, giving to "fictive" the following meaning: the mode of being of an object that elicits from the imagination an attitude "indifferent to the real existence of the object of this representation" (§2.43, *41*). For such forms no concept can be found. This condition applies most cogently to poetry, where, according to Kant,

everything is straight and above board. It shows its hand: it desires to carry on a mere entertaining play with the imagination, and one consonant, in respect of form, with the laws of understanding; and it does not seek to steal upon and ensnare the understanding with a sensuous presentation. (§53.193, *184*)

Lessing is generally of two minds on the question of what poetry wants, as I have suggested in the course of reading the "Thirtieth Piece" as a text of wit. Lessing, we recall, envisages the artwork as an intentional representation of a natural, orderly movement of life, perceptible to the genius (and to the spectator) as "chains of causes and effects." In this sense, of course, the work of art is an interesting affair, calling for verification by empirical judgment of the natural and necessary character of the order constituting it. This way Lessing is able to lay witty em-

phasis on the difference between a work of art of genius and the only artificial character of the product of wit. But the status of these "chains of
causes and effects" was hybrid from the start.[61] Indeed, the "Thirty-
Second Piece" states plainly that the poet's concern is with "*inventing*
[*erfinden*] a sequence of causes and effects" (my emphasis). The constructed character of such aesthetic fictions—"poetic inventions," *Er-
findungen*, or *Erdichtungen*, as Lessing also calls them—is plain, for their
status as possibilities is based above all *not* on "mere historical truth [*der
bloßen historischen Wahrheit*]" (32, 47).[62] If, then, on the one hand, such
constellations are offered to empirical judgment for verification, on the
other hand, as invented fictions for which there is no model, they escape
judgment. As "poetic truths" they can be verified by feeling but not empirically judged.[63]

Consider, now, the different types of judgment called for, first, by
the artwork whose task, according to Lessing, is to imitate nature, even
if an only selective nature true to the "nature of our feelings and emotions [*Seelenkräfte*]"; and, second, by the artwork whose task, according
to Kant, is to bring the cognitive faculties into harmony with one another through a play of fictive forms. In the first case, that of imitation,
judgment is concerned with the object for its fidelity to an original—
even when the so-called original is an "abstraction [*Absonderung*]" from
raw nature, a sort of silhouette ("Seventieth Piece," 171, 276–77).[64] In
the second, in the case of the fiction, judgment is concerned with the
object solely for its attunement to attributes of the subject: namely,
those governing the possibility of the cognition of any object whatsoever.

The passage from the aesthetics of Lessing to the aesthetics of Kant
leads away from a principle—dominant in Lessing's view—of discursive fidelity to exemplary nature. This fidelity is based on a perceptible,
causally structured sequence of actions. The passage leads toward a pleasure principle, based on the fitness of an object to produce a felt *Stimmung* of the cognitive faculties, a sort of *sentiment de l'existence intel-
lectuelle*.[65]

I hope also to have defined in the aesthetic superstructure a moment
of radical fictionalization of the aesthetic object intimately tied to an
unheard-of valorization of mood. Kant concedes to mood, in the
words of Walter Biemel, "a function of disclosure that had been attributed only to logical cognition. Kant implicitly gives mood a significance

that, only recently, in the work of Heidegger and Scheler, has received the explanation that is its due."⁶⁶

We can stop to review the stages of the aesthetic and epistemological self-consciousness that have prepared this moment and made it necessary. In passing from wit to logical judgment to aesthetic judgment, we pass from the pseudocognitive ("the bungler"), to the logically cognitive (Lessing), to the nonlogically cognitive (Kant)—from flat resemblance via a logic of causes and effects to a subjectively purposive play of images and concepts, whose distinction is not the uptake of cognition but rather the aesthetic (and hence political) pleasure of imputing consensus. Wit, as the faculty producing cognitive judgments on the basis of similarity, is put into question, tested, and rejected. In a countering movement in Lessing, that judgment is valorized which aims to verify the plausibility of causally structured sequences of actions on the basis of empirical norms. This activity is consistent with the principal function of judgment—with *Mutterwitz*—which subsumes particular effects under causes as their genera. The stability of this aesthetic state of affairs, however, is threatened in Lessing by the basically hybrid character of the work of art. For its being extends from the one pole of the natural product, which tends to remain true to its origin, to another, a poetized nature, which is without a model. Out of this tension arises Kant's act of clarification and concentration by which the aesthetic object is defined as fundamentally fitted only to a subjective judgment founded on moods.

We conclude by turning to the place in Kant's *Critique of Judgment* where the power of wit is most plainly diminished. Here we should recall the Enlightenment insistence on the labor essential to the pursuit of truth. At first Kant defines the activity of aesthetic judgment as being without cognitive interest: it involves only "the feeling which the subject has of itself and of the manner in which it is affected by the representation" (§1.42, *40*). But such quietude does not extend far in the exposition of the aesthetic judgment, and an (unwarranted) impression of its unworldliness or otherworldliness can be obtained by abstracting from the *Critique of Judgment* but not by actually reading it. At the end of the "Dialectic," Beauty is graduated with the degree of Symbol of Morality. And indeed it has been plain, from as early on as the "Analytic of the Beautiful," that the Third Critique is mediated by the primacy of practical reason within Kant's system as a whole. The logic, indeed, the drama of the *Critique of Judgment* is of the moral education of the infant aesthetic judgment. A being conceived as pure, contemplative, and disinterested is increasingly burdened with empirical and practical duties.

The aesthetic judgment may not work—at first. In aesthetic experience, the cognitive faculties celebrate Sabbath—for a time.[67] The aesthetic judgment is allowed to play but not for long and never entirely. For already in the Second Moment of the "Analytic of the Beautiful"— in §8 and then explicitly in §9—aesthetic judgment is assigned the task of constituting the entire human community while it plays. In the aesthetic judgment society resurges as the constituted object of a presumption—of an *Ansinnen*. No such thing as aesthetic pleasure could arise unless that pleasure can be imputed to every other rational human being: "it looks for confirmation, not from concepts, but from the concurrence of others" (§8.56, 54). This imputation is in Kant the social work of the solitary, the "*Hausarbeit der Seele* [the soul's domestic duties]." Kant's aesthetic judgment is the tribute paid by the lonely man to sociality. Here, then, *pace* Grimminger, Kant's aesthetics displays its non-aristocratic character. Indeed, Kant's insistence on the communally creative function of aesthetic judgment is so important that he is willing to make this point even at the cost of violating the logical coherence of his demonstration. (The apparent contradiction is taken up in detail in Chapter 2.) Logically speaking, Kant can hardly impose on aesthetic pleasure the precondition that it be generally imputable at the same time that he defines it as a feeling which gives pleasure immediately—without concepts and interests. This moment marks the onset in the *Critique of Judgment* of a growing intellectualization, and moralization, of aesthetic experience. Kant has postponed for as long as he can attaching work-ethical values to aesthetic experience. But now, the wit, who flaunts useless wordplay, is simply banned from the community of ethical-minded critics:

For where civil laws, the right of individual persons, or the permanent instruction and determination of men's minds to a correct knowledge and a conscientious observance of their duty is at stake, then it is below the dignity of an undertaking of such moment to exhibit even a trace of the exuberance of wit and imagination. (§53.192, *183–84*)

The *Critique of Judgment* prescribes the conditions for the coexistence within aesthetic activity of (1) an autonomy,[68] arising from the fictive character of the work of art, and (2) a productive, socially useful character. This connection of ideas, which could sound paradoxical, acquires a solid existence in eighteenth- and nineteenth-century literary self-consciousness, in (1) the development of *l'art pour l'art* and the sense of "writing" as an intransitive verb, along with (2) the developing social consciousness implied by the replacement of the term *Dichter* by *Schriftsteller*. Gerhard Kurz stresses the "work character, the labor character [*Arbeits- und Mühecharakter*] of art" in the nineteenth century: "'Writing [*Schreiben*]' is at once the most materialist and the emptiest definition of literature, defining literature in its aspects of *poiesis*, artistic production, and labor."[69] (Kurz could well be thinking of Flaubert.) At this point the concept of a self-sufficient wit is finished.

Later aesthetics develop a dimension that I have not yet profiled in the aesthetics of Lessing and Kant: namely, a heightened sense of the temporality and historicity of the work of art and its reception. The beginning of this consciousness is already present, however, in Lessing's and Kant's repudiation of wit. Lessing arraigns wit for its blindness to its object, which, in its exteriority, like the "rushing away of a fatal current," is a temporal movement—"a natural movement"—and in its interiority, for Lessing, a movement of "pity and terror." For Kant it is a temporal play of moods constituting the "historical identity" of the subject.[70]

This crucial heightening of temporal and historical consciousness is won at the cost of the *similitudo*, the cognitive figure that once shaped, through essentially spatial resemblance, the syntax of wit. Supposing it fruitful to want to go on repeating this rejection, what hope would there be of achieving a logic consistently transcending correspondence?

Futile or not, this intention informs the effort repeatedly made to think past *adequatio*, past correspondence, as the model of truth. Indeed, one could characterize many of the major thought-adventures of the twentieth century as attempts to think in a way radically different from a thinking by correspondence.[71] Heidegger's *Being and Time* is in various ways an encyclopedia of the types of critique leveled at the syntax of wit: consider, for instance, Heidegger's category *Dasein*—the radically individual existent, cast wholly back onto itself—and Heidegger's critique of truth as *adequatio* and his pushing back of the "as"-structure to a precognitive level.[72] Consider, too, the passage of Wittgenstein of the

Tractatus to Wittgenstein of the *Philosophical Investigations*, a movement meaning to resist thinking in symmetrical and analogous models. Consider, further, Benjamin's valorization of allegory over symbol in the *Origin of the German Mourning Play* and Kafka's "sliding paradox," which proceeds not "by making comparisons [*vergleichsweise*]" but "allusively [*andeutungsweise*]" and hence expresses Kafka's aversion to the "metaphors that cause [him] to despair of writing," as well as his "repugnance for antitheses."[73] More recently, of course, there is Derrida's assault on thinking in structures of binary opposition. About the style of all these writers—of Heidegger, Wittgenstein, Kafka, and Benjamin (omitting *One-Way Street*) or Derrida (before 1972)—few readers would be inclined to say that it is basically "witty."[74]

These rigorous thought-experiments, which continue to attack resemblance as the foundation of truth, derive important impulses from Kant without following him. For, unlike Kant, they tend to undo even the minimal systematicity of intelligible discourse as well as to devalue a sense of the primacy of interpretive communities. Of course, it is plain that such demolition work must follow from a critique of the cognitive model of correspondence. For, how, indeed, could there be a general intelligibility if not on the basis of resemblances, and how could there be society, if not as the place where such resemblances are instituted and maintained? It would also seem impossible to get beyond the invasively witty structure of polemical writing against wit. Each effort to purge language of metaphors and analogies generates a few new ones; no degree of vigilance is proof against the fascination of similitude. This point will come as no surprise. How can knowledge be understood if not as the assimilation of disparities—as the imposition of identity, by means of resemblance, so as to create uniformities?[75]

But we should reflect again on this effort to resist the creation of identity by the imposition of resemblance on what is disparate, that is, to resist the colonization of differences.[76] For this resistance, Lessing's and Kant's critique of wit is exemplary. Consider the misery of a leveling thought when the well-being of society depends on the right of everyone to make a difference—to "distinguish" himself or herself and in this way "be different."[77] Too many crimes, not just of rhetoric, have been committed in the name of the logic of wit for the sake of extirpating the individual. The play with assimilation easily runs wild, and hence wit is no laughing matter. Fortunately, however, when we grow careless, wit itself takes pains to show up the reckless assertion of resemblances as some sort of a joke.[78]

• ⟞ •

"No society could exist without rhetoric," notes Hans-Georg Gadamer, in a remark that could serve to head a postscript to the foregoing.[79] But it is clear that there is one sort of rhetoric our academic community means to do without: the discourse of wit. Richard Rorty's famous citation of the values key to the moral constitution of postmodern society—Irony, Contingency, Solidarity—is striking for the parts of the Kantian enterprise it leaves out.[80] Kant's dislike of one common meaning of rhetoric as the "exuberance of wit" would exclude irony from the social order of law, rights, and education. The attempt to drive out contingencies from aesthetic experience by means of the logic of judgment has a purpose: to maintain such experience as the source of a feeling of solidarity. But if by irony Rorty means basically a consciousness nurtured by aesthetic play, his program is the same as Kant's: to find a reason for solidarity where one seems hardest to find.

The project of reconnecting art and the feeling of human solidarity, after the loss of the Enlightenment's generalized man, is a pressing one. The thing this task is up against, however, is a two-centuries'-long misreading of Kant as a formalist in aesthetic matters. I say this in a critical atmosphere laden with the charge that the serious misreading of Kant is the politicized one, which makes the alleged perfection of aesthetic disinterestedness a way-stage to the absolute state (the much-decried aesthetic ideology). But this concern, in its eagerness to play a rigorous Kant off against a muddled Schiller, erases from Kant's text even nonincriminating traces of political thought. In doing so, however, it overlooks the main point: for Kant aesthetic form is a function of feeling, and this feeling cannot be what it must be unless it is imputed to every one. This is the empathetic, politically constructive function of Kant's aesthetic form.

The Third Critique functions as a wider source of aesthetic thought than the one thing that the formalist perspective makes of it. What is at stake is a view on the self-reflexive character of art other than that put forward, for example, in the early work of Paul de Man. For him the "self-reflecting mirror-effect" in "a work of fiction" "asserts" a certain awareness of its own "fictional nature"—of its "separation" and its "divergence" from "empirical reality." The distinction of aesthetic form is its consciousness of the disparity between itself, "as a sign, from a meaning that depends for its existence on the constitutive activity of this sign."[81] Since this awareness is one that reproduces itself in the alerted reader, the outcome is a sense of the solitude of the fiction—of its standing-apart from socially constituted reality—and hence of the reader's own solitary inhabitation of a void. For "literary language"—as another, related essay of de Man has it—"does not fulfill a plenitude but originates in the void that separates intent from reality."[82]

It is otherwise for Kant. Certainly, for Kant, the awareness produced by the work of beautiful art is self-reflexive; the work moves the spectator into an inescapable attitude of self-reflection. He reflects on and finds a pleasurable attunement of the conceptual faculties, which he must then attribute to every other spectator. The thrust of the experience of fiction is consciousness of a moment generally imputable; the factor of imputability is the enabling condition of aesthetic experience. We could speak here of the "bliss of imputation." The goal of aesthetic self-reflection is the experience of virtual community; the beautiful fiction conduces the spectator to a self-reflection in the mirror of an *a priori* enabling experience of other spectators.

In this light de Man's view of the solitude of aesthetic self-reflection appears to be an aberration of an impulse of the greatest importance in Kant. De Man's bias is so pronounced that his later work—the essay on Kleist's *Marionette Theater*, for example—in effect redefines the literary fiction that produces, or is said to produce, social cohesion as the (bad) *aesthetic* pure and simple (leaving room in his system only for the literary fiction that is principally nonaesthetic). He now considers the bearing of the aesthetic inescapably social—and pernicious; it is literary fiction in bad faith, attempting, precisely, to close the distance genuinely constitutive of literature: namely, the distance between the fiction, as purely and simply the nonexistent, and empirical reality. But Kant's example shows us, at the origin of the thesis of the self-reflexivity of fiction, how self-reflection might and indeed must contain a bearing on social reality. It evokes in every reader of the beautiful fiction the existence of fellow consciousnesses entirely sane, a whole society of such consciousness, all the time preserving in aesthetic awareness a dimension of irreducible solitude. Its social dimension exists as an imputation;

it is not an empirical certainty that might be won on the basis of individual experience. It is hypothetical, it is communal, it constitutes the individual consciousness; without it there could not be an experience of the beautiful, and without it no human being could suppose he were at home in the world.

2

WHAT IS RADICAL IN KANT'S "CRITIQUE OF AESTHETIC JUDGMENT"?

The Thorough Who Get to the Bottom of Things
A scholar, I? Oh, hold this word!—
I'm merely *heavy*—weigh many a pound!
I fall, and never cease to fall
Until I finally hit the ground!
—Friedrich Nietzsche, *The Gay Science*

What is radical in Kant's "Critique of Aesthetic Judgment"?[1] This is not an easy question to answer. For in trying to get to the root of Kant's essay, we come up against a text deeply resistant to such a thrust, a work whose refrain throughout is: "Since taste [is] at bottom [*da aber der Geschmack im Grunde*] . . . something *else*, taste must be supplied with yet another ground.

The particular phrase I've quoted, "since taste [is] at bottom," is found in §60, where it is important by virtue of its position. This section concludes the "Critique of Aesthetic Judgment"—or, to be more accurate—at once concludes it and doesn't conclude it, for what it concludes is actually an *Anhang*, a supplement, and it is not certain that a "supplement" concludes anything. This section goes on to say that the ground of the aesthetic judgment is the "making-sensory [*Versinnlichung*]" of moral ideas. Kant puts forward this claim even though all the candidates for the founding position up until this point have been nonmoral. Thus, as we read in sequence from the beginning of "The Critique of Aesthetic Judgment" past the "Analytic of the Beautiful," we find the basis of the aesthetic judgment defined, first, as the form of an object as it is "estimated on mere reflection" (43, *40*); then, more radically, as the "form of the finality [*Zweckmäßigkeit*] of an object" (62, *59*); then, more radically still, as the activity of the subject with respect to the enlivening of its cognitive powers (143, *137*). This deepening of the basis can be extended further—via a reflection on the fundamental attunement of the cognitive powers required for concept formation; via a reflection on the pleasurable awareness of the unimpeded imputability of such harmonies to fellow judgers—until this sequence, not as deep or radical as it might be, circles round back to that "basis of unity [*Grund der Einheit*]" alluded to at the outset in the "Introduction"—to that "ground" of unity or substrate of the supersensible, unifying the supersensible that underlies the concept of nature with the supersensible that underlies the concept of freedom (14, *11*).

This circular journey is certainly one revolution in Kant's aesthetics, but it does not really provide a new beginning. That is because, in the "Introduction," Kant defines this very "field of the supersensible" as the "inaccessible" field wherein "we find no ground [*Boden*] for ourselves" and to which "our theoretical knowledge" cannot in the slightest be extended. So, if the idea of finding a radical foundation means searching forward for a ground for aesthetic judgment, we would then have to begin all over again and search forward, so to speak, in the opposite direction. That is, we would have to hearken back continually to the "Introduction," where we've been alerted to the relentless provisionality of each proffered solution.

Even so, this impasse is in many ways instructive. It reminds us, first of all, that Kant's various foggy bottoms, in their variety and in their heterogeneousness, cannot finally be fitted into one another; they cannot be subsumed. The "Critique of Aesthetic Judgment" is too internally various, complicated by concerns too disparate. The disparity is especially evident in the gap between the epistemological question of judgments and their validity (with its own interesting, worrisome inconsistencies) and the systematic and foundational question of the position of judgment (the faculty) within the project of all three Critiques. This second question involves the relation of the faculty of judgment to the concept of nature and the concept of freedom.[2]

The search for the bottom goes awry, because to inquire into the metaphysical substrate of judgment is to seek to penetrate what Kant has determined to leave "obscure [*unbekannt*]"—"obscure" being the way in which "in the supersensible the theoretical faculty gets bound up into unity with the practical" (224, *214*). The substrates of freedom and nature are radically joined "in an intimate and obscure manner." This obscure manner therefore constitutes the ground—and grounds it, one could say, by keeping it obscure.

The question of what is radical in the "Critique of Aesthetic Judgment" has to be understood differently. Here we could try to catch at the elusive character of this work on the very model of the Kantian *aesthetic idea*. The Critique, we recall, does not produce a concept of the beautiful form; instead, it "opens out for the mind [*Gemüt*] a prospect onto a visually indeterminate, unsurveyable field [*ein unabsehbares Feld*] of associated ideas" (177–78, translation modified, *169*). In the region of aesthetic judgment, the "aesthetic idea" environing it "allows a great deal that is unnameable, to be thought onto [. . . the concept] [*die ästhetische Idee läßt viel Unnennbares hinzudenken*]" (179, *171*). Hence, the more appropriate figure for the radicalness of Kant's "Critique of Aesthetic Judgment" might be this infinitely extensible field of associations—without borders—rather than the vertical vector of movement toward a bottom. My title might therefore better read, "What Is Radically Associable in Kant's Third Critique?"

Now, one important association, one that cannot be overlooked or go unfelt, links what Kant says is "the key idea" in the Critique of Taste with how Kant *goes about arguing* for it—in short, how the intelligibility of the key to the Critique of Taste is itself keyed to the kind of intelligibility that goes with the circular manner in which Kant defines aesthetic judgment in the course of the Critique.

According to Kant, the key question of the Critique is, "In the judgment of taste, is the feeling of pleasure posterior to judging the object?" And the answer, for Kant, in §9, is yes, the feeling of pleasure is posterior, although this posteriority, as we shall see, is at bottom circular (though by no means meaningless).

This is the place where I intend my associating to get radical, for here I shall try to enlarge and complicate this key to the Critique of Taste, which has to do with the succession of moments within the judgment of taste.[3] This key to the Third Critique will fit no doors unless it is itself fitted out with an awareness of the circular way in which it has been produced. But things get truly radical when this doublet of associations is introduced into another field that crosses through the entire Critique of Taste and which, in my view, is finally the most irresistibly associable of its moments. It takes us to the center of Kant's argument. I am concerned with the question of the intentionality of the aesthetic judgment, the question of that disposition or intent that produces, in response to an object, a "form" fitted to subsumption in aesthetic judgment rather than a "manifold" fitted to subsumption in a conceptual judgment or concept.

This most compelling question in and about the critique reads: Why, in relation to something other than itself, does the mind seek and find disinterested, animating pleasure rather than the sobering labor of the concept—a question about intentionality that can and must arise because both aesthetic and conceptual subsumption involve exactly the same faculties (of conceptuality and imagination), faculties that, for both types of subsumption, are mutually attuned in exactly the same (optimal) way; or, in other words, they share the same mood (*Stimmung*). No ascertainable quantity or quality in the aesthetic object determines the manner in which it is "read," whether as an object of conceptual understanding or a form giving aesthetic pleasure. It is true that "the *beautiful* . . . requires the representation of a certain Quality of the Object, that permits also of being understood and reduced to concepts, (although in the aesthetic judgment is not so reduced)" (§29.117, *113*). But the decision about whether to read this quality of the object conceptually or aesthetically is not itself determined by a quality of the object. The thrust, the decision, comes from the subject; hence the judgment must be guided by a certain disposition and anticipation, by temporal tension.

We are (in Heidegger's words) addressing the fore-structure of the aesthetic judgment. Can the difference between the activities of conceptual judgment and aesthetic judgment be defined essentially in terms of temporality? What is the temporal character of the fore-structure of the aesthetic? Can it be clarified by reference to the circular temporality of Kant's narrative?

Before attempting to answer these questions, we should be sure we have a good grip on them. So let us go over once again the various fields, unlimited spaces, and circular modes of thought they involve. I am proposing to associate two moments of circularity in the Third Critique in order to think of them together as heuristically potent. The first is found in Kant's claim in §9 of the Analytic, which he terms the "key to the Critique . . . , worthy of all attention." Here Kant argues that aesthetic pleasure *follows* rather than *precedes* an act of reflective judgment—an act that occurs with respect to the attunement of imagination and understanding. The validity of aesthetic judgment (the legitimacy of bliss) is based on an awareness of the harmonious attunement of the cognitive faculties—of a self, in Walter Benjamin's phrase, "at one with itself in its consciousness [*mit sich selbst einstimmend in Bewußtsein*]."[4] This attunement (*Einstimmung, Stimmung*) of the faculties arises as a state of mind imputable to every other rational being. And it is only with the discovery that this judgment on harmony can be generally imputed that aesthetic delight arises unchecked.

The validity of the aesthetic judgment is grounded not on the quality of an inaugural delight but rather on a reflection on the attunement of the faculties. This attunement is the condition of the aesthetic and therefore imputable to every beholder capable of judgment. The aesthetic judgment projects a time of complex pleasure, one that follows the judgment and finally validates it.

So much, so far, for §9. But what we are now getting involved in is the circularity constituting the famous "contradiction" in the Third Critique. For, from the outset, Kant has affirmed the firstness, and not the secondariness, of the sentiment of delight (*interesseloses Wohlgefallen*), its immediacy with respect to the aesthetic form-object. The possibility of delight depends on a detachment from interest, on disinterestedness. No particular judgment, no particular interest, may intervene between the apprehension of a form and the sentiment of delight on the basis of which aesthetic judgment arises; and it is just because of this nonintervention of moral or cognitive interests that pleasure can be validating.

Such is the perplexity that Kant now puts before us. Aesthetic delight is immediate—preceding and giving a basis to aesthetic judgment. How, then, can it also be conditioned, made to arise only from the judgment as to the universal imputability of an attunement of imagination and understanding?

Walter Biemel asserts that we really have no reason to be disconcerted by this apparent breach in the logic of successiveness. For Kant's aim—he declares—in this disputed §9 is to organize aesthetic judgment not principally in terms of successiveness but in terms of "structure." "The procedure," writes Biemel, "is not intended temporally—Kant is not concerned with a psychological analysis of what comes 'earlier' and what comes 'later.' The analysis is structural; it deals with the question of the condition of the possibility of the judgment of taste."[5]

Thus, in the late 1950's, as we now know well, "the condition of possibility" went structural. But even structures, if they are to be intelligible, must be organized on lines of generality and hierarchy. Something must still come "first," have priority by virtue of the factor of inclusiveness. Something, however, in the aesthetic response initially stated in the Critique to be foundational has turned out to be secondary and derivative.[6] Kant now wants pleasure to follow the general imputability of a state of mind.

Like every attentive reader of the Third Critique, Biemel is captivated by the initial economy of Kant's argument and then disconcerted by the reshuffled primacy of its moments. He recovers his footing by proposing, so to speak, a sublime category: pleasure can still be assured of its prime status if grasped as a "mediated-immediate reflection-pleasure [*vermittelte-unmittelbare Reflexionslust*]."[7] But, we mutter, if mediated, it isn't disinterested. Biemel's answer is called "solution by neologism": it cannot lead us out of this impasse into the pleasure of the sublime.[8]

In an important book, *Kant and the Claims of Taste*, Paul Guyer proposes several different solutions to the difficulty.[9] One is to dismiss the paradox altogether. In this troubling §9, Kant gives prime place to the moment of communicability, the imputability of a state of mind. This is simply a mistake, says Guyer; it does not fit in with the rest of the Critique. It is there only as a remainder, an obsessional holdover from Kant's philosophical immaturity, when Kant made all civilized pleasure dependent on that sociability allowing for "the communication of a 'perfection.'"[10] This would leave the initial moment of spontaneous, immediate delight the exclusive determining factor of the judgment.

But this is not the conclusion that Guyer wants to arrive at, since it says exactly the opposite of what Kant says in §9. Guyer needs to show that Kant's own account is coherent, and so he writes, more interestingly, that the contradiction does not have to be eliminated since it is only apparent. It can be explained away by trisection.

Consider the determining moments of the aesthetic judgment—(1) "simple" or "mere" reflection, with its attendant pleasure; and (2) the judgment as to its imputability, whose equivalent sentence is "This form x is beautiful, and you will think so." The reflective judgment—item (2)—is not really one thing, says Guyer; it is two-sided; and so the relation between it and item (1), which is crucial, involves not two but three terms. To judge from Guyer's remarks, the reflective judgment would look like the last page of a closed book, printed on both sides. Recto, facing inside, is its reflection on what has gone before, item (1), the simple bliss of immediate perception. Verso, facing outside at the bottom of the page and concluding the whole movement of aesthetic reception, is the complex pleasure that guarantees the judgment. What Kant means to say, according to Guyer—and what he could have said more plainly—is that while (1) "simple" or mere reflection is accompanied by pleasure and hence, in a certain sense, pleasure precedes the aesthetic judgment, as foreplay, it is finally only (2) the complex reflection on the social communicability of that pleasure that produces the judgment proper. This, in turn, gives rise for the first time to the real, complex pleasure, the big bang whose posteriority Kant calls the "key" to the Critique. This model of reflection, continues Guyer, explains the "key to the critique of taste."[11]

But I cannot agree that splitting up the pleasure of reflection into types (1) and (2) "removes the appearance of paradox,"[12] for this step devalues, etiolates, or occludes the first moment of pleasure. The allegedly first, simple reflection is more than the prod of pleasure. It is an already fully charged epiphany of pleasure; it is, in the words of an expert reader, Richard Acquila, a reflection "internally involved in aesthetic pleasure."[13] For in this same §9, Kant fundamentally identifies the harmonious activity of the faculties producing aesthetic pleasure with that pleasure itself. Kant writes: "The quickening of both faculties (imagination and understanding) . . . is the sensation whose universal communicability is postulated by the judgment of taste" (§9. 60, 57). It is clear from this passage that the attempt to situate decisive aesthetic pleasure *posterior* to the quickening of both faculties in reflection is high-handed.

We have been returned to the paradox of §9. Using Guyer's own language against him, I hope not churlishly, it appears that Kant would indeed have complicated matters inextricably in making pleasure "the consequence of the judgment of communicability even though that judgment must in fact presuppose the feeling of pleasure in order to have any subject at all."[14]

Aesthetic feeling comes first. But then, according to the Kant of §9, something called aesthetic feeling emerges in second place. Aesthetic feeling constitutes a circle, producing by means of *its own narrative* an "*unabsehbarer* [visually indeterminate, unsurveyable]" space. For on the circle as a figure of thought, propositional moments, like points on the circumference, lose the elementary distinction of sequence. Kant's narrative points up the simultaneously backward-and-forward-tending movement of aesthetic pleasure. His demonstration is circular, because points on a circle are not intrinsically first or second: their position in a sequence depends on the direction in which reflection goes around the circle, a movement that reflection is always free to reverse. There is no natural beginning point to the reading of points on a circle—hence no natural first or second position. Any point on a circle, and therefore, in our example, either point of pleasure, can be read as the starting-off point; hence, any point on a circle (or either point of pleasure) can be in first position. Because the movement of aesthetic reflection runs backward and forward fundamentally, one can understand how the pleasure of reflection may be supposed to come into its own only in becoming self-conscious within the pleasure-producing judgment on its imputability. It begins there where it comes into its own. It could now seem interesting to associate the circular character of Kant's demonstration with our sought-after intentional character of the aesthetic judgment.

In one sense a circle having a finite radius is visually graspable, hence spatially determinate. In another sense it is not, since the mind cannot grasp spatially a relation of points the direction of whose sequence runs simultaneously forward and backward. In the latter sense, this model of thought, not being spatial, suggests that it should be conceived temporally. Kant's §9 invites us to think the aesthetic intention as a temporal movement—more than this, to rethink in a fundamental way the kind of temporality it possesses. Furthermore: the way we should proceed to rethink it is to recall the kind of analysis that Kant performs on the aesthetic judgment, and we are to endow the aesthetic judgment itself with the temporality that goes with this analysis. This suggests a temporality that cannot be conceptualized but only narratively performed. But if this temporality is, according to Kant, the *crux* of the demonstration of the aesthetic judgment, then neither can the aesthetic judgment be conceptualized: it can only be narrated.

The temporal structure of the aesthetic judgment cannot in principle be clarified in terms of succession or even in terms of structural priority and secondariness. In making succession a temporal mode inadequate for the aesthetic judgment—that entity reflecting the fundamental attunement of imagination and understanding necessary to any cognitive or aesthetic judgment—Kant reaches toward another sense of the temporality of self-reflection.

In §9 the optic of successiveness is suspended. Here Kant proposes a narrative principle different from the one apparently employed at the outset of his demonstration. He disrupts the coherence of a *sequence* of intelligible moments; he invokes the circular temporality of self-reflection and its representations. The temporality of the aesthetic judgment discloses the circular temporality of self-reflection. And insofar as self-reflection in the instance we are considering aims to discover the intention informing aesthetic judgment, we are brought to this conclusion: aesthetic judgment arises from the mind's intent to manifest itself as aesthetic pleasure.

Consider now the relation of the subject that seeks itself to the subject that it finds. Does it find a subject other than the subject it has constituted in the seeking? But is not the constituting subject itself constituted by the subject that it seeks?

What is the relation of reflection on the cognitive faculties to the mood of pleasure it finds there? The act of reflection, and its particular intentionality, cannot be without power on the mood of the faculties. Is not the "mere reflection" itself the creation of the mood it finds? Heidegger, for one, thinks of reflection (*theōria*) as a mood, the mood of "letting [something] . . . come toward us in a tranquil tarrying alongside."[15] Such tranquility does not rule out bliss. These relations suggest an associative and circular movement and not a discursive logic.

Kant's aesthetic judgment produces the sense of another temporality, whose chief "ecstasy" is the suspension of serial consciousness. If, as Lacan writes, "*le vrai serieux c'est le serial*," Kant provokes playfulness by means of this rupture. The assignment of successiveness to moments of experience occludes their character as fascination and play. Aesthetic play acts to suspend the consciousness of successiveness in a manner resembling Rousseau's *sentiment de l'existence* (in the Fifth Reverie), where the consciousness of consecutive wave motion gives way to a "play" of the mind with itself, a play without consciousness of serial time, an intensification of self-affectivity without awareness of regular sequence, a mood marked not by a succession of concepts but by a fittingness of virtualities, a playful attunement (to return to Kant's own language) of the faculties of images and concepts. This is a play whose character as power and pleasure exceeds its rule-bound character;[16] it suspends a consciousness of temporal successiveness for states of mind that abolish the subject's inculcated intention to find itself only via a (necessarily systematic) succession of concepts.

The thing that can be imputed to every beholder is the formal attunement of the faculties of imagination and conceptuality. Such proportion, requisite to any cognition, goes unfelt in ordinary cognitive activity: it is lost in the experience of particular concepts. A certain daily practice of concept-formation obstructs the possibility of "pure" reflection on its enabling condition. The work of concept-formation consumes, as it were, the raw material, a sort of nature ["*die Natur (des Subjekts)*"], which enables it. Concept-formation exacts a continual sacrifice of reflective bliss.

That the aesthetic should provide a kind of relief from the sober labor of the concept has a strong precedent in Lessing's notion of aesthetic abstraction:

> In Nature . . . everything is connected. . . . Its infinite multiplicity, however, is a theater that only an infinite spirit could enjoy. If finite spirits are to find pleasure in it, they must . . . be able to abstract from it [*abzusondern*] and to direct their attention to it at their own discretion. . . . The purpose of art is to relieve us of this work of abstraction . . . , to make it easier for us to aim our attention.[17]

Kant, too, describes the aesthetic as a type of relief from the abstraction that goes with ordinary perception and experience. But he adds a crucial clarification about what the labor of abstraction is supposed to accomplish. The kind of relief granted is specifically relief from concept formation. Aesthetic abstraction liberates for the first time what is always overwritten and obscured in the conceptualizing abstraction of ordinary experience. Furthermore, what it then directs our attention to are not things in the world but the internal conditions of conceptual experience as such.

I have proposed as the key question of the Third Critique the type of intentionality informing the aesthetic judgment. The answer is supplied by what Kant calls the "Nature (of the Subject)" bent on self-reflection—a Nature that is a kind of bliss, Kant says, of incomparable quality. It is one best modeled on the circular temporality of the herme-

neutic process by which a subject engages in self-reflection, a process intrinsically circular, as necessarily producing an uncertainty about agent
and end: "Who of us [when a self reflects on itself] is Oedipus here?
Who the Sphinx? It is . . . a rendezvous," writes Nietzsche, "of questions and question marks."[18]

When a subject undertakes to feel itself, it cannot bracket out in advance of its first take on its "object" the abyssal logic of that constitution. It cannot be certain of having avoided all the ways that make of the
object its only illusory double. Even the factor of duplication varies;
"the point of view of art and that of life are different even in the artist
himself," wrote Kafka, a difference I understand as itself different.[19] The
identity of subject and object in the hermeneutic process is suppositious
and ineffable—necessarily, if the hermeneutical is founded chiefly on
the claim "that every starting point is subject to reinterpretation":[20]

> The subject that poses itself as an object of reflection encounters itself in ways
> presumably always different. . . . That is precisely why all self-reflection is an ex-
> perience of thought and not a logical operation, and every attempt to think
> through such experience is a hermeneutic, where what is at stake is indeed de-
> tecting in the object, through a sort of empathic coincidence, those features of
> the human subject it inadvertently contains. That, furthermore, is why all de-
> scriptions of such subject-object relations internal to consciousness cannot find
> a beginning point, cannot decide what is first and what is second in such experi-
> ence, cannot fail, it would seem, to contradict themselves.[21]

The more precise form of the question raised by Kant is, does aesthetic pleasure arise as a consequence of a reflection constrained by the
formal features of an object? Or does bliss, being impacted in the cognitive faculties and pressing toward self-evidence, invent the aesthetic
form as the occasion of its own showing-forth? This would appear to be
the answer—radically so, despite the perplexities of §9. There is a pleasant irony in J. M. Bernstein's conclusion: "Hence, it must be assumed
that both the grounds for attributing universal validity to aesthetic
judgments, and the pleasure that results from aesthetic reflection, derive
from sources that do not belong exclusively to the faculty of knowledge."[22] Bliss, being impacted in the cognitive faculties and pressing toward self-evidence, invents the aesthetic form as the contingent occasion of its own showing-forth. It is this bliss-impacted being that
glimpses itself when the aesthetic judgment is imputed to others as the
final condition of its validity.

3

HÖLDERLIN'S "SWIFT CONCEPTUAL GRASP"

This power to live, to make decisions, to set one's
foot down joyously in the right place.
—Franz Kafka, *The Diaries of Franz Kafka, 1910–1913*

Whom then are we able to need?
—Rainer Maria Rilke,
The Duino Elegies

Faust, a tragic poem, is "incommensurable," said Goethe, because it is produced by "the imagination," which "has to abide by laws of its own." Rational understanding cannot—and should not—get hold of them. The products of the imagination thus "remain eternally problematic to reason," and here poetry parts company from prose, where reason "is and may and should be at home."[1]

One of the most salient features of Hölderlin's modernity is the impertinence of the distinction between his poetry and prose. For Otto Pöggeler, "poems of Hölderlin set beside poems [of Celan] clarify a basic feature of the modern lyric—a new structure striven for in strange works that look like prose."[2] For Pierre Bertaux, "Hölderlin, with few exceptions, expresses himself completely and thoroughly in 'emmetric' (poetic) diction—in his novel *Hyperion* too, and even in his letters. Every single sentence displays rigorously correct prosody."[3] Equally, Hölderlin's novel *Hyperion* and his prose writings on poetics generate a reservoir of problems provoking "eternal" reflection. His notion of "*schneller Begriff* [swift conceptual grasp]" exhibits this sort of productive complexity. It lays impassable problems at the door of rational understanding, just as the dilemma from which it arises strained Hölderlin's existential powers to the breaking point.

The notion starts up a path of reflection that can be traced through the essays Hölderlin wrote in Homburg v.d.H. during spring and summer 1799. At that time he was planning to publish a literary journal— "a journal with aesthetic subject matter" called *Iduna*—containing poems of practical benefit ("*auszuübende Poesie*") as well as essays on the "history and evaluation of art."[4] Success in his plan was crucial: it promised a practical foundation for his life as a poet, which lacked material support.[5]

From a number of loose pages composed during summer 1799, we can get hold of Hölderlin's own views on the "history and evaluation of art"—thoughts probably intended to be published in *Iduna*. The fortunes of his own swift conceptual grasp are complex and troubled, and the serenity he required to formulate and pursue it was undoubtedly disturbed by what was to be the failure of *Iduna*.

The densest of these short texts—the fourth of seven *Maxims*[6]— speaks of "*die wahrste Wahrheit*," the truest truth:

Only that is the truest truth wherein error too becomes truth, because truth places [*setzt*] it in the whole of its system, into its time and place. Truth is the light that illuminates itself and the night too. This is also the loftiest poetry, where the unpoetic also becomes poetic because it is spoken at the right time and at the right place. But here swift conceptual grasp [*schneller Begriff*] is most necessary. How can you make use of something at the right place when you still shyly tarry [*verweile*] over it, and do not know how much meaning it has, how much or little to make of it? That is eternal serenity, divine joy—one's putting everything particular in its place, in the whole where it belongs. Therefore, without understanding or a thoroughly organized feeling, no excellence—no life. (14:59)

The maxim is organized around a series of apparent oppositions: truth versus error; light versus night; poetry versus the unpoetic. A principle of antithesis appears to divide the system truth/light/poetry from that of error/night/the unpoetic. But the maxim means to overcome principles of opposition and exclusion in poetry. It advances a kind of thinking beyond antithesis—a responsiveness to the dimension that holds entities together and makes them graspable through the opposition that distinguishes them. This synthetic judgment subsumes each minor antithesis under a superior term: it places the opposition of truth and error under "the truest truth"; light and the night, under "the light that illuminates both light and the night"; poetry and the unpoetic, under "the highest poetry," which, even if it speaks falsely or erratically or eccentrically, does so at the right time and in the right place.

As the aphorism advances, Hölderlin rapidly adds on superior terms, sublating the initial antithesis, without adding further oppositions, under ever more comprehensive categories. The highest truth, light, and poetry arise amid "eternal serenity" and "divine joy," until they too are finally encompassed by "excellence," by "life."

This critique of particular binary oppositions entails the critique of the atomism that underlies them, since binaries purport to function as inexplicably self-contained essences. What is not immediately evident, but what Hölderlin draws out, is the fact of the mutual dependency of these terms, by which (in the words of Terrance King) "each of the terms simultaneously excludes yet invokes its companion." Hölderlin's view affirms that "there is everywhere operative a principle of continuity in which nothing is so discrete and distinct from something else that it can symmetrically implicate it as an unexplainably absolute opposite."[7]

I want to stress from the outset that this gesture of subsumption, redeeming the apparently negative, is not itself provided by a concept. Hölderlin's phrase is "*schneller Begriff*"; and while "*Begriff*," in current German, means "concept," it means something else in Hölderlin's phrase: it means "facility in comprehending." The term "*Begriff*" defined as conceptual grasp sounds antiquated, but in Hölderlin's usage, emphasis goes on the process of conceptualizing, whose active character is stressed by the qualifier "swift." We see here Hölderlin's *activation* of the concept: stress falls on the mode of action, not on the concept moved about or the concept obtained; and as a result both object and end are physicalized—made, through their mode and quality, analogous to body. In the literal meaning of the phrase, "swift conceptual grasp" is an aesthetic category. In this way, as including the "unpoetic," it is constituted by conflict and physical pain and hence includes a trace of negative pleasure on the model of the Kantian sublime.[8]

The gesture of swift conceptual grasp is found in many places in Hölderlin's work around 1800. Among his major themes are ostensibly alien, recalcitrant moments subdued by wider contexts. In the second verse of "Brod und Wein," for example, the night, unpoetic—"*die zaudernde Weile . . . im Finstern* [the tarrying while . . . in gloom]"—is celebrated "*weil den Irrenden sie geheiliget ist und den Todten* [because it is sacred to those who go astray and the dead]" (6:258).[9] Such disturbing, painful states must be endured, again and again, by the poet; indeed, they must be solicited. They are part of the poetic rendering of being and must be acknowledged.

Elsewhere, in *Hyperion*, a footnote specifically identifies an un-truthful moment in Hyperion's reflections. Hyperion has had a para-doxical thought that troubles him: Why isn't the world even more im-poverished than it is? For if it were, man would be entitled to seek a di-vinity outside it as well, a transcendental god above that nature which manifests itself immanently as "quietness" and "life." But the narrator continues: "It is hardly necessary to recall that assertions of this sort should not by rights scandalize anyone, for they are the *mere phenomena* of the human spirit" (emphasis added).[10] Hyperion's effort to motivate the invention of a Father God, a Creator, by appealing to an exorbitant poverty of the human condition is not so much heretical or cynical, Hölderlin says, as inevitable. It is also false. Like many of Hyperion's thoughts and projects, such moments are errors, although they are nec-essary ones. They are exemplary errors which, within the system of truth belonging to "the human spirit," occur at the right time and in the right place and which therefore, in a work of art, must be tactfully placed.[11] Perhaps this awkward footnote itself might be accounted a de-liberately unpoetic moment, the aesthetic exigency of which exceeds even the ethical exigency of defending against scandal, for the novel means to assimilate this footnote at the right place and time, very likely on the example of Rousseau's *La nouvelle Héloïse*, a work that Hölderlin knew well and which contains such authorial intrusions.[12]

"Divine joy" and "life" are the principles of the mind that can subor-dinate the particulars of its experience. What is at stake is a certain ex-emplary exercise of judgment. Just as Kant, in his analysis of taste, finds at its root the harmonious attunement of the faculties of conceptuality and imagination required for any cognition, so too Hölderlin explores the condition of the possibility of artistic judgment, a judgment that os-cillates between reflective and determinative modes with the rhythm of the hermeneutic. And if the artistic judgment of swift conceptual grasp is to be like Kant's judgment of taste, we would expect it to be accompanied by a certain type of disinterested pleasure. Indeed: Hölderlin calls it "eternal serenity," "divine joy," "life." Except for "eternal" and "divine," these qualities match perfectly those of the quickening pleasure of Kant's judgment of the beautiful.

In the right hermeneutic rhythm the mind may not tarry (*"verweilt nicht"*) on the detail, which would mean to succumb to a form of the Faustian temptation to say, "Tarry awhile, thou art so fair! [*Verweile doch / du bist so schön!*],"[13] though here the detail is sooner a matter of the curtailed sublime than the beautiful, since its charm is the charm of irritation. To stay put here would be to admire single moments that fascinate, disturb, and obscure a wider vision—the sorts of experience that Mephisto is good at supplying to Faust. In the Faustian perspective, Hölderlin's swift conceptual grasp amounts to a precision tool, or to tact, a type of judgment, serving to articulate a totality of experience—a scanning tool to bring about, without loss of particular distinction and without one's being overwhelmed, a differentiated unity of the life and of the work. The mind informed by superior principles (such as the truest truth and the truest poetry) knows at once when to dwell and when to flee, it can grasp relations swiftly. Though Hölderlin's essay identifies the difficulty of such comprehension and indeed the inconceivableness of it in its absence—for, to represent properly this sort of facility, swift conceptual grasp would be necessary, but swift conceptual grasp is difficult to achieve—nonetheless, the maxim tries to conclude on a note of full recovery of the truest truth and the loftiest poetry. At the close the speaker bathes in the light of the truest truth.

It is, however, precisely at this pleasant place that readers of the maxim cannot tarry. I have stressed its ostensible parallels and symmetries and the regular sublation of oppositions under superior terms. But this, of course, is to make the maxim all-too-readable. In such a light, understanding is blind to its own problematic character. Other difficulties start to appear when one looks more closely at its sequence, which reveals important differences at the level of actor, act, and product of subsumption. A number of questions arise: Who, when swift conceptual grasp is spoken of, speaks? Who plays the lead in this drama of system-building?

The maxim consists of three different formulations of a movement posed at the outset. In the first, the actor is "the truest truth" itself, its action a placing or "positing [*Setzen*]" and its product the totality of its system. This subsumption is also represented as the light that illuminates the night and itself. The second version introduces an important change; the role of the actor—"the truest truth"—is now played by poetry, and the action of truth—a positing—is redefined as *poetic* saying. The outcome, therefore, is no longer a system of truth but a work of art, reminding one of Hölderlin's inclination to constellate activities of natural and poetic creation—poetry being for Hölderlin (in Gerhard Kurz's phrase), "a universal ontological determination."[14] The agencies of nature and poetry are engaged in the same activity, *poiesis*. Positing, or *Setzen*, equals poetizing, or *Sagen*.

If, however, *poiesis* is to be accomplished, "swift conceptual grasp is most necessary." Only where inductive judgment is at work can natural and artistic production be thought together. At this juncture, however—as a certain tension begins to make itself felt—Hölderlin registers a heightened sense of personal responsibility. He is the one to perform this task. The third formulation of the scene of swift comprehension addresses the agent as "Du." The *Du* who is this being is supposed to shape its immediate poetic experience by deciding how much or how little to make of the recalcitrant element that needs to be assimilated to the poem.

Now the maxim starts to make its trouble plain. Swift comprehension soon seems to have been less fully realized when it is conceived ideally—as tireless judgment—than when it is actually experienced, *through its absence*, as hesitant tarrying, as the failure of an organizing feeling. Given this uncertainty, isn't it the mark of an only mythical leap out of danger when the author, in a final formulation, elevates the poet's achievement to a hyperbolic totality of life? Swift conceptual grasp, hard to come by, appears to have done its work—at least at the order of the verbal imagination—by an act of poetic will. But at this peak moment, who does Hölderlin now say possesses this ability? Whose swift conceptual grasp has done this work? Like "the truest truth" at the outset, an agent posits a totality—an agent, however, who is now not *Du* but *man* ("one"). The fusion of the powers of the truest truth and those of the poet occurs at the cost of an annihilation of personal identity. "Du"—the poet—is erased as the "one." Poetic success is cast as an event effacing an empirical subject. From the standpoint of the subject, this successful conclusion runs contrary to fact; the aphorism speaks of being "*without* understanding or a thoroughly organized feeling," "of *no* excellence—no life" (my italics). Where is such facility to be found? The condition of its being present is that no feature of subjective personality also be present: the skill of swift comprehension lies outside the order of personal experience. Indeed, it might be said to require its sacrifice.

This result is confirmed by a moment in the First Version of Hölderlin's verse drama *Der Tod des Empedokles* (The death of Empedocles), written in 1799, the same year as the *Maxims*. Empedocles' disciple Pausanias reminds his teacher, the exiled and hunted Empedocles, of his old achievements in statecraft and pedagogy:

> . . . and didn't you draw
> The great lines of the future
> Before me, as the sure glance of the artist
> Links a missing member to the whole form.[15]

These achievements of recollection and divination belong to Empedocles' past; he has ceased to be himself. Hence, so does the cogency of the analogue, which likens the seer to the artist, belong to the past. The analogue makes a precise reference to the product of a proper use of swift conceptual grasp, which here, too, must be thought of as a lost historical possibility.

Hölderlin's readiness to posit a usable swift comprehension is the reverse ideal side of his inability to get clear of the all-arresting negative impression. To an immeasurably deep degree he is marked by his inability to "process" a memory of suffering.[16] He tarries hesitantly, petrified by meanness. Here we're reminded of the meaning that the word *Scheue*, or shyness, timidity, has for him. In a delicate spirit of justification, in 1797, Hölderlin wrote to Schiller of his "metaphysical mood, . . . a certain virginity of the spirit," equating it with a "shyness toward the material side [*Scheue vor dem Stoff*]," a "flight from determinate relations [*Flucht bestimmter Verhältnisse*]."[17] He knows, of course, that poetry must draw an "indispensable material [*unentbehrlicher Stoff*]" from what is "mean and ordinary in real life [*vom Gemeinen und Gewöhnlichen im wirklichen Leben*],"[18] from "the ice-cold story of the day [*die eiskalte Geschichte des Tages*]."[19] Hence the absence of swift conceptual grasp runs two sorts of risk. The first is an unnatural, a "virginal" ascesis; the second, unquestionably worse, an attachment to the crude facticity of the everyday—a danger that Hölderlin had long been aware of. His epigram "Die beschreibende Poesie" (Descriptive poetry) reads (with some inevitable roughening of tone): "Get this! Apollo has become the god of the journalists, / and his boy's the one who gives him the facts straight."[20]

These earlier texts profile a superb spirit of resistance. The danger of getting stuck in daily meanness, to which the poetic spirit is as if lured, haunts Hölderlin as a virtual melancholy. The danger is precisely identified at the time of the composition of the Fourth Maxim in a letter, dated June 4, 1799, which Hölderlin wrote to his brother:

> I am not entitled to complain about nature, which heightened my sense of the shortcomings of things [*das Mangelhafte*], in order to make me all the more intensely and joyously aware of what is excellent. Once I have arrived at that point of mastering the knack [*Fertigkeit*] of feeling and seeing in things that fall short less the indefinite pain that they often cause me than precisely their special, momentary, particular lack, and thus also of recognizing their beauty, their characteristic good—once I have achieved this, then my spirit will become calmer and my activity make a steadier progress. For when we experience a lack only infinitely, then we are naturally inclined, too, to want to repair this lack infinitely, and then our strength often gets entangled in an indefinite, fruitless, exhausting struggle, because it does not know definitely where the lack is and how precisely to repair and supplement this lack.[21]

"But here," as Hölderlin will add, "swift conceptual grasp is most necessary."

This exacerbated sense of lack, this failure of the energy of specification, is, for Lacan—we could also note—the product of an unconscious that is without a certain decisive regulatory function. "By means of the hole which [this absence] opens in the signified, [this absence] attracts the cascade of revisions of the signifier, whence proceeds the increasing disaster of the Imaginary."[22] It is certain, however, that Hölderlin did not experience this absence as merely personal and in this sense as unconscious, let alone reified as a "hole." One mode of this absence belonged to his time: during at least one stage of his writing, the composition of *Empedocles*, Hölderlin began to center his fury on the dissonance of his age, which assailed him as Empedocles' time did him—the conflict between the paralyzed forms of a traditional political state and a "defiant, anarchic life" (13:876). "In our imperial cities," Hölderlin writes, "the republican form has become dead and meaningless, because men there are not so constituted that they have any need of it."[23]

"Death and meaninglessness"—did he take on his madness as their simulation? This idea will concern us.

• ⌒ •

Our second reading of the maxim brought to light features of unmastered conflict and asymmetry. This dissonant character reflects the practical difficulty or even the impossibility of exercising swift conceptual grasp. The difficulty is crucial, since swift conceptual grasp is the enabling condition of full *poiesis*; this trouble will point toward painful tensions in Hölderlin's subsequent writing, thinking, and social existence.[24] There will be other, I hope fruitful ways of further defining this difficulty, which is written into the maxim by a problematic imagination.

So I turn first to another writer—a Hölderlinesque one—in the hope of providing an illuminating counterexample.[25] His words also describe a live totality as the form imposed by an artist-type who has "the ability to organize."

Wherever [such artists] appear, something new soon arises, a ruling structure that *lives*, in which parts and functions are delimited and coordinated, in which nothing whatever finds a place that has not first been assigned a "meaning" in relation to the whole.

This is Nietzsche's description of that "creation and imposition of forms" instituting the first "state," which also happens to be the work of "some pack of blond beasts of prey, . . . the most involuntary, unconscious artists there are. . . . These born organizers . . . exemplify that frightful artists' egoism that knows itself justified to all eternity in its 'work.' "[26] As an operation of the very same heliotropism informing Hölderlin's valorization of the light, the blondness of these beasts can be taken as the warrant of their success. Their blondness "illuminates" the untruth of their cruelty (Hölderlin's phrase is "the light that illuminates both light and the night").

Nietzsche's aphorism accentuates a certain repressive dimension of Hölderlin's own. The figure of the state—the *polis*—is precisely the one seductive figure of totality missing from all seven of the *Iduna*-maxims. They are all concerned with structures of totality, yet not one contains a metaphor of political organization. This absence is suggestive.

We could put the omission in a more nuanced form. One of the most impressive features of Hölderlin's swift conceptual grasp (*"schneller Begriff "*), unlike Nietzsche's swift attack (*"schneller Angriff "*),[27] is its sensitivity to the vulnerable humanity of the material it organizes. It places *error*—human error—in the whole of its system, in its time and place. Indeed, if the repetition of the word "its" in the first sentence refers back to "error," the value of this weaker term is heightened, for then swift conceptual grasp would have to place error in the time and place that *error* constrains.

The divergence between Hölderlin and Nietzsche can be seen, too, as Hölderlin's development of an important argument in Schiller's *On the Aesthetic Education of Man* (1795). In the Fourth Letter Schiller distinguishes the artist from the educator and the statesman, types that he calls "the pedagogic and political artist."[28] The artist cannot but do violence to his raw material in the course of imposing form onto it. The sculptor chisels stone, the writer inscribes paper or does violence to the conventional unity of the sign, and then hides this violence behind the appearance of the beautiful work. But, says Schiller, Hölderlin's teacher, never may the pedagogic or political artist (that is, the statesman) do even initial violence to his material, because this material consists of human subjects. In this sense, it could still be said that Hölderlin's maxim is implicitly intersubjective—and hence political. It deals with error, human error, with all the ways, in a word, in which human beings engender conflict because they are not truthful or reasonable beings. But this is so merely implicit and tenuous a political dimension that we can still speak with justice, thinking of Hölderlin in Homburg in the summer of 1799, of a repressed political consciousness. A letter written by Böhlendorff, the unhappy friend of Hölderlin and Sinclair, makes a point of distinguishing the politics of the two: Here in Homburg, writes Böhlendorff, "I have a friend [Sinclair] who is a republican in body and soul and also another friend [Hölderlin] who is one in spirit and in truth," that is, *merely* in spirit and in truth.[29] Hölderlin's politics are underrealized.

It is remarkable, though, that even the implicit politics of the Fourth Maxim is one of benevolent autocracy. The *Du* concedes authority to the weaker parties in its system only after arrogating to itself the central, privileged, all-seeing position from which an act of positing or correct saying is performed. As an individual, the *Du* posits itself as in no way constrained. Precisely the difference in the systematic positions of power (better, powerlessness and contingency) in Hölderlin and Nietzsche calls for comment.

In their representation of power one difference of structure and emphasis is most striking—the "involuntary and unconscious" character of Nietzsche's political artist. This phrase heightens by contrast the conceptual, appraising, system-generating character of Hölderlin's artist-politician. His action is, precisely, meditated—it is conscious, even hyperconscious, of complexity. The poet's relation to the truest truth, like the apostle's relation to his God, is more "mediate," is "highest intellect in highest spirit."[30] As the term reminds us: swift, *conceptual* comprehension is essential.[31]

Now the point is more than that Nietzsche has projected in the instinctive activity of the blond beast a provocative metaphor for the spirit of poetic organization. After all, in "Patmos" Hölderlin conjures eagles building light air-bridges joining the peaks of his sacramental history of the poetic spirit, eagles who "go over and return" with swift conceptual grasp. What is more revealing is that Nietzsche's figure of instinctive life allows him to leap out of a circle of difficulty that girds Hölderlin's maxim and that can be termed the ontological circle. I mean by this the aporia that arises when a self, by the lights of its own individual activity, attempts to posit and define being. In the course of Hölderlin's aphorism, the active, governing factor slips more and more out of the "whole of the system," the work of totality. If at the outset the term "truth" is presented with seeming assurance as self-identical, at once product and agent, at the close it can be self-identical and at once product and agent only by means of a metaphor: that of the "light that illuminates itself and the night too."

But how good is this metaphor? The light with which light illuminates itself could not be self-identical; it would have to be different from the light it illuminates.[32] How otherwise could this active light come·to light? But what status and what temporal position would such a light have within the system? Would not the factor producing the difference between the two kinds of light in fact unsettle a system founded on "*the* light"?

The dissociation of agent and product is even plainer at the second stage of the aphorism, when the product is called "the loftiest poetry" but the agent left nameless and unspecified and the widening gap between them rhetorically marked for emphasis. The agent is occluded

within a passive, agentless verbal construction ("the unpoetic also becomes poetic because it is spoken at the right time and the right place").
And with the introduction of a hesitant *Du*—indeed, what place has
hesitant tarrying in the system, since it does not belong either to the
truth or quite to error?—the organizing factor begins less and less to resemble the "system" of truth, and in no obvious way has "being." "Eternal serenity, divine joy" openly belong only to "one" (*man*). At the close
of the maxim, truth, the agent of totality, has declined into the quite
fragile figure of an "organized feeling." No being goes to this agent to
guarantee its mythic potency.[33]

The ontological circle emphasizes the fragility of the consciousness
that means to determine being. Nietzsche wants to escape from this circle, but to do so he must mythicize simplicity of instinct.[34] In this way
he guarantees the instituted work, the real institution correlative with
instinct, as an ordered totality having being, quite apart from the experience that any finite consciousness could have of it. Hölderlin, on the
other hand, returns to a figure of hermeneutic regress, a bare mood of
intelligibility, whose ruling logic states: "A totality is whatever feels organized." This logic has to guarantee the production of the highest
truth. Hölderlin's agency of totality remains an only subjective, reflective judgment, once more like the aesthetic judgment of Kant's Third
Critique.

What a weight of responsibility, therefore, falls onto this fragile, subjective agent! Without such swift conceptual grasp there is only endless
indetermination and endless revision—permanent error at the order of
the signifier, the order of work, and the order of self-making, of *Bildung*. Without swift conceptual grasp, there can be no system, no "ruling structure," no understanding, and no art, as a result of which each
particular part can claim with equal justification that it already occupies
the proper place in a system of truth. If considered as a political allegory,
the outcome would be disastrous.

In another essay written in summer 1799 for *Iduna*, Hölderlin responds to this very question. The article, "The Perspective from Which
We Have to View Antiquity [Der Gesichtspunkt, aus dem wir das Al-
tertum anzusehen haben]," acknowledges the fragility of swift conceptual grasp while addressing the shape and the emergency of contemporary Western culture. Hölderlin writes, underlining the entire passage:

There is a difference whether the drive to self-cultivation [*Bildungstrieb*] operates blindly or with consciousness, whether or not it knows what its source is and what it is striving for, for one mistake human beings make is that their drive to self-cultivation goes astray [*sich verirrt*], assumes an unworthy and utterly false direction or—what amounts to the same thing—misses the mark of its special place, or, when it has found it, remains stuck in place, in a half-way house [*auf halbem Wege*], arrested by the very means that were supposed to lead [. . . human beings] to their goal. (14:95)

How, then, we are obliged to ask, in the absence of swift conceptual grasp, can this missing of the mark be averted? Hölderlin's answer is certain and confident: protection comes from knowing in advance the source and goal of that drive, the essential direction it takes in proceeding toward its goal, and the detours or false turns that confront it— a knowledge accessible from the fact that the drive "springs forth from a common primordial basis [*gemeinschaftlichen ursprünglichen Grunde*]" (14:95).

Hence this essay, "The Perspective from Which We Have to View Antiquity," introduces another term into the argument—a "basis" or "ground" comprehending truth and error, light and night, poetry and the unpoetic. This third term is an already subsistent totality, a universal being guiding swift conceptual grasp and guaranteeing its efficacy. But in introducing this term, Hölderlin does not register the essential question—namely, what access could human beings have to such a ground? Hölderlin's conception of a common primordial basis in this early essay is, uncharacteristically, neither tragic nor dialectical. It is not conceived in relation to a time in which the basis could become a destiny—could, in other words, sink out of the range of representation; or grow chaotic from excessive contradiction; or in other ways, difficult to specify, become finite and impoverished in the absence of something essential to it.

To find the strongest exercise of Hölderlin's historical imagination, we must go to an explicitly political essay, the "Foundation of *Empedocles* [Grund zum Empedokles]." This remarkable work, written in Homburg in the fall of 1799, between the second and third versions of the Empedocles tragedy, allows one to grasp through the figure of Empedocles the failure of swift comprehension. It allows one to see this failure as an aporia arising from the shattered relation of the representative individual to his basis.

The "Foundation" is preceded by an "Allgemeiner Grund" (General Foundation), which speaks of the deepest inner intensity, or *tiefste Innigkeit*, initiating tragic writing. Hölderlin is discussing its transformation into a poetic work:

The feeling [the deepest inner intensity] no longer expresses itself immediately, it is no longer the poet and his own experience that comes to light—even if every poem, the tragic as well, must have come forth from poetic life and reality, from the poet's own world and soul, because otherwise the right truth is everywhere lacking, and nothing at all can be understood or given life, if we are not able to carry over our own sensibility [*Gemüth*] and our own experience into a strange, an alien analogous material. (13:869)[35]

"The right truth"—the truest truth—is again a function of the poet's own world and soul. In a state of excessive intensity, that world and soul, Hölderlin says, requires protection in a strange, an alien, analogous material. This term can be clarified: the "strange, alien analogous material," the medium of the right truth, is a subject-matter for poetry.

Now, what makes a poetic material suited to linguistic elaboration, like the historical subject matter of Empedocles—or, for that matter, the Greek text of *Antigone* or the mountain Tek or the river Ister—is the promise of organization. It could be "analogous" to experience by virtue of its implicit organicity, in the Hölderlinean sense of the term: its susceptibility to organization. But the law of tragic composition requires that "the more infinite, the more ineffable, the closer to the *nefas* [injustice, outrage] that inner intensity is," the more severe, cold, strange, and audacious that material must be. The tendency of tragic composition is thus literally to alienate personal authenticity in its myth: "The tragic poet, because he expresses the deepest inward intensity, wholly denies, disowns his person, his subjectivity . . . ; he carries it over, metaphorizes it into strange, alien personality" (13:870). Almost immediately thereafter the "General Foundation" breaks off.[36] And when it picks up again, it does so in an obscure and negative manner, as it describes in drastic language a destructive and adverse process. It is as if, for the reader, its breaking off were due less to the necessity of postponing reflection than to a loss of belief in the possibility of a tragic writing that could indeed carry over anything of the poet's spirit. It speaks of "miserable success," "a mind contested [thereafter, "disturbed"] through its own autonomous activity," finally, "a violent reaction." What brings about this reaction? We will understand this crisis better in passing over to the next portion of the essay, entitled "Grund zum Empedokles" (Foundation of *Empedocles*), an essay more pertinently about the representative individual, the poet Empedocles. As the son of his period, Empedocles inherits powerful oppositions between nature and art:

> a man in whom those oppositions are so intensely united that in him they become One, casting off and reversing their original form as agents of distinction, so that which in his world counts as more subjective . . . —the activity of distinguishing, thinking, comparing, forming, organizing and being organized—is in his very self more objective; with the result that he distinguishes more, thinks more, compares more, forms more, organizes more, and is more organized *when he is less self-possessed* [*bei sich selber*] *and in so far as he is less conscious of himself.* (13:872)

Evidently, Empedocles' sense of self and those activities that his world counts as more subjective—thinking and judging, for example—do not function cooperatively. Hence, when Empedocles is more nearly self-conscious and self-possessed (literally, at home with himself), he is further from having swift conceptual grasp, his effect on others being more incomparable, shapeless, aorgic, and disorganized.

A plain back-link to the Fourth Maxim is forged when Empedocles himself is described as

> by all appearances born to be a poet. This means: in his subjective, more active nature . . . he appears already to have that uncommon tendency toward generality, which under different circumstances . . . would develop into that quiet meditation, that fullness and thoroughgoing definiteness of consciousness, with which the poet aims at *totality* [*ein Ganzes*]. Equally, there appears to lie in his objective nature . . . that happy facility which, even without industrious, conscientious ordering and thinking and forming, is inclined to order and think and form—that plasticity of the senses and the spirit that in a quick, lively way [*leicht und schnell*] takes up everything easily and swiftly as a totality [*in seiner Ganzheit*]. (13:873)

Hölderlin is plainly redescribing "swift conceptual grasp." But

> the fate of [Empedocles'] time, the powerful extremes in which he grew up, did not require song— . . . which lies between the structure of fate and originality . . . ; neither did the destiny of his age require the authentic deed, which certainly has an immediately beneficial effect but is also more one-sided, and all the

more so the less it *exposes* the whole man: this destiny demanded a sacrifice.
Here the whole man becomes truly and visibly that being in whom the destiny
of his age appears to be dissolved, where the extremes appear to become really
and visibly united in One, but precisely for that reason are too intensely and in-
wardly united: in an ideal deed the individual therefore perishes and must per-
ish. (13:873)

The figure of Empedocles enables Hölderlin to pose the question of
swift conceptual grasp in its most general form. Where, in an ill-fated
age, might the tragic poet, full to excess with inward intensity, take his
stand, or from what other source find the power to organize his own
world and soul upon a strange, an alien, analogous material? The contradictions of Empedocles' age have so fully penetrated him that for
him to be a conscious self (*bei sich selber*) is to be least capable of organizing, be most without swift conceptual grasp. How, then, could the
poet keep his footing on a ground itself torn, in a time in which beginning and end do not rhyme, while carrying over his own world and soul
into its proper time and place? In such a time, the age itself appears to require an exemplary sacrifice of its own contradictions, which in the
poet have grown prematurely unified and objective. Empedocles' sacri-
ficial death, afterwards contemplated by his survivors, might restore, in
conceptualizable outline, the extremes of violated feeling and technical
knowledge in his age. His predicament requires, more than the timeli-
ness of the organizing Word, the Deed—more than the Deed, the Sacrifice. In this way Hölderlin enlarges, and shatters, the hopeful thrust of
Faust's Bible translation in the first "Studierzimmer" scene of *Faust*.[37] It
is no longer the productive Deed that enables Hölderlin's Faust-figure to
tarry no longer.[38]

Empedocles' time, like Hölderlin's, is dissonant and divided. If once
a type of self-conscious, conceptual *Bildung* was possible through the
poet's swift conceptual grasp, such development becomes impossible
under the force of a tearing destiny. Might that lack be translated into
public action? Now public action is too one-sided and must be translated into sacrifice: the self takes hold of the inflicted fragility and torn-
ness of its own self-consciousness and disowns it.

The "organized feeling," the mood of the intelligible subsumption
of parts under a whole, became for Hölderlin unthinkable except by an
act of ascetic self-disowning.[39] Put plainly, the poet perceives, with
dread, the necessity of his own translation into a foreign, analogous

stuff. In the letter to his brother of June 4, 1799, quoted earlier, Hölderlin defines the fundamental obstacle to swift comprehension. The stability of particulars and generals is unsettled by a chaos of things that refuse to be beings of any categorical kind. Undermining the poetic play of particular and general is the anxiety of a world grown infinitely uncertain. The field of swift conceptual grasp passes into obscurity.

In the letter to Böhlendorff of December 4, 1801, Hölderlin strives to address what matters universally in art, namely "living proportion and order [*Geschick*]." In his historical scheme, the patrimony of Western art, and hence its origin, is "Junoian sobriety," a term valorized as the condition of poetic order. In the Western tradition sobriety comes first, is at the origin; this discriminating consciousness is properly its own, unlike the "sacred pathos" it acquires by mastery of what is alien to its composure. But whatever is one's own, says Hölderlin, is not for that reason any easier to employ, for "the *free* use of what is one's *own* is most difficult."[40] (I would inflect this phrase to say the "swift" use of one's "own soul and world" is most difficult.)[41]

Of Hölderlin's own part to play within the enterprise of a new "Western" (*abendländisch*), national poetry, he writes, "Once, I could rejoice over a new truth, a better view of what is above and around us; now I fear lest it come to pass in the end with me as it did with old Tantalus, who had from the gods more than his fill."[42] One could rewrite this sentence, thus: "Now I fear lest it come to pass in the end with me as it did with old Empedocles."[43] For, Hölderlin continues,

I do what I can, as best I can, and think, when I see how I, too, must, on my way, depart like the others, that it is godless and mad [*rasend*] to seek a path that would be safe from all attack.

Now I am full of parting. . . . It cost me bitter tears when I decided to leave my fatherland even now, perhaps forever. For what is dearer to me in the world?[44]

"But," he concludes, "*they* [*the poets*] *cannot use me* [*sie können mich nicht brauchen*]." I underscore this phrase: "they cannot use me," which is the national counterpart of a moment in the definition of "swift conceptual grasp":

But here a swift conceptual grasp is most necessary. How can you make use of something in the right place when you still shyly tarry over it and do not know how much meaning it has, how much or little to make of it?

The problem of swift conceptual grasp comes back, inevitably, as the problem of a lifetime without a center. Hölderlin stands opposite to the ".truest truth" of his epoch, as the error in its system that must be used but cannot be used. As long as he lives his isolation is certain.

In Hölderlin's model of swift conceptual grasp there was no explicit provision for conflict; no obstacle was specified in the maxim. And yet now the individual poet is conflicted. He has become the medium of the contradictions of his time. He is disorganized; in the language of the first model, center and periphery collide in him. He becomes an unusable error with respect to the perspective of the center. By thinking the crisis of his age and at the same time becoming the most intense experience of it, Hölderlin moves closest to it; but in so doing, according to the Empedoclean paradox, he also moves furthest from its center as that center might become conscious of itself.[45] His position shifts from agent to candidate for sacrifice.[46] The individual Hölderlin himself prematurely unifies and illustrates the contradiction of live feeling and technical skill in his age; like Empedocles, "the more his age individualizes itself in him, the more necessary his fall [*Untergang*] becomes" (13:874).

In autumn 1802, remembering his life in the south of France, Hölderlin writes, in the draft of a letter to Böhlendorff, "The mighty element, the fire from heaven, . . . absorbed me continually." His thoughts turn to separation and death, as the act by which truth and error, center and periphery, can again be distinguished. Hölderlin considers himself the casualty of a time of national poetry that does not yet exist; he consents to be the casualty of the "philosophical light" that "shapes forms . . . as a principle and mode of destiny [*Prinzip- und Schiksaalsweise bildend*]."[47] (Recall that the "truth" of "the loftiest poetry" is "the light that illuminates itself and the night too.") Neither he nor Böhlendorff "will come into use [*wir werden nicht aufkommen*]," and so he now has "no thoughts for himself," wanting to "belong" wholly "to the sacred image that we are shaping." This image is the fate of poetry, which he means to foster as, discerning the beginnings of a new poetic character, he disappears.

It is as a madman that he disappears, and there attaches to his fate a shadow of decision, which could make it seem deliberate, an organized fall, less an alienation from his conflict than its metaphor. This disappearance does not have the magical power of sacrifice in the sense of an (illusory) union of man and god; it does not have the heroic, the titanic aura of Empedoclean suicide. Perhaps it was an intuition as to its metaphorical flatness that prompted Benjamin to read the moment of the death of the poet in "Timidity" as the center of a flat mosaic. The crux is the expendableness of Hölderlin's empirical being; he persists as the form of a man in whom the riven character of a historical period could be read. That form is madness.

From our own standpoint, it is hard to descry a German poetry arising in the first decade of the nineteenth century that needed Hölderlin enough to warrant a belief that his madness was a sacrifice to it. Had he known this, Hölderlin would have died mourning.

On the other hand, if one thinks of Hölderlin as the modern poet who more completely than any other lived the contradictions of his culture—amid outbursts of violence and melancholy creating works from the omnipresent conflict of feeling and skill—so that in him these contradictions became objective with a definiteness of outline heightened by his abrupt end, his madness does become the philosophical sacrifice he contemplated. And then he would not have to mourn.

Indeed, in the following maxim, Hölderlin asks that others be understood in joy [*aus Freude*], for

love enjoys making delicate discoveries (when the spirit and the senses have not grown timid [*scheu*]) . . . and is not inclined to overlook anything, and where it finds so-called errors or mistakes—parts—which because of what they are or their position and movement momentarily disrupt the tone of the whole, feels and views the whole only all the more intensely. . . . That man or woman has achieved a great deal who can understand life without mourning. (14:71)

Such insight is the fated form of Hölderlin's swift conceptual grasp, which urged him not to linger, not to tarry on "the special, momentary, particular lack," for this would be a kind of mourning.

Thinking himself useful to the philosophical light, Hölderlin does not mourn. Nor would we mourn if we could "feel and view . . . more intensely" through the pieces of his shattered nation, another whole, in which all parts are attuned. This would be the only forgiveness for the self-inflicted inability to mourn. The task comes forward—in the words of a writer of like poetic intensity and dedication—of practicing a "special method of thinking. Shot through and through with feeling. Everything that has access to itself as feeling, even what is least definite, becomes thought."[48] That author is Kafka. The vision is also Hölderlin's, who in the Third Maxim wrote: "Surely feeling is the best sobriety" (14:69).[49] Hölderlin's and Kafka's worlds fuse palpably in the Square of the Old Synagogue in Aschaffenburg, Germany, whose synagogue was incinerated in the pogrom of November 9, 1939, and where words of Hölderlin have been inscribed: "Ach, töten könnt Ihr, aber nicht lebendig machen, wenn es die Liebe nicht tut [Oh, you can kill but not bring to life, if love does not do it]."[50] "Love" is another, a perhaps more accurate word for Hölderlin's swift conceptual grasp. It accords with Kant's view of the beautiful, which "prepares us to love something, even nature, apart from any interest."[51] Hölderlin and Kafka share this view. It is the most desperate and hence the most realistic form of swift comprehension—the love that "delicately discovers" a single indestructible whole.

4

NIETZSCHE'S MOODS

> You ask me where I get my ideas from? . . . They come
> unbidden . . . , as clear as day, in the open, in the woods,
> on walks, in the still of the night, at dawn, aroused by
> moods, which for the poet transform themselves into
> words, for me into sounds, that ring, roar, storm until
> they finally stand before me—in notes.
>
> —Beethoven, in Oscar von Pander, *Beethoven:*
> *Der Künstler und sein Werk*

The existential category of mood, or *Stimmung*, according to Walter
Biemel, acquires in Kant's *Critique of Judgment* "a function of disclosure
which, before Kant, had been attributed only to logical cognition. Kant
implicitly gives mood a significance that, only recently, in the work of
Heidegger and Scheler, has received the explanation that is its due."[1] No
one would dispute the reasonableness of situating Nietzsche (1844–
1900) in the arc of reflection on art, aesthetics, and play that leads from
Kant through Heidegger and Scheler (and in which accounting Walter
Benjamin needs to be reckoned).[2] Furthermore, if that arc, as Biemel
suggests, describes a major line of philosophical reflection on art because it involves art in mood, then it is important to know Nietzsche's
views on mood.[3]

The term appears in a number of decisive contexts throughout
Nietzsche's early work, especially preceding and including *The Birth of
Tragedy* (1872). By the mid-1880's, however, with the writing of the ma-
jor essays of the axial period—*Thus Spoke Zarathustra* (1883–85), *Beyond
Good and Evil* (1886), and *The Genealogy of Morals* (1887)—the term

"mood" nearly disappears. This is a fact, I think, of considerable interest. The importance of Nietzsche's abandonment of mood is highlighted by the importance it had for him up until the early 1880's.

The first mention of mood in Nietzsche's work occurs in a letter to Wilhelm Pinder on August 21, 1861, in a context that forecasts Nietzsche's habitual use of the term. Pinder, a school friend at the Schulpforta with whom Nietzsche had close intellectual ties, had written Nietzsche a letter describing a journey through the Bavarian Alps. Pinder lingers on his first encounter with Alpine scenery:

> Ever more powerfully the rocky masses of the high mountain chains jut out; ever lovelier, the lower ridges, with their greening meadows, spread out below. . . . So we lived in the beautiful Alpine valley, now in joy, now in sorrow— in joy, when the friendly sun shone down from the blue sky, in sorrow when clouds veiled the mountains and the sky turned gloomy.[4]

The moods of this passage from Pinder's letter are literary, their source almost certainly Hölderlin's novel *Hyperion*—as in "Oh come! In the depths of the mountain world the secret of our heart will rest. . . . I mourned. . . . It was the harbinger of joy—this sorrow."[5] Nietzsche wrote back:

> My warmest thanks for your lovely, detailed, interesting letter from the Tegernsee. . . . You will have got home safely even while I am writing this letter. Perhaps you've already read my letter of August 3, and perhaps your moods are like the ones I had at the end of the vacation.[6]

If the pattern of probable influence holds, then the moods that Nietzsche asks Pinder to acknowledge are also Hölderlinean in inspiration. We do in fact know that the philosophical debating society Germania—founded by Nietzsche, Pinder, and a certain Gustav Krug—had by this time acquired a copy of Hölderlin's poems.[7] More to the point is that Pinder's letter is itself a response to a letter Nietzsche wrote on August 3, 1861. This letter has disappeared, but its outline survives: "End of the vacation. / Nuremberg. / Pain is . . . / Ustaj. / Shipment. / Bookbinder. / Hölderlin. / What are your plans tomorrow? / Missed the Founders' Celebration. / Write soon."[8] At the end of the summer of 1861, having been especially preoccupied with Hölderlin, Nietzsche recorded his distinctive moods, which were almost certainly modalities of the joy and sorrow inspired by his reading. Nietzsche's letter to

Pinder marks the earliest association in Nietzsche's oeuvre of the category mood with a Romantic-Idealist source.[9]

Nietzsche's first long text on mood has powerful implications for his mature thought. In spring 1864, while still a schoolboy at the Schulpforta, Nietzsche composed an entire essay on the subject.

ON MOODS[10]

Imagine me sitting at home, wrapped in a dressing gown, on the evening of the first day of Easter: outside a fine rain is falling; no one else is in the room. I stare for a long time at the white paper lying in front of me, pen in hand, angered by the confused crowd of themes, events, and thoughts all demanding to be written down; and a number of them demand it in a very stormy way, because they are still young and in ferment, like must [new wine], while a number of old, mature, clarified thoughts resist, like an old gentleman gauging with an equivocal glance the strivings of the world of youth. Let us say this plainly: our frame of mind is determined by the struggle of the old with the young world; and we call the state of the struggle at each moment "mood," or else, somewhat contemptuously, "whim."

As a good diplomat, I hold myself somewhat aloof from the contentious parties and portray the condition of the state with the impartiality of one who day after day inadvertently attends the sessions of all the parties, employing in practice the very principle which, when he is on the podium, he mocks and jeers at.

Let us admit that I am writing on moods because right now I am in a mood, and it is a good thing that I am just in the mood to describe moods.

Today I spent a lot of time playing Liszt's *Consolations*, and I feel how the sounds have penetrated into me and, having become spiritualized, echo inside me. And a little while ago I had a painful experience and went through a parting or a nonparting, and now I note how this feeling and those sounds have fused together. I don't think I would have liked the music if I had not had this experience. Thus, it is similar things that the soul seeks to attract; and the current mass of feelings squeezes out, like a lemon, the new events that touch the heart, yet always so that only a part of the new fuses with the old. Therefore, a residue remains that has so far failed to find anything kindred in the household of the soul and hence lodges there alone, quite often to the displeasure of the old residents, with whom it often finds itself quarreling on this point.

But look! here comes a friend; there, a book is opening; there a girl is passing by. Hark! sounds of music!—Already new guests are once again streaming in from all sides into the house, which is open to everyone, and he who was just now living by himself finds many noble kindred.

But it is strange; it is not that guests come because they want to or that they come as they are; rather those come that have to come and only those which have to. Whatever the soul *cannot* reflect does not touch it. Since, however, it is a function of will power whether the soul reflect or not, only that touches the soul which the soul desires to touch it. And this seems absurd to many, because they remember how they resist certain feelings. But what finally determines the will? Or how often is the will asleep, and only drives and inclinations keep watch! One of the strongest inclinations of the soul, however, is a certain curiosity, a taste for the unusual, and this explains why we often let ourselves be put into unpleasant moods.

But it is not only via the will that the soul takes on things; the soul is made of the same stuff that events are made of, or of something similar, and so it happens that an event that does not touch any kindred string nonetheless with its burden of mood lies heavy upon your soul and can gradually become so predominant that it cramps and compresses the other contents of the soul.

Thus moods come either from inner battles or from an external pressure on the inner world. Here a civil war between two army camps—there oppression of the people by a caste, a small minority.

It does often seem to me, when I overhear my own thoughts and feelings and silently attend to myself, as if I heard the buzzing and raging of those wild factions, as if a rushing went through the air, as when a thought or an eagle flies up to the sun.

Struggle is the soul's constant nourishment, and it knows how to take from it quite enough sweetness and beauty. It annihilates and thus gives birth to the new; it battles fiercely and yet draws its opponent gently to its side into an intense and inward union. And the most marvelous thing is that it never pays attention to externals—to names, persons, countries, fine words, flourishes; all this is of lesser value to it—but it values what lies within the shell.

What now is perhaps your utter happiness or your utter heartache in a short time perhaps will be only the garment of a still deeper feeling and hence will disappear when the higher one comes. Thus our moods grow deeper and deeper; no single one is exactly like any other one, but each is unfathomably young, the offspring of the moment.

I think now of much that I loved; names and persons changed, and I do not want to say that their natures had really become more and more profound and beautiful; but it is probably true that each of these kindred feelings means a step forward for me and that it is intolerable for the spirit to pass once again through the same stages that it passed through; it wants to go on expanding into the depths and heights.

I greet you, dear moods, strange alterations of a stormy soul, manifold as nature, but more splendid than nature, because you are growing ever more intense, ever striving upward, whereas the plant still smells now as it smelled on Creation

Day. I no longer love the way I loved weeks ago; at this moment I am not in the same mood I was in when I first began to write.

Easter, 1864

In 1864 Nietzsche was still a student at the Schulpforta; by then, however, he was almost twenty years old and ready to graduate from that formidably rigorous college. Only four years later he would be professor of classical philology at the University of Basel. Thus, in 1864, at the time of composing "On Moods," he was three years older than he had been when he wrote his celebrated schoolboy essay on Hölderlin[11] and the same age as Rimbaud when, in 1873, *he* wrote *Un Saison en enfer*. "Schopenhauer as Educator," the third essay in Nietzsche's *Unfashionable Observations*[12]—a text we would certainly want to take very seriously—was partly written in the winter of the very next year, in 1865. These facts suggest that "On Moods," although the work of a schoolboy, might justify an attentive reading.

· ᴧ ·

In speaking, human existence *ex*presses itself, not because it has, first of all, been encapsulated as something "internal" over against something external, but because as Being-in-the-world it is already "outside" when it understands. —Martin Heidegger, *Being and Time*[13]

Nietzsche's essay on moods enacts the being "outside" of articulated understanding. More than this, the essay suggests that mood is the very basis of this exteriority.[14] Nietzsche represents his topic by means of a continuous movement toward an outside—a conception remarkable enough because in the Romantic-Idealist tradition before Nietzsche, mood is regularly viewed as "inside," as inside as possible. Certainly this is true of Kant's beautiful mood of cognitive attunement (between the faculties of imagination and concepts), which possesses no correlative domain of objects. No object-thing corresponds to the mood that founds the judgment of beauty.

From the beginning, Nietzsche's essay transposes the scene of understanding mood to an outside. The scene is staged, envisioned *elsewhere*— otherwise than as the intuition of an inner event. From the start, the mood-project requires the orbit of an unnamed other person. The apparently naive, phenomenological (but actually overdetermined) starting point—the author is in his dressing gown, pen in hand, staring at the white paper lying in front of him—arrives already bled of immediacy, for it has been preceded by the disruptive fiction of its frame. This frame is the fable that Nietzsche's act of writing "On Moods" is an intersubjective event, even a theatrical one. The fiction advances by means of the claim that an other will supply this scene with the presence it does not possess by itself: "[Let someone] imagine [me] [*Man vergegenwärtige sich*] as I proceed to understand mood" is the first proposition of an individual understanding of mood.

Within the field of the unnamed other, the subject matter of "On Moods" unfolds, whose fable is that a text on moods is being composed. And yet each attempt to project this subject matter as a visualizable image or event encounters complicating obstacles and has to begin all over again. For "outside," the scene suggests, is also a domain of obscurity and invisibility: it is night, "outside a fine rain is falling." And even the room environing the act of writing contains nothing visible beyond the halted pen. An act of perception—a stare—"takes place," yet it encounters a blank page. Mood requires an other's imagination if it is to be theorized. Mood is . . . somewhere else as someone else's understanding.[15]

Under the pressure of this exterior imagination, inwardness "expresses" itself as a mob in turbid agitation, a "confused crowd."[16] The essay's task is now to contain or situate this mob, but can it? This complex belongs to the common imagination of political life, but it is also the metaphor of any unruly abundance of things—here, of mental events, mainly "thoughts." More precisely, only some of the mob are thoughts and some are themes and events in a domain going beyond thought, neither inside nor, certainly, outside in the sense of being perceptible to an observer; they are sheerly excessive. Conceptual thought resists them and will not admit them. They crowd backwards and forwards over the border between more familiar domains inside and outside the psyche, seeking a path to "being written down" that evades the resistance offered by "old" thoughts. Through the mingling of its literal and figurative senses, the image of the mob precipitates a second complex of political, generational, and also intrapsychic conflicts.

It is interesting how, throughout the essay, Nietzsche complicates the status of the subject that, assailed by moods, aims to understand mood. He suspends the decision about how its operations are to be grasped. Is it that thoughts on mood must appropriate events in order to grow definite enough to be understood (to be written down, as articulate expression)? Or is it that these thoughts are themselves events, arising from a source external, willful, and adversarial? In other words, when a thought is understood, is it that an event captured in the thought (*noema*) is understood? Or is it that, in understanding a thought, we understand rather the kind of event (*noesis*) that thought is?[17] This interinvolved but indeterminate character, as it connects the inner and outer elements of experience, is the main dimension acquired by mood in the course of the essay. The precise nature of mood, Nietzsche says, is a disposition, logic, or rapport in the state of the struggle between the thrust of event en route to thought and the thrust of thought en route to (capturing) its own event. For throughout this essay, Nietzsche's understanding of mood, eventuating as writing, must itself travel a route exterior to introspection, in a gesture anticipating something of Foucault's account, according to which "today's writing has freed itself from the dimension of expression: referring only to itself, it is . . . identified with its own unfolded exteriority."[18] Understanding, continues Nietzsche, is articulated expression or writing; it is not the same thing as "having the concept for," which his highly rhetorical attempt at conceptualizing mood pragmatically demonstrates. The virtual concept is metaphorized, as it strives to include the experience of the becoming that lies before or outside the concept.

The mob of thoughts, themes, and events consists of all the contending parties, but the mob is internally separated into fractions only at the moment that some of its members are said to be "stormy" (*stürmisch*). This word, which produces a separation, does not come from the metaphorics of politics but from the metaphorics of nature—a return surreptitiously guided by the initial given of foul weather. The outside (the political struggle) that exteriorized the inside (thoughts on mood) is itself exteriorized by the term that invokes the natural world of weather. And it is again this natural order, at once outside and inside the political order, that generates the mob of predicates distinguishing the party of the young from the party of the mature. "Stormy" functions altogether as a rhetorical leitmotiv. With its final appearance as predicate of choice, it closes the entire essay, identifying the "soul" of the narrator: "I greet you, dear moods, strange alterations of a stormy soul." At the same time, this essay can also be said not to have "closed" but only to have been broken off by a change in mood; expression is governed by a wayward temporality that is not its own thing to control. The indeterminate, unfinished character of expression is in fact made graphically plain in the Hanser edition of the text "On Moods." After a few blank lines, another untitled text begins, which might or might not be read as part of "On Moods" and is itself saturated with the metaphorics of stormy weather.

In "On Moods" the polarity of the predicates "youthful" and "mature" typically resists a definite assignment of value. The young have the vigor of new wine but also have all the turbulence and turbidity of must: indeed, as must, they are not yet wine. And their opponents—mature (they are *ausgereift*) and settled (they are *geklärt*, clarified, "fined down")—appear to be no longer ripe. At what point does such ripeness, which amounts, in this context, to "being aged," begin to suggest, "like an old gentleman," chemical stoniness?

Indeed these "wines" are either already old, or else they are not yet wines at all: the essay opposes must—something short of wine—as the property of youth, all in a ferment, to *eau de vie*, something past wine, as the property of balky old men casting unfocused glances. And so it isn't possible to assign a definite predominance of value to either figure. Indeed one could just as soon characterize grapes on the vine as *ausgereift* (ripe) as characterize wine or (aged) spirits this way; and we now increase the turbulence of exchange when we realize that it is these fully ripened grapes that must be trampled—"annihilated," *in sich verschwinden*, Nietzsche will write, at the end of the essay—in order to produce stormy, juvenile must.

The initial scene is thus a continual movement of metaphors—"a mobile army of metaphors and metonymies"—none of which can be contained by the scene of mood. None of these figures conjures a firm tenor or significance; each conjures instead entire orders of associated vehicles or signifiers, whole metaphorical domains. The essay advances by always attaching a contestatory image to the elected metaphor, the polarity of image and metaphor then precipitating the polarity of entire systems of metaphor. Thus ferment opposed to fining down conjures the whole of oenology; storminess opposed to serenity, the whole of meteorology; youth's conflict with age, the whole of the struggle for survival—biology.

·~·

If we were to continue to read this essay closely, we would go on emphasizing its rhetoric in excess of doctrine. And supposing that Nietzsche's rhetoric is, precisely, in genuine touch with its topic, then this excess will suggest the insatiably ("ever young") constructive power of mood. And yet, however secondary the essay's doctrine of mood, it will be interesting, nonetheless, to set it down. In doing so, one has to be guided by a preconception of mood, as I am guided by Heidegger's discussion of mood in *Being and Time*.

The point for mood of Nietzsche's little drama of the deluded diplomat—of the reflective self-consciousness blind to the interests it prejudicially seeks to maintain (the search for the self being self-seeking)—is this: Consciousness is always moodfully attuned, and so-called reflective consciousness is itself attuned by a mood, even if this mood be that of *theōria* (a tranquil tarrying-alongside), the mood that resists strong coloration. In the figure of the diplomat, Nietzsche describes the observer who supposes himself disinterested but who is actually the naive partisan of all those representatives of old and new experience, mood being the index of this struggle for hegemony. The "principle" that the observer derides is partisanship, but this is the very principle of his practice—and even of his practice *as* observer, for, says Nietzsche, he is only "somewhat" aloof. The condition of writing on mood is the attunement by some other mood, which, here, for the young author, is the mood of writing.

The inevitable, classically grounded metaphor of mood is musical resonance—a point famously elaborated by Leo Spitzer in *Classical and Christian Ideas of World Harmony: Prologomena to an Interpretation of the Word "Stimmung."*[19] The musical metaphor is apt, because it evokes a comparable kind of attunement, a reciprocity of disposition that puts the responsive subject outside, in events—in real harmonics—before the subject appropriates inner events as thoughts. It is via a musical association that young Nietzsche acknowledges the power of affectionate feeling (afterwards, "love") to enter him, to overcome psychic resistance. Music pierces him and resonates in the train of feeling, its passage eased by the vulnerability that feeling opens up. But music also has a fundamental importance within the fable because it is mentioned ahead of love.

Nietzsche can be seen at work composing a kind of ranked list of experiences according to their power to overcome resistance and to enter him. In this way they bring about (good) moods as changes in the disposition of forces in what is already inside vis-à-vis what is newly arrived from the outside. First position means least resistance encountered and, hence, the best mood; this goes to sympathetic feeling. The next position, the next best mood, goes to music ("I don't think I would have liked the music [of Liszt] if I had not had this experience"). The succession of moods is facilitated by the power of assimilation through resemblance, Nietzsche says—a thesis enacted in the overture to his essay, which abounds in associations of images with metaphors. "New events" "touch the heart" only as feeling discovers in them resemblances to objects already appropriated.

This is Nietzsche's Romanticism of moods—I mean, the fact that he gives a privilege to "love" as the agent most immediately able to produce mood-changes by its power of metaphorical appropriation. In Nietzsche's adolescent lexicon of metaphors for the activity of love, the first mental power is neither mirror nor lamp but juicer ("expresser"). But there is also a competent logic at work in this figure, because Nietzsche proceeds, faithful to his opening, to identify the specific factor of mood production as not only the ready assimilation of metaphorlike experiences but also the thrust to consume them even in their otherness, to leave nothing over, to squeeze them dry. No mood change, then, without the experience, too, of something alien to consciousness; and if what is resistant to consciousness is finally assimilated, then the play of (good) moods is affective testimony to the power of this unconscious practice.

The dominance of affectionate, sympathetic feelings and music marks the overcoming of moods produced by disparity in favor of moods inflected toward—I must use the German word—*Heiterkeit* (gaiety, serenity), although the word does not specifically appear in "On Moods." Nietzsche does employ the congeners *Unbefangenheit* ("nonchalance," which I've translated as "impartiality") and also sets in motion the words "unconstraint" (that is, *not* being *zusammengedrückt*, *not* being *eingeengt*) as well as "sweetness" and "beauty." *Heiterkeit*, of course, will be an important value throughout Nietzsche's writing. As the name of a mood it is suggestive of *theōria*, of doing philosophy, in which light the expression "the gay science" could actually seem pleonastic, for gaiety is as such philosophical. And the word *heiter* also describes fair weather—the weather one could find especially in Athens and Jerusalem, cities productive of genuine—hence, fair-weather—philosophy.

Throughout "On Moods" Nietzsche stresses the factor of intentionality. Since what comes in, comes in only as a function of the mind's disposition to double itself (in metaphors), it follows, from Nietzsche's little parable of the mind as social gathering, that only some "guests" are invited whereas others are turned away ("Whatever the soul does not reflect cannot touch it"). And if Nietzsche also puts the matter as "those come in which must come," attributing intentional thrust to the *noemata* of intentional consciousness, this is rather a part of his relentless exteriorizing of the act of expression (of having moods) throughout the essay. A further observation: if Nietzsche's discussion of mood began by emphasizing as mood-engendering the disparity of resistance to metaphorical appropriation, his essay must and now does dwell on the mystery of disparity, the otherness in experience. How could what is Other be accommodated by the Selfsame? Here Nietzsche posits a primordial inclination, curiosity for the unfamiliar, forecasting, perhaps, his entire mature philosophy of self-contestation, of self-overcoming in the name of a sought-after otherness of experience. Here, too, is Nietzsche's antimentalism, his refined materialism: world events, he says, are made of the same stuff as the soul; the experience of things actually "weighs upon" the soul. And there is, especially at the end of his essay, an example of his characteristic figure of armies in combat.

At this point, two models of the underlying structuration of mood have emerged, both dependent on war: one is a war more nearly within—a civil war of the already interiorized against what's newly arrived from the outside. The other is a foreign war pitting what's inside against what weighs upon it from the outside as an alien disparity, a dangerous clique—the image of an oppressive elite. Nietzsche projects what is new, inassimilable, and other as elite oppressors of the ordinary, anticipating the violent originators of new states and classes in *The Genealogy of Morals*.

Nietzsche attends to and valorizes mood (the index of contestatory states of mind) by likening moods to acts of writing such as his own essay. These acts, it is important to note, more nearly resemble "events" of the "soul" than projects of the willing ego; it is important to stress this point about the productiveness of unconscious states of aesthetic mastery and not triumphs of design.[20]

Finally, Nietzsche's conclusion speaks of *Steigerung* (intensification), of rising moods. It is Easter! The risen Christ resonates as the high mood of an essay written through the night. Forever after, Nietzsche vows, moods will be tokens of his development, of journeys taken, of vertical flights. "I feel that I can prove," wrote Gaston Bachelard, "that Nietzsche is the typical *vertical poet*, the *poet of the summits*, the *ascensional poet*."[21] As such tokens, moods have a distinctively nonnaturalistic side—more like script than pathos, "the secret alphabet-script" of the body (I:1090) and a language, moreover, blessedly without Indo-European grammar. Nietzsche's own essay, which has followed its trajectory "like an eagle flying up to the sun," amounts to a confirmation of a pledge, a vow of continual evolution, of intensification.

· ᕬ ·

One could and should reread this text with a better eye for detail. Among other gains, close reading would bring to light conflicts and shortcomings of adequate *ex*pression—would describe more and different figurative thrusts toward exteriorization that fail to hit the mark. But descriptions of this rich fault do not obviously take us closer to an answer to the question posed at the outset: why, to judge from Nietzsche's oeuvre, does his preoccupation with mood have so relatively short a shelf-life? In what other ways does the early work so dwell on mood that Nietzsche has to reject it by the early 1880's?

We have not so far considered the appearance of the category of mood in any text that Nietzsche intended to publish; but now we shall see that the term produces powerful effects throughout his first work— *The Birth of Tragedy.* Wherever the term "mood" occurs we find an especially significant intellectual context. The appearances of the term are mediated by the intellectual system of Romantic-Idealist aesthetics, for they almost always occur in contiguity with canonical writers (Kant, Schiller, Schopenhauer) and with key terms from their discourse. This is the logic governing the use of mood in its first appearance in Nietzsche's letter to Wilhelm Pinder in 1861.

The first mention of Schiller in *The Birth of Tragedy* is remarkable, because it already includes an anti-Romantic point. In Section 3, Nietzsche writes apropos of the Will's longing for Apollinian existence:

Here we should note that this harmony which is contemplated with such longing by modern man, in fact, this oneness of man with nature (for which Schiller introduced the technical term "naive"), is by no means a simple condition that comes into being naturally and as if inevitably. It is not a condition that, like a terrestrial paradise, *must* necessarily be found at the gate of every culture. Only a [romantic] age could believe this, an age which conceived of the artist in terms of Rousseau's *Émile* and imagined that in Homer it had found such an artist Émile, reared at the bosom of nature.[22]

(This hint of anti-Romantic polemic provides a precedent for Nietzsche's 1886 critique and retraction of everything Romantic in *The Birth of Tragedy*.) In case this point needs stressing, from now on there will be as much Schiller on the face of this work as Schopenhauer. The first actual appearance of the word "*Stimmung*" in *The Birth of Tragedy* occurs in Section 5, where Nietzsche quotes Schiller's remarks on the role of mood in poetic activity.

Schiller has thrown some light on the poetic process by a psychological observation, inexplicable but unproblematic to his own mind. He confessed that before the act of creation he did not have before him or within him any series of images in a causal arrangement but rather a *musical mood*. ("With me the perception has at first no clear and definite object; this is formed later. A certain musical mood comes first, and the poetical idea only follows later.") (*BW* 49)[23]

Nietzsche is attracted to this argument, of course, since it adumbrates the ontological "anteriority of the Dionysian [the musical mood] in relation to the Apollinian [poetical idea]."[24] Later in the same section, Nietzsche goes to Schopenhauer's *The World as Will and Idea* for an idea that enlarges this argument—the claim, namely, that the lyric subject is never continuous with the "subject of the will," the empirical self. Nietzsche quotes Schopenhauer:

It is the subject of the will, *i.e.*, his own volition, which fills the consciousness of the singer, often as a released and satisfied desire (joy), but still oftener as an inhibited desire (grief), always as an affect, a passion, a moved state of mind. Besides this, however, and along with it, by the sight of surrounding nature, the singer becomes conscious of himself as the subject of pure will-less knowing, whose unbroken blissful peace now appears, in contrast to the stress of desire, which is always restricted and always needy. The feeling of this contrast, this alternation, is really what the song as a whole expresses and what principally constitutes the lyrical state. In it pure knowing comes to us as if it were to deliver us from willing and its strain; we follow, but only for moments; willing, the remembrance of our own personal ends, tears us anew from peaceful contemplation; yet ever again the next beautiful environment in which pure will-less knowledge presents itself to us lures us away from willing. Therefore, in the song and the lyrical *mood*, willing (the personal interest of the ends) and pure perception of the environment are wonderfully mingled; connections between them are sought and imagined; the subjective *mood*, the affection of the will, imparts its own hue to the perceived environment, and vice versa. Genuine song is the expression of the whole of this mingled and divided state of mind. (my emphasis; *BW* 51)

One aspect of this passage is of immediate interest for our entire discussion of the value of aesthetic feeling. It is the fact that the concept of mood appears within a double register. On the one hand, mood is apt to describe the lyric state constituted by the tension *between* the pure knowing subject and the empirical willing subject. On the other hand, it is also attached entirely to the subject, the affection of the will, in what appears to be a degradation of its status. But how can mood characterize the disclosure of the essential tension *between* the self of pure perception and the contingent, conative self and also be equated with a mere contingent "affection of the will"?

What Schopenhauer calls in the first instance the lyric mood—stressing its tension, its diacritical character—matches well what I have been calling "complex pleasure." What he aims at in the second instance, however, is mere fugitive, opaque feeling. With this contradiction, he offers a prime illustration of the aporia that bedevils the history of aesthetics: is a disclosure accomplished by mood (whereupon mood needs to be something "higher"), or is it accomplished in a field in which mood is only associatively, contingently present? It will prove impossible to disentangle this double valuation of mood and all its feeling congeners, but we shall observe Nietzsche making the attempt by finding truer names for feeling.

Further along, in Section 6 of *The Birth of Tragedy*, Nietzsche additionally takes up Schopenhauer's categories. Having posed the question: "As what does music *appear* in the mirror of images and concepts?" Nietzsche replies, "It *appears as* will, taking the term in Schopenhauer's sense, i.e., as the opposite of the aesthetic, purely contemplative, and passive mood." I have modified Walter Kaufmann's translation of Nietzsche's (and also Schopenhauer's) word *Stimmung* in this passage as "frame of mind," although previously Kaufmann has consistently rendered it as "mood." But this deviant translation of Nietzsche's category as it is taken from Schopenhauer could be read as also marking the more significant deviation of Nietzsche's argumentative thrust, for it is precisely at this point that Nietzsche for the first time explicitly resists Schopenhauer, remarking: "Here, however, we must make as sharp a distinction as possible between the concepts of essence and phenomenon; for music, according to its essence, cannot possibly be will. To be will it would have to be wholly banished from the realm of art—for the will is the unaesthetic-in-itself; but it *appears* as will" (*BW* 55).[25]

The next appearance of "*Stimmung*," in Section 7, is especially productive, conforming remarkably to the logic of mood in Nietzsche's schoolboy essay "On Moods." Mood—especially foul moods—is the index of the resistance posed by an established (because valuable) state of mind to unfamiliar experience—to themes and events. In this passage Nietzsche writes powerfully about the experience of falling back from Dionysian states into ordinary reality:

For the rapture of the Dionysian state with its annihilation of the ordinary bounds and limits of existence contains, while it lasts, a *lethargic* element in which all personal experiences of the past become immersed. This chasm of oblivion separates the worlds of everyday reality and of Dionysian reality. But as soon as this everyday reality re-enters consciousness, it is experienced as such, with nausea: an ascetic, will-negating *mood* is the fruit of these states. (my emphasis; *BW* 59–60)

This passage is obviously important as much for what it says as for its position within the argument of *The Birth of Tragedy*. In general it is an important document marking the route of Nietzsche's separation from Schopenhauer; look how Schopenhauer's privileged mood—"an ascetic will-negating mood," the peak of wisdom for Schopenhauer—is represented here: as the reflex of nausea, as the frustration of what is evidently a love of "that life . . . at the bottom of things, . . . indestructibly powerful and pleasurable" (*BW* 59). This anti-Schopenhauerian habitus follows hard upon Nietzsche's celebration of the joy and wisdom of "true tragedy," an affirmation impressive enough to prompt Kaufmann to speak here of "Nietzsche's emancipation from Schopenhauer. . . . Nietzsche writes about tragedy as the great life-affirming alternative to Schopenhauer's negation of the will" (*BW* 59n). Obviously Nietzsche cannot settle for the "fruit" of nausea—a will-negating mood. The passage unfolds into a powerful celebration (and a sexualization) of the Dionysian reality, accessible through the tragic chorus: that reality is called "ecstasy," "rapture," "reverence," "wonder," "wisdom," "sublimity," "jubilation," "reality," "eternal life," "unvarnished expression of the truth."

Now, it turns out—not trivially, I think—that precisely here through Nietzsche's first uncited use of the category of mood in this essay, his own first use, that he conveys the enthusiasm of the full human subject. "The reveling throng, the votaries of Dionysus jubilate under the spell of such *moods* and insights whose power transforms them before their own eyes till they imagine that they are beholding themselves as restored geniuses of nature, as satyrs" (my emphasis; *BW* 62). If, from "On Moods" forward, "mood" (principally life-enhancing moods) means the unencumbered advent to the old self of the fullness of analogous experience—especially, what can now be made analogous—then, humankind being at core this Dionysian reality, all mood, so to speak, aspires to the condition of the Dionysian.[26] And, quite consistently, affection and music are the great stimulants to mood.

These relations can be put semiotically, and Nietzsche does so. For the crowd, who, through satyric provocation, have become "poets," all meanings are images; "for a genuine poet, metaphor is not a rhetorical figure but a vicarious [*stellvertretendes*] image that he actually beholds in place of a concept" (*BW* 63).[27] Schiller's and Schopenhauer's language of mood helps Nietzsche to his own formulations of such "intensification"; and toward the end of this very Section 8, mood again appears in Nietzsche's own inflection, torn from its Schopenhauerian link with the spirit of world-denial. Nietzsche suggests that the Dionysian is indeed itself a mood (as then the Apollinian would have to be, by dependency and contrast, the original of the mood of contemplation noted above):

Now the dithyrambic chorus was assigned the task of exciting the *mood* of the listeners to such a Dionysian degree that, when the tragic hero appeared on the stage, they did not see the awkwardly masked human being but rather a visionary figure, born as it were from their own rapture. (my emphasis; *BW* 66)[28]

The Dionysian use of mood at the close of Section 8 is the perfect symmetrical pendant to the rejected mood (indeed, the nausea) of will-negation associated with Schopenhauer at the conclusion of Section 7. The use of "mood" to describe Dionysian states is the most vivid marker of Nietzsche's leave-taking from Schopenhauer. Finally, the next and last appearance of the category occurs altogether appositely in Section 17, refining the character of the Dionysian mood as all-annexing. The Dionysian mood marks a maximum of appropriation by the subject of something crucial in experience—of "theme, event, thought."[29] From "On Moods" forward, all experience, in Nietzsche, involves assimilation on the model of the introjection of metaphors. In *The Twilight of the Idols*, for example, the "art of communication commanded in the highest degree by the Dionysian type [is] marked by the ease of metamorphosis; it is impossible for him to overlook any sign of an affect."[30] But we must be quite clear about what is metaphorized in the Dionysian mood. This scene of appropriation is opposed to the scene of the New Dithyrambic poetry, which completes a so-called decadence of the tragic vision—a fall inaugurated by Socratic irony and Euripidean theater. Nietzsche writes:

In this New Dithyramb, music is outrageously manipulated so as to be the imitative counterfeit of a phenomenon, for instance, of a battle or a storm at sea; and thus, of course, it has been utterly robbed of its mythopoeic power. For it seeks to arouse pleasure only by impelling us to seek external analogies between a vital or natural process and certain rhythmical figures and characteristic sounds of music; if our understanding is to content itself with the perception of these analogies, we are reduced to a mood [*Stimmung*; Kaufmann again gives "frame of mind"] which makes impossible any reception of the mythical; for the myth wants to be experienced vividly as a unique example of a universality and truth that gaze into the infinite. The truly Dionysian music presents itself in such a general mirror of the universal will. (*BW* 107)

The kind of metaphorization of new experience underlying mood is not distinctively suggested by an art of phenomenal analogies, in which sign (mode of representation, for example, "musical figure") and meaning (for example, phenomenon, "natural process") are, so to speak, consubstantial. Even in "On Moods," where Nietzsche speaks of "the soul [. . . as made] of the same stuff [*Stoff*] out of which events are made or *something similar*" (italic added), he does not *equate* "stuff" or "phenomenon" with "event," *Ereignis*. Indeed, at the outset of that essay, he was quite careful to distinguish stuff or theme from event; and he noted there, not how musical sounds and phenomena fuse, but rather "how this *feeling* and those sounds have fused together" (my emphasis). "The soul seeks to attract" things similar to itself (a "mass of feelings" to which no phenomenon is essentially similar); it attracts "new events that touch the heart" but not phenomenal things that are similar to one another. It is essential to what is seized as a metaphor that it leave at the limit an unmetaphorized remainder—the "shell [*Hülle*]." The mind annexes a complex of likeness and disparity but evidently finds its deepest counterpart in the tragic myth, "which can be interpreted only as a manifestation and projection into images of Dionysian states, as the visible symbolizing of music, as the dream-world of a Dionysian intoxication" (*BW* 92).

What Nietzsche also accomplishes at this point is to produce a vivid and powerful definition of myth. Conjuring the satyric crowd risen to the level of the poet—metaphor, for them, is a vicarious image that they behold in place of a concept—Nietzsche poses as the extreme test of their vision the capacity to view the "musical" image in place of an idea that is more than a concept, importing "a universality and truth" that gaze into the infinite. Myth is a painless sublime, the Kantian sublime relieved of its initial constraint and negativity—indeed, an ecstatically pleasurable sublime that will be melancholically avenged only *afterward.*[31]

What Hegel called "the task of art: the sensuous representation of a spiritual idea,"[32] Nietzsche calls myth: the confinement of an infinite gaze in an image, which, as the making-visible of music, is its one apt medium.

Nietzsche's next use of *Stimmung*, occurring in his succeeding work, *Unfashionable Observations*, suggests that it is right to connect distinctive moods with the art-divinities Dionysus and Apollo. In "On the Utility and Liability of History for Life" (the second of the four essays), Nietzsche writes: "Through this excess [of history] an age lands in the dangerous mood of self-irony."[33] In *The Birth of Tragedy* the agency of Socratic irony has the power to contest, and surpass, the hegemonic authority of the Dionysian: one mood displaces another, at the order of the subject and at the order of an entire culture. The point appears to be confirmed by Nietzsche's following use of mood in "On the Utility and Liability of History for Life," which speaks of the destructiveness of the "historical sense" when it goes unchecked: it can exhaust "the creative instinct." "The reason for this," he writes, "is that every historical audit always brings to light so much falsehood, coarseness, inhumanity, absurdity, and violence that the pious mood of illusion, in which alone everything that wants to live is actually capable of life, vanishes" (131). Nietzsche's evocation of a mood of illusion as the precondition of life is reminiscent of passages in *The Birth of Tragedy*. In this case, in "On the Utility and Liability of History for Life," a mood so opposed to the historical consciousness of inhumanity and violence suggests the mood of specifically Apollinian illusion. Furthermore (to speak of the utility of this essay for mood), it contains the first notation of the name Hölderlin in any work that Nietzsche intended to publish. (Recall that Hölderlin was Nietzsche's Romantic "Lieblingsdichter" and that in the letter to Pinder discussed above, the figure of Hölderlin is a kind of placemarker for mood, the first in Nietzsche's writings.) Fittingly, the mention of Hölderlin in "On the Utility and Liability of History for Life" occurs as "Hölderlin's *mood*" (my emphasis; 135).

This lexical drama that will lead to Nietzsche's abandonment of mood comes to a head in the third and fourth essays of *Unfashionable Observations*. The third essay, "Schopenhauer as Educator," criticizes Schopenhauer's own mood as one "that may seem too caustic and sometimes all too pugnacious (191)"; and when the term resurfaces in this essay, it is again with the negative connotations of a certain Rousseauistic "popularity," with self-despising and "frightful decisions" (201). But it is the fourth essay, "Richard Wagner in Bayreuth," that is most strikingly mood-conflicted—a fact that will not come as a surprise since from the beginning Nietzsche has cast music as mood's double.

It is in this essay that mood enters into a crisis. Accordingly, the direction of Nietzsche's thought is not clear or single-minded: it becomes puzzling and ambivalent. For, on the one hand, Wagner is characterized as someone who has taken intense pleasure in his own exalted moods (263); and furthermore, a passage of Wagner's music (Brünnhilde's awakening by Siegfried, in the *Ring*) is praised for the "loftiness and sanctity of its mood" (265). On the other hand, and this is decisive, these references are followed by a single page in Section 9 (I:418) on which the term "mood" appears six times—seven times on the corresponding page of the English translation (*Unfashionable Observations* 314–15). Mood turns out to be the precise feature characterizing music *before* Wagner and marking, through Wagner's surpassing of it, his originality. Until Beethoven and Wagner, mood had been music's source and goal—the element that music reveals and the element into which the listener is transported. Now Nietzsche writes, "Wagner's music is *never* mood-like" (my emphasis). In his music mood has been replaced by "passion" and "will" (316).

In this passage Nietzsche has indeed departed from the distinctions of *Birth of Tragedy*. It must be an only devious compliment to Wagner to say that he abandons a music of mood, a Dionysian category, for a music of affect, marker of the scorned Euripidean. The passage functions as an altogether surprising resuscitation and defense of the Euripidean.

Faced with these conceptual puzzles, I think it less urgent, for the moment, to decide (it is undecidable!) whether in this text Nietzsche chiefly identifies Wagner as the artist of moods or as the artist of the decisive rejection of moods; it may be enough to register the crisis in the form of the vivid association of Wagner with this category. Their bond sets up the argument for rejecting Wagner if he should one day be judged to fall back into the indefinite, uncontoured "mood-like" music that Nietzsche calls Romantic (though not Beethovenesque!). And if, one day, Wagner were to be rejected, so too, with greater scorn, would the entire discourse of moods—mood having become Wagner's casualty.[34] It is no secret that Wagner could not sustain the trajectory that Nietzsche codes as the passage from mood (Romantic) to affect (modern). If Wagner, on Nietzsche's account, once rejected mood for affect, he thereafter fell back into typically Romantic moods of metaphysical homesickness (in *Parsifal*, for example).[35]

The category of mood continues to appear, though with dwindling frequency, during the years of Nietzsche's composition of the "free-spirited" texts—*Human, All-Too-Human* (1878–1880), *The Dawn* (1881), and *The Gay Science* (1882). Here mood is treated as an explicit object of *psychological* analysis. In the orbit of *Human, All-Too-Human*, for example, Nietzsche speaks of "those who write on inner motives," which is to say, of good psychologists: they must be "artists [skilled] at representation so as to awaken the memory of this or that . . . mood."[36] In another place, the "value of a depressed mood" is said to be its "inclining human beings to excesses—also of thought" (Musarion 9:402). "Sentimental moods (about the transitoriness of all joy or the melodic sighing for liberation from prison) [are] always the expression of *depressed* nervous activity. The greatest part of the joy of music comes under this heading" (Musarion 9:417). In *The Dawn* mood appears as an "argument": the decision to undertake some action is confirmed by the mood that accompanies it, which once was thought of as a manifest sign of divine favor (I:1033). Finally, in a striking passage in *The Gay Science*, "high moods" of "long duration" suddenly, but briefly, forecast the full human type. A future history will recurrently produce human beings "embodying a single, great mood" (II:168).

These scattered passages enrich the trajectory of uses which the category mood takes but add little to the question of why Nietzsche abandons the term. So let us propose an answer. In *The Birth of Tragedy* mood always appears with considerable importance and, unlike the categories "emotion" (*Gefühl*) or "affect" (*Affekt*), is never denigrated. The contexts in which mood appears in *The Birth of Tragedy* are furthermore saturated with references to Kant, Goethe, Schiller, and Schopenhauer; the work as a whole is far less a fundamental critique of Idealist aesthetics than Nietzsche's declaration of indebtedness to it. *The Birth of Tragedy* is the only place, not counting *Unfashionable Observations*, where Nietzsche writes, typically, of "the extraordinary courage and wisdom of *Kant* and *Schopenhauer* [who] have succeeded in gaining . . . the victory over the optimism . . . that is the basis of our culture" (*BW* 112). By such associations, *The Birth of Tragedy* appears (to Nietzsche and to his critics real and imagined) as an affirmation of Romantic-Idealist thought. Given, then, the contiguity of the appearances of mood with key authors and terms of Romantic-Idealist aesthetics, mood takes on a Romantic-Idealist connotation in Nietzsche's lexicon. Is it not probable that Nietzsche's rejection of Romantic-Idealist aesthetics dictates his abandonment of the category mood? This reversal can be read in his subsequent writings, in which Kant, Schiller, Hölderlin, Schopenhauer—and especially Wagner—are treated harshly. Nietzsche's attack on Wagner's music is an attack on Romantic music, and "German philosophy as a whole—Leibniz, Kant, Hegel, Schopenhauer, to name the greatest"—appears as "the most fundamental form of *romanticism* and homesickness there has ever been."[37]

In this perspective, it is rewarding to review Nietzsche's critical preface to *The Birth of Tragedy* (added on in 1886). Nietzsche's attack on German music, particularly Wagnerian music, means to attack Romantic music. The critique is addressed to the concluding sections of *The Birth of Tragedy*, which speak of "a yet-impending rebirth of Hellenic antiquity [through Wagner]; for this alone gives us hope for a renovation and purification of the German spirit through the fire magic of music" (*BW* 123). This critical preface is a tour de force for the decisive way in which it clarifies uncertain points in *The Birth of Tragedy*. First, it strengthens the fundamental opposition of Dionysian and Romantic: "Romanticism [is] through and through the most un-Greek of all possible art forms" (*BW* 25), Nietzsche writes, in the course of attributing to Romanticism not ecstatic states but a low power to stupefy and console. The task of a musical culture is to arise not, like the German, in conformity with a Romantic origin but in a Dionysian manner. It is true that

Romanticism—like any serious metaphysics of art or, better, any essentially artistic metaphysics—aims against what is "now," against "reality," against "modern ideas." But there is a key distinction to be made in the matter of the principle to which *The Birth of Tragedy* opposes the reactive art of the moment. Nietzsche takes seriously the charge that the text of *The Birth of Tragedy*, while speaking for Dionysus, could actually seduce listeners to Romanticism, to consolation, to Christianity. He conjures a speaker, not altogether wrong, who objects to this confusion, saying: "Is it not a deep bass of wrath and the lust for destruction that we hear humming underneath all of your contrapuntal vocal art [*Stimmen-kunst*] and seduction of the ear, a furious resolve against everything that is 'now' " (*BW* 25, I:17). And would not, therefore, *The Birth of Tragedy*, in its loathing of modernity, amount to Romantic pessimism and "the art of metaphysical comfort" (*BW* 26)? Nietzsche replies in another voice by shaking up the suspect text with Zarathustra's paean to laughter as the repudiation of metaphysical comfort—indeed, of any sort of metaphysics whatever.

The critical preface is additionally interesting for the way in which Nietzsche avoids the word "mood" (*Stimmung*) at a place where its use could seem attractive. I think of the neologism "*Stimmen-kunst*" as such a circumlocution. This omission is significant as a gesture of distancing. If once Nietzsche had understood Dionysian and Apollinian "voices" as types of mood, that category has now been annihilated or displaced.

I will sum up my argument at this point.

1. Even though Nietzsche, in his Second Preface to *Birth of Tragedy*, distinguished between Romanticism and Dionysianism, it is clear that he was not able to succeed in doing so decisively enough: the speaker who speaks on behalf of this distinction is himself troubled. Hence the discourse of mood remains Romantically contaminated.

2. Within my argument, the key aesthetic distinction in the *Birth of Tragedy* is that between mood (associated with Dionysus) and affect (associated with the pseudo-pantheon of Euripides). If Nietzsche abandons mood, he is to a certain extent obliged to sup with its counterpart: affect.

3. With the abandonment of Wagner as mythical continuer of a (lost) Dionysian culture, as poles of a metanarrative suspended over mere historical contingency, Nietzsche is plunged into factical, degraded modernity, in which only will to power without anchorage and

stations in the metanarrative is available to him as a way out. We could anticipate a linkage of the terms "affect" and "will to power."

The most striking evidence of this displacement is found in Nietzsche's account of the will to power. Nietzsche, it seems, wants a harder, more painful body language than mood.[38] In the discourse of the will, moods give way to affects, which constitute more readable signs in the alphabet-script of the body—a language without conceptual grammar. "Affect" is also the word that goes with Euripides' modernity: affect is the inescapably modern case. If Nietzsche gives away mood for affect— gives away a word associated with an original state of affairs dominated by the Dionysian and the Apollinian, for a word associated with its suicide—then in abandoning "mood," we may see him as "caustically and pugnaciously" acknowledging what cannot be otherwise, namely, the modern world, with all its realism, false fire, and psychology. (Acknowledgment doesn't mean *accepting* the momentary configuration!) The thrust of mood for Nietzsche over time is finally too much opposed to the biological will, the will as causal principle stripped of Schopenhauerian metaphysical connotation.[39] Recall that even in the early essay "On Moods," mood, *rather than will*, was defined more nearly in terms of "drives and inclinations," a distinction that can be grasped along the lines of Nietzsche's distinction between "appearance" (consciously apprehended drives and inclinations) and "essence" (allotropic will). Here we might recall further Freud's distinction in *The Interpretation of Dreams*: "A dominating element in a sleeper's mind may be constituted by what we call a 'mood'—or *tendency to some affect*—and this may then have a determining influence upon his dreams" (my emphasis).[40]

In *The Birth of Tragedy* Nietzsche describes the alienation of the Dionysian precisely as the eclipse of ecstatic moods by Euripidean affects. At the end of his life, however, Nietzsche does prefer the term "affect" (with all its lexical and conceptual baggage) as the truer name of the agent of knowledge. "The force, the power of the will" (notes Alphonso Lingis)

does not come out of the sovereignty of an ego, the sovereignty of self-consciousness; rather, it comes out of the fact that the will to power is fundamentally receptive and continually draws force from the universe, from the dispersed, the distant, the different, and the beyond. It owes its force not to the sovereignty of the self-conscious ego-formation but to its essentially receptive, affective nature.[41]

This observation explains the association of will and affect; in the lexicon of the will to power, affect displaces mood as the feeling mode of disclosure. Indeed, as Nietzsche wrote, the will to power is "the primitive form of affect."[42] "Who interprets?—our affects [*Wer legt aus?— Unsere Affekte*]."[43]

But this granted, one might finally ask, is there anything more at stake than a terminological change in the shift from mood to affect? Doesn't "affect" now mean what "mood" once did? The answer is that mood does not mean the same as affect, because affect is linked to will to power. The terminological shift now retrospectively stains an entire narrative.

The question of power was for Nietzsche an affair of feeling and sensibility before it was an affair of the will. "Pleasure," he notes, "as a feeling of power . . ."[44] This point is stressed by Gilles Deleuze, who cites Nietzsche: "So that will to power can manifest itself, it needs to perceive the things it sees and feel the approach of what is assimilable to it."[45] *We* can now perceive, with some enthusiasm, that "[the] feel[ing of] the approach of what is assimilable to it" are Nietzsche's very words, in 1864, to define mood. But with the will to power he now no longer needs this category; affects, like moods, are indicators of incipient and relentless appropriation. Recall the powerful apothegm from *Twilight of the Idols*: "The art of communication commanded in the highest degree by the Dionysian type," Nietzsche wrote, is "marked by the ease of metamorphosis; it is impossible [for this type] to overlook any sign of an affect."[46]

In *The Birth of Tragedy* the term "affect" suggested a state of mind too coarse, particular, and unlike knowledge—too little a feeling mode of disclosure—to accomplish what mood accomplishes. The thrust of Nietzsche's entire enterprise, with respect to the knowledge that consciousness has, is to subordinate it to some other category of action or exteriority, with a view to showing how conscious, cognitive states are always themselves a play of the thing they mean most to alienate.[47] Nietzsche would take satisfaction from showing that consciousness— the Romantic-Idealist category par excellence—was itself a product of affect. This reversal could readily include mood as too nearly a fiction of consciousness.

5

TELLING SADISM IN MUSIL'S 'YOUNG TÖRLESS'

> The bad conscience of the novel—the bad
> conscience of love. (& of the hero. Hence
> the more or less worm-eaten hero).
>
> —Robert Musil, "Aus einem Rapial"

A logic of justification informs Robert Musil's novel *Young Törless* (1906).[1] The novel appears to do everything in its power to ward off moral criticism. It is doubly, triply insulated against it. In this chapter, I want to explore the various strategies of narrative and persuasion by which the novel achieves a dandylike countenance of impassiveness and superiority. I do not believe that Musil consciously set about constructing fortifications around his work in order to defend against scandal, yet it is as if *Young Törless* had in fact been constructed that way. Pursuing its defensive design ought to throw new light on some of its well-known psychological and narratological salients. One of the reasons for giving importance to its defensive work, its *resistance*, is a certain effect that the novel produces—an effect less of truth in narration than of a subject matter that has been bled of life and given artificial strength through excessive protection.

The narrative mode of *Young Törless* shapes and is shaped by the matter it conveys—Törless's risqué experiments on the mind and body of his fellow pupil Basini.[2] The narrative mode—its situation-cum-perspective—is anomalous, no doubt. In order to get hold of it, we could proceed by trying to approximate it to a model of real speaking. So I shall identify the basic narrative situations that the novel at times assumes but from which it then systematically and significantly departs.

Let us consider a narrative mode that the novel describes and evokes though never assumes as its own. This is the situation of the *direct report*: on this model, Törless, as author, would state his present confusions directly to a reader. He would describe his preoccupations while he is involved in them, and we would read them with the anxious sense that even as we were reading them, these adventures were proceeding to their dismal conclusion.

The novel gives us a close approximation of this model when Törless's thoughts about Basini are literally reproduced: " 'I feel something in me,' he wrote, 'and don't quite know what it is. . . . I must be ill—insane!' "[3] At this point, somewhat like Törless's parents, to whom he writes, we are receiving a direct report of his experience. For in one letter he has told them in an immediate way "about his peculiar states of mind, though this was before he had been drawn into the sexual adventure." Perhaps because of this omission, their reply strikes him as "boring" and "prosaic," advising him "to get Basini to give himself up and thus put an end to the undignified and dangerous state of subservience he was in" (196, 128★). In an earlier letter Törless had written "all about [Basini's disgrace]; the only thing he [had] passed over in silence was what he himself had felt at the time" (69, 51★). The mode of direct report is not congenial to him. Understandably, on receiving a temperate reply advising charity to Basini, Törless "tor[e] the letter into shreds and burned it" (71, 52★): his parents' failure to acknowledge Basini's outlandishness makes him a less fascinating object. We do not hear further of any letter Törless wrote, so he has presumably failed to spell out details of his acceptance of Basini's love-making, his inquisition of Basini in the attic, and the contempt with which he has then discarded him, having no further experimental interest in him. Such reports, especially as they might seem to be composed by a real adolescent, would be bound to provoke a show of scandalized authority. This is a truth that Törless himself registers at a time when he is most fascinated with Basini. Glad that his parents will not spend the holidays with him, "he knew . . . that it would have been almost an interruption—at least it would have perplexed him considerably [*es hätte ihn arg verwirrt*]—if he had to face . . . [them] just at this stage" (142, 94★).

He is right. For anyone for whom Törless matters, his stance of voyeuristic superiority will set off an alarm. At the very least his attitude falsifies his experience: it blinds him to his felt but repressed feelings of affinity with his victim.[4] His superior stance conceals a certain truth of sympathy—"this secret sympathy for Basini" for which, for a time, he "suffers ceaselessly" (165, 108*). But his actual behavior is appalling. Törless capitalizes on the anguish and confusions of Basini, who makes his body available for sadistic abuse. In the narrative situation of the direct report, we would have a mode almost completely bare of the mediations of elapsed time (between the events and the reporting of them) and of differences of personality (between the moral personality of the doer and his deeds and that of their narrator). *Young Törless*, I conclude, cannot be cast in such a mode, because the author of such confessions would be implicated in his story (if a legal personality, he would be incriminated in the legal sense). Few readers, I think, would bring to such a story the obligatory suspension of disbelief without noting the cost of a disturbing impulse to intervene. They would be inclined to shout at such a narrator: "Break off your story and save Basini instead! . . . And I will help you simply by breaking off sympathy with your story." This is exactly the effect that the novel needs to defend against, but it is an effect that, whatever its complications of form, it tends to produce because of its peculiarly repellent subject matter.

Young Törless, however, is strictly speaking never a direct report of experience, since even Törless's literal report of his reflections earlier quoted is bracketed as a citation (132–34, 88*–89*). I think that bothering to consider this form if only to discard it serves to highlight the actual complications of the narrative. *Young Törless* is told by an authorial intelligence vastly more articulate than the adolescent pupil at the boarding school. This is the intelligence of a considerably older person; the full range of narrative differences mentioned above are in play.[5] As I proceed to construct the narrative mode of the novel, I want to put forward not so much empirical descriptions as constitutive "takes"—the stratified succession of profiles on narrative perspective that every reader reading in the mode of the Hegelian "philosopher" would have to make.

To grasp the narrative intelligence of *Törless* on the model of a real speaking situation, we will imagine it as that of the adult Musil, the author of this novel. This is a hypothesis no longer obviously contrary to fact; as Eric Miller remarks, "The third-person narrative situation makes it more difficult to insist on a distinction between the narrator and the author."[6] This way of formulating the narrative situation has the merit of a long-standing and satisfying convention.

We are not now considering that Musil only lends his authority to a fictive narrator who is his representative—as, for example, the grown-up Törless or a confidant of his. The claim I am now making alleges an authorial presence more impressively immediate than that of the fictive narrator representing aspects of the sensibility of an empirical author.[7]

As the real, empirical narrator of *Young Törless*, Musil would then be reporting on either (1) a fictional episode, (2) an episode from the youth of someone known to him, or indeed (3) an episode from his own youth. Hypotheses (2) and (1) actually merge, because if the subject matter of the novel is the sensibility of someone other than the pupil Musil, then, considering the degree of its refinement and intricacy and the fact that it cannot be remembered, it cannot have been reproduced as original experience. It would have to have been imagined. But I believe it is correct to assume that for most readers, the adventures recounted in *Young Törless* have an undeniably personal character. They seem to constitute an acquist of true experience which has then been embellished.[8]

According to the hypothesis of the real autobiographical narrator, then, "Törless" is only a disguised name for the sinisterly adventuresome pupil Musil was. In the English-language version I am using, there is at least one plain textual fact to justify this surmise: the note "About the Author" preceding the novel declares that "Musil . . . attended military academy at Mahrisch [sic]-Weisskirchen in Moravia" (my emphasis; ii). Readers will draw the obvious conclusion when they read, on page 2, that "in this town there was a celebrated boarding-school . . . ; it was a particular advantage to have been educated at *W*" (my italics).[9] Furthermore, the boarding school W.—it is at least suggested—has "a military bias" as well,[10] since "it was here that the sons of the best families in the country received their education"—some of them then going on into the army (2, 8★). The school library consists of "drearily humorous tales of army life" (10, 13★). As Törless begins his dismal walk with Beineberg to the prostitute Bozena's hovel, his "sword," we read, "clattered on the stones" (31, 26★). Finally, Beineberg, in whom "the image of his eccentric father [the general] lived on in a kind of distorted magnification" and in whom "every feature [of the general] was preserved," would pre-

sumably have gone on to a military academy (20, 20*). But this identification is only a hovering suggestion; and that league of critics and cover
illustrators who depict the boarding school at W. as a military academy[11]
must have been bedazzled by Volker Schlöndorff's movie.[12]
The note "About the Author" additionally contributes the impression that the narrative intelligence is Musil's personal best, since Musil,
we learn, went on "to study experimental psychology in Berlin" (ii).
The words "experiment" and "psychology" easily function as predicates linking the behavior and attitude of Törless toward Basini with
that of the narrator toward Törless and his world. An early passage asserts, for example, that the bond of animal spirits between Törless and
his friends at the time of the Basini episode constituted a phase, but neither Törless nor his parents could "recognize [in it] the symptoms of a
definite psychological [*seelische*] development" (5, 11*). Of Törless's
entire captivation in "the narrow, winding passages of sensuality," the
author writes: "It was all the result not of perversity but of a psychological [*geistige*] situation in which he had lost his sense of direction" (173,
114*). Indeed, the psychological character of the work seemed so pronounced for Musil's readers that Musil had to fight to have its art character acknowledged. Psychology, he wrote, is supposed to be in the service of a fiction; you take a wagon to explore a landscape, but you do not
look for the landscape in the wagon.[13] The experimental character of
Törless's behavior toward Basini is part of the narrator's claim that what
Törless wants from Basini is not the sensation of sex or power but psychological knowledge.
I shall not discuss all the other reasons a specialist reader would have
for identifying the narrator's values and concerns with those affirmed
and elaborated in the novels, stories, and essays of Robert Musil. Here,
though, is just one example of a permanently Musilian trope. It is found
in the aperçu that concludes *Young Törless*: "Any great flash of understanding is only half completed in the illumined circle of the conscious
mind; the other half takes place in the dark loam of our innermost being. It is primarily a state of soul, and uppermost, as it were at the extreme tip of it, there the thought is—poised like a flower" (210–11,
137*). Musil is throughout the pupil of the Nietzsche who wrote, "[By
assuming] that really words exist only for *superlative* degrees of [inner]
events and drives, . . . we misread ourselves in this apparently clearest
letter-script of our self [*Buchstabenschrift unseres Selbsts*])."[14]

In the narrative situation we are considering, the language with which this narrator (Musil) tells Törless's (Musil's) adventures would have to be Musil's chosen diction. He is responsible for it, and the description and explanation of Törless's motives are Musil's best justification and defense of his own experience—experience that, as the novel repeatedly reminds us, requires one. But then, if we are not satisfied with this defense, Musil himself (in 1906 and all the days of his life and reputation thereafter) would expose himself to the charge of bad faith: that he has constructed in this novel an exquisite but impotent alibi for his youthful abuse of a certain Basini. Such a reaction would be intolerable for the author. It would point up his need to substitute fictional representatives for himself at the level of both theme and narrative structure. The complications of the latter, with their inevitable power to inform everything they touch with a profound and inescapable fictionality, are especially evident through striking breaks in narrative perspective, to which I shall soon return.

In the novel the pupil is called "Törless"—with its overmarked connotation of "Türlosigkeit" (the being from which there is no exit)—and not "me" (young Musil).[15] This is the main index of the substitution of a fictional subject-matter for a real one at the center of the novel. The pattern of substitutions at the order of narration is subtler and more engaging. The author Musil, although he once says "I" early in the novel,[16] in fact conjures a narrator who by no means has to be the empirical personality Musil or even to represent aspects of him. Who then is this "I"? The shifter "I" encourages the attempt to identify personally a speaker even thus minimally embodied.

The narrator, I have suggested, could seem throughout much of the novel to be the fictive Törless grown up.[17] In offering this equation seriously, I do not mean to ignore bits of evidence scattered throughout the novel that contradict any such strict identification. And yet a fictive narrator can be more or less uniformly identified and still be meaningfully identified. The narrator of Kafka's *Metamorphosis*, for example, narrates from a perspective congruent with Gregor's own—with the exception of the coda following Gregor's death and with the exception of a minute break or two. Yet, even though in at least one small scene the narrator speaks from a perspective wider than that of Gregor, it will certainly not do to describe the perspective as therefore authorial rather than figurally congruent. What is crucial in such judgments is a sort of narratologist's tact, which examines breaks in perspective for the importance of the information they convey at the moment they occur.[18] In *Young Törless*, such breaks arise whenever the narrator, putatively the older Törless, describes with confidence the innermost sensibility of someone whom he cannot have known personally—for example, Beineberg's father—without offering even the suggestion of a "perhaps" or "as it were" ("Only occasionally did his [General Beineberg's] thoughts lose themselves in a twilit state of agreeable melancholy," 19, 19*). In another case, he describes events which befall the pupils at academy W. during the time that Törless has run away ("Basini was still paralysed with terror from his experiences of two days earlier, and the solitary confinement in which he was kept . . . was in itself a tremendous relief to him," 205, 133*). It is true that a mature Törless writing a history of himself as a younger man could be imagined as having taken pains to find these things out, but the effect is still of a break in perspective, though an unimportant one.

Finally, in a very important and controversial passage two-thirds of the way into the novel, the narrator starts out abruptly from a temporal standpoint much in the future of the events narrated. Here he is very likely saying explicitly, and for the first time, that he is not Törless. The passage begins, "Later, when he had got over his adolescent experiences, Törless became a young man whose mind was both [very] subtle and sensitive" (169, 111*). While all through this passage it is possible to suppose that the grown-up Törless is referring to himself even under the alias "Törless," it is implausible, I think, to imagine him describing his own mind as "[very] subtle and sensitive." This would make him an impossible prig. True, the passage goes on to describe the mature Törless as an impossible prig, but such a hypothesis, aiming to preserve at all costs the coherence of the fiction that the narrator is Törless, would then also succeed in abusing the reader. Yet the whole purpose of Musil's narrative strategy must be to avoid abusing the reader while continuing to preserve the advantage of an intimate and hence authoritative perspective. The narrative must find the right play of distance from the character and sympathy with him, without duplicating the discreditable play of invasive intimacy and intellectual contempt that young Törless maintains for Basini.

Considering these various breaks, one must conclude that in a strict sense the narrator is not Törless grown up. But one should not leave this assumption behind before drawing all conceivable profit from it. That is because the text gives eminent grounds for finding the assumption interesting and valuable. Here are several.

The narrative is a work of art, and it lies well within the thrust of Törless's depicted development that he is to become an imaginative writer.[19] Thus, we hear that if he has not given evidence of literary abilities while a pupil at W., it is only because of the impoverished literary education he receives there: he has not been acquainted with the literary examples ("Goethe, Schiller, Shakespeare") that a student at a Gymnasium would have been able to emulate (9, 12*). At the same time the pupil Törless is a writer—of letters and psychological notations—and the bliss of writing to his parents at the beginning of his stay at W. is intense.

He wrote letters home almost daily, and he lived only in these letters; everything else he did seemed to him only a shadowy, unmeaning string of events. . . . But when he wrote he felt within himself something that made him distinct, that set him apart; something in him rose, like an island of miraculous suns and flashing colors, out of the ocean of grey sensations that lapped around him, cold and indifferent, day after day. And when by day, at games or in class, he remembered that he would write his letter in the evening, it was as though he were wearing, hidden on his person, fastened to an invisible chain, a golden key with which . . . he would open the gate [*Tor*] leading into marvelous gardens. (3, 8*)

The access he thus obtains to these arcane recesses of the "inner life" (170, 111*) is "novelistic," because it is the entire project of the novel *Young Törless* to provide such access generally. Furthermore, it is habitual with Törless, when he has to "do some hard thinking about himself . . . to do it with pen and paper" (130, 87*), and it can seem that the text we have in front of us is the direct descendent of such spiritual-artistic exercises: "He had worked out, during the course of the day, what it actually was he wanted to make notes about: the whole series of those particular experiences from the evening with Bozena on, culminating in that vague sensual state which had recently been coming over him" (132, 88*). Indeed, as he watches Basini during an entire day's vigil in the study hall, Törless "seemed to himself as one elect—like a saint, having heavenly visions. For the intuitions of great artists was something of which he did not know" (137–38, 92*). Törless is allowed to think of himself as elected; the moment in which he gazes with muddled lust at

Basini constitutes (he thinks) a consecration, an initiation into a religion of sensibility. Are we to criticize the exaltation in this moment? The narrator prefers to read it without irony, as an intuition into the moods of great artists—an intuition that he presumably does not deny to himself as the narrator of this work of obvious intellectual power.

There are many different kinds of evidence for the continuity of subject and narrator. In the important interpolated passage that introduces the mature Törless, he is described as an "aesthetically inclined intellectual" with "creative talent" (169–70, 111*). The suggestion that this very book *Young Törless* is his own work continues to be appealing. As young Törless glances at Basini, "something instantly began in him that was like the crazy whirling of a top, immediately compressing Basini's image into the most fantastically dislocated attitudes and then tearing it asunder in incredible distortions, so that he himself grew dizzy. *True, these were only figures of speech* [*Vergleiche*] *that he found for it afterwards*" (my emphasis; 134, 90*). The conclusion reads like a self-reflexive gesture, directed toward the thick abundance of figures of speech ("those obscure metaphors [*Gleichnisse*]," 213, 138*) that arise and grow in the narrative in proportion to Törless's increasing preoccupation with Basini.[20] Furthermore, the novel continually thematizes "changes in perspective" (159, 105*)—including, especially, the alternation between the sunlit perspective of psychological science and the "dreamy" perspective; and this prevailing reality, the Törless-reality, re-emerges in the "behavior" of the narrator, who, in this sense, is iconic with his subject as a bundle of heterogeneous perspectives. "It was this mental perspective that [Törless] had experienced, which alternated according to whether he was considering what was distant or what was nearby; it was this incomprehensible relation that according to our shifts of standpoint gives happenings and objects sudden values that are quite incommensurable [*unvergleichlich*] with each other, strange to each other" (216, 139*).

Here is another striking detail helping to confirm the association of Törless sufferer-poet with Törless narrator-poet. "It was a pet notion of his that the capacity for enjoyment, and creative talent, and in fact the whole more highly developed side of the inner life, was a piece of jewelry [*ein Zierat*] on which one could easily injure oneself" (170, 112*). It is hard to understand the sense of "a piece of jewelry on which one could injure oneself," but it is much easier and richer to understand if it is read as referring to the Maeterlinck quote that appears as the epigraph of "Törless's" novel.[21] This famous passage describes having experiences of the inner life—of "the abyss"—as a kind of diving for jewels. Yet when they are brought to the surface, they seem like only poor chips of glass. The jewels on which one could injure oneself (lose one's sanity) are all the fascinations of the inner life, which harm in the sense of their imperviousness to articulation and use in the sunlight world: their otherness, their mystery, their lure is an impediment to good conscience. Nevertheless, says Törless, it is expected of the proud possessor of such jewels that he will "make exquisite use of them afterwards" (170, 112★), and the novel *Young Törless*, requiring courage to publish, is exactly the use that Törless has made of them. But they are also pieces of jewelry on which one could injure oneself.

Finally, one could note the obsessive images of web (79, 57★), veil (89, 63★), and net (132, 82★) that mysteriously cover Törless's vision. If we pursue this image over its various appearances, I think we will understand it as a pattern formed from the superimposition of the two modalities of vision—outer and inner, lighter and darker, science and "tensed image."[22] This play of texture—a "bewilderingly close-knit [*verwirrend eng*] mesh" of moments of disjunctive intersection between these orders of word and thing, husk and gleam (90, 64★)—could seem to be the very text that we have before us. Törless's veiled vision becomes this book. And the veil having been fully drawn, the knots situated, there could be a beginning to the legitimate and regulated distinction between disjunct worlds, which is the sense of Törless's final perception: "He now knew how to distinguish between day and night" (216, 140★).

In the type of narrative structure I have been discussing, the modalities of intimacy and distance in the attitude of Törless toward Basini tend to shape the attitude of the narrator (Törless) toward Törless, even though, for obvious reasons, it cannot be advantageous for this to happen. The events of Törless's relation to Basini prove to Törless that his sense of adventure can flourish only as he imagines at a contemplative distance from the real Basini what it is to be Basini and be in his predicament. To come too close to his object—to "become" Basini—is to risk an identification that destroys a necessarily imaginary rapture. This set of injunctions could answer well to the program of the narrator, who as Törless 2 intuits the perplexities of a young Törless (Törless 1) whom he no longer strictly resembles, having come the length of the journey on which Törless has just embarked.

But, paradoxically, as the resemblance of these two stances grows more pronounced, the narrator risks a kind of inculpation. Even as a fictive personality, in appearing to employ Törless's intellectual discovery, he assumes the profit of the vanity and cruelty of the young man he was. And if the youthful Törless seems discreditable, despite the narrator's efforts to do everything in his power to secure a good opinion of him, then Törless's older ego stands condemned by a sort of condemnation forward. Would not a young man so precocious at hypocrisy and at the construction of elegant alibis have contaminated the narrator he was to become?[23] They are not a good or reliable pair, this Törless 1 and Törless 2. And this may be why the narrator has to make such lofty claims for the dignity of Törless's sensibility, pleading more and more urgently, as the novel proceeds, for the importance of his adventures to his and indeed any person's development.

So it seems as if the assumption of a fictive narrator—Törless 2—were not defense enough. As if determined by this flight from a moralizing reading of his novel, Musil must further complicate the narrative position. The narrator keeps all the values of Törless grown up—for who else could report reliably, in mature language, moods of such intimacy? But it is no longer obligatory to assume that the narrator is telling a story about himself in order to disburden himself. Earlier, I noted that the narrator describes Törless's evolution into an aesthetically inclined intellectual whose feelings were "[very] subtle and sensitive." This is praise that would be vaunting and indiscreet in the mouth of the mature Törless. Hence the phrase only really seems possible on the lips of an observer not personally involved—one who "knew" the real Törless as a friend or confidant. Musil winds up—in what is essentially the most adequate fictive model of the narration—speaking as "the friend" of the mature Törless who has heard his story (*"jemandem, dem er die Geschichte seiner Jugend erzählt hatte,"* 170, 112*), even though there cannot be such a friend, with such powers of recall, in real experience. To refine this impossible instance of the "witness biography" still further: the narrator of *Törless* is retelling the story he overheard Törless telling himself.[24] The degree of reciprocal intimacy implied by this model becomes even more intriguing in light of the description of consciousness as such provided by Stephen R. L. Clark on Julian Jaynes's account: "a matter of overhearing oneself repeating to oneself what one heard others say."[25]

By means of the "friend," the external double, the work takes on the steadiness and objectivity of psychonarration even as it preserves the intimacy and psychological realism of the fictive autobiography (here narrated from the third-person perspective)—a fictive autobiography apparently animated by the motive of catharsis and exculpation. Moralizing readers are thus disarmed. If, captivated by the pathos of a novelized confession, readers nevertheless refuse their sympathy, they are immediately corrected. After all, the exculpation is being performed by an omniscient narrator who is not Törless and has no discernible axe to grind. Interestingly, the clearest signs of the case that the narrator cannot be Törless, because he knows more than Törless can know, occur during the late chapters of the work, when the expectation might be highest that the reader will turn in disgust from Törless as not worth saving.

This discussion of the narrative structure of the novel so far aims to articulate just that judgment on Törless's vanity and cruelty which the novel attempts to hide *and* reveals through the mechanism of its denegation (*Verneinung*).

The exculpatory narrative structure is also involved in the great theme of *Young Törless*—the richness of the "inner life." This follows as a consequence of Musil's chief psychological postulate—the resistance of this inner life to verbal representation. One special way of showing its resistance is by the complexity with which motives are represented. What is striking, again and again, is the intricate *dis*continuity of the arc leading from motive to expression, from intent to deed. Musil writes, typically: "Even as . . . [Törless] talked he could feel that he had nothing but irrelevant points to bring up, and that his words were without any inner substance, having nothing to do with his real opinion" (62, 47*). Of course, this is a novel not rich in event but rich in the elliptical representation of what underlies event. The novel proves the standard claim of *Lebensphilosophie*, especially in its decisive formulation by Dilthey: the deed is a poor thing next to the imagination that gives rise to it. In Dilthey's words,

Through the power of a decisive motive, the act emerges from the fullness of life into one-sidedness. However meditated, it nonetheless expresses only a part of our being. Possibilities which lay in this being are annihilated by it. Thus the act detaches itself from the background of the context of life. And without clarification of the way in which in it circumstances, purpose, means, and life-context are connected, it does not allow a full-sided definition of that inwardness from which it sprang. Quite otherwise the objectivation of experience![26]

"Objectivation," for Dilthey, means, chiefly, artistic expression.[27]

These passages will make us think of Törless. "An idea wakened him . . . : what in the distance seems so great and mysterious comes up to us always as something plain and undistorted. . . . What . . . approaches from a long way off is like a misty sea full of gigantic, ever-changing forms; what comes right up to any man, and becomes action, and collides with his life, is clear and small, human in its dimensions and human in its outlines" (159–60, 106*). It goes without saying that all Törless's actions can be detoxified (exculpated, palliated, deconstructed) by reference to the complex originality of their motives.

This is only one part of the thematic logic of Törless's justification. The true subject matter of the novel—Törless's felt perplexities—is informed by two apparently conflicting claims. One is moral, though it might be unconvincing; it asserts the value for the hero's development of his experiment in sadistic cruelty. The other claim is cognitive; it is made about moods, asserting that they are valuable for their distinctive power of disclosure.[28] Typically, we learn that Törless's pained mood "touched his inmost balance at a much deeper point than any moral consideration could" (158, 105*).

On the face of it, these two claims do not have much in common. Yet in *Young Törless* moral and cognitive claims are connected, and their covert linkage shapes the novel in important ways. In a word, Musil's cognitive claim on behalf of moods comes as a lucky find for the novel's apologetic, justificatory intent: Because the narrator needs to come to terms with acts of sadistic cruelty, he can shift the moral gravity of interpersonal action onto the aura of the mood that accompanies it. The narrator's repeated assertion of the cognitive dignity of moods effectually serves to justify his hero's sadism. It is as if Musil had taken up again Nietzsche's abandoned category of mood to reacquaint himself with its powers of cognitive disclosure and, satisfied that they are there, intuited their plot function.

There may be another, more interesting way of putting this appropriation, and reversal, of Nietzsche by Musil when we reflect that by the time of *The Genealogy of Morals* at least two crucial thought-events have occurred. First, Nietzsche has rejected "mood" as the right sort of feeling word, as the word for the kind of feeling capable of being the strongest illustration, of making the most important disclosure; and second, Nietzsche glorifies cruelty. Hence, what Nietzsche definitively puts asunder—mood and cruelty—Musil recombines: cruelty *because* it is the strongest propagator of moods.

The plainest evidence for Musil's general claim about moods is the statement that Törless's sadistic adventure was the necessary product of a time of experiment marked by the cultivation of outré states-of-mind. In later life, we are told, Törless was to grasp this experience as beneficial, if not indeed redemptive—as heightening and refining his capacity for experience.

Therefore, claims that are put forward as discrete actually intersect— "unconsciously," one could say, because the idea of their interinvolvement and reciprocal motivation (which is a true idea, in the sense that it is able to organize disparate themes and rhetorical features of the novel) is never explicitly asserted to be the case.[29] At the same time, we find in the novel the expected effects of the unconscious denial of such motivation—namely, signs, at levels of rhetoric that seem least under control, saying the opposite of what the narrator says most plainly: that Törless, despite and indeed because of his power to experience the world "moodfully," is not different from and not superior to the victim of his sadism. That is because the condition of the experience of moods is a certain passivity.

From the start, Törless is defined through his susceptibility to moods. He gives himself up, with the sense of danger attendant on cultivating passive states-of-mind, to moods, which are revelatory though they cannot be translated into discursive language. "The more accurately . . . [Törless] circumscribed his feelings with thoughts, and the more familiar they became to him, the stranger and more incomprehensible did they seem to become, in equal measure" (28, 25★):[30]

Törless's taste for certain moods was the first hint of a psychological development that was later to manifest itself as a strong sense of wonder. The fact was that later he was to have—and indeed to be dominated by—a peculiar ability; he could not help frequently experiencing events, people, things, and even himself, in such a way as to feel that in it all there was at once some insoluble enigma and some inexplicable kinship for which he could never produce any evidence. . . . The severity of these struggles [to resolve his feelings into words and ideas] was indicated only by a frequent sudden lassitude, alarming him, as it were, from a long way off, when ever some ambiguous, odd mood . . . brought him to a foreboding of it. Then he would seem himself as powerless as a captive, as one who had been abandoned and shut away as much from himself as from others. (28–29, 25★)

Afterwards we read (just to give a few salient examples) that Törless "was in that state of more psychic than bodily fever which he loved. The mood went on intensifying" (136, 91★). He reacts to his having thought something out all too carefully in advance: "It was too unspontaneous, and his mood swiftly lapsed into a dense, gluey, boredom" (144, 95★; cf. 88★).

Törless has a marked consciousness of boundaries and frontiers without being able to map the zones that they define; having moods, he escapes consciousness of the disparity between zone and limit. Typically, in the attic,

he saw people in a way he had never seen them before, never felt them before. But he saw them without seeing, without images, without forms, as if only his soul saw them; and yet they were so distinct that he was pierced through and through by their intensity. Only, as though they halted at a threshold they could not cross, they escaped him the moment he sought for words to grasp them with. (76, 55★)

Moods themselves, like a darkness populated with shapes that hold him fast (65–66, 49★), are subliminal or superliminal. At a certain stage they are attractive, and Törless clings to them, because they pass over and erase boundaries, even in their negative modality fusing inner and outer worlds, like that "same dreadful indifference that had been blanketed over the surrounding countryside all that afternoon [and which] now came creeping across the plain." Törless's act of marching along behind Beineberg through the indifferent mist reinscribes a boundary— "and he felt it as though it must be so, as a stony compulsion catching his whole life up and compressing it into this movement—steadily plodding on along this one line" (14, 16★). The marking of the boundary line is painful. As for his fascination with Basini, "Shut up!" he cries, in self-defense, "It wasn't me. It was a dream. A mood [*eine Laune*]" (187, 123★). Afterwards, "he now knew how to distinguish between day and night; actually he had always known it, and it was only that a monstrous dream had flowed like a tide over those frontiers, blotting them out" (216, 140★).

The painful deficit of Törless's openness to moods is the passivity he has identified in Basini and which is literally poisonous. The image of one who administers and/or takes poison amounts to a link between them. Poison is at first associated negatively with Basini: "He had no power of resisting anything that occurred to him and was always surprised by the consequences. In this he resembled the kind of woman . . . who introduces doses of poison into her husband's food at every meal and then is amazed and horror-struck at the strange, harsh words of the public prosecutor and the death-sentence pronounced on her" (69, 51★). Törless's weak target here figures as a subtle and dangerous avenger—author, as well as victim, of a fatal sentence. But, when the poison image resurfaces in the later passage to justify Törless's behavior, it is homeopathic. In his case, he alleges, the poison he took became a factor that improved him—"that small admixture of a toxic substance which is needed to rid the soul of its over-confident, complacent healthiness, and to give it instead a sort of health that is more acute, and subtler, and wiser" (171, 112★). But the defense is compromised for being spoken, not by the narrator, but by the mature Törless, in his very own words.

The thing that the novel needs fundamentally to defend against is not only or chiefly Törless's sadistic experiments with Basini. It is the possibility that even in asserting his superiority to Basini, Törless is essentially like Basini; that even and especially in tormenting his victim, he is exhibiting his identity with him. If it is true that *for Törless* to be a girl is to assume the passivity simultaneously craved and feared, then the preconscious meditation in which he rediscovers his "unspeakable longing to be a little girl" is revealing, for it culminates in the figure of Basini: "Today for the first time he felt something similar again—again that longing, that tingling under the skin . . . and then, last of all, there was only the pleasant warmth that lapped him . . . like a bath and a stirring of the senses . . . but no longer conscious to him as that, only in some utterly unrecognizable but very definite way being linked with Basini" (128–30, 86★–87★).[31] From the outset, Törless has "yearned to feel . . . definite needs that would distinguish between good and bad, . . . and to know he himself was making the choice, even though wrongly—for even that would be better than being so excessively receptive that he simply soaked up everything" (54, 42★). But in Törless, little better than Basini, "the moral force of resistance . . . was not yet developed either" (172, 114★).[32]

If, now, the young Törless is to escape whipping, then the narrator of *Young Törless* must himself be the moral force. In reproducing Törless's confusions (and illuminations), the narrator must fight clear of identity with Törless the sadist, voyeur, and collector of poisonous moods. Put otherwise, young Törless's fear of being exposed as Basini's accomplice (195, 128★) may be supposed to haunt the narrator: he must not be exposed as Törless's accomplice. Only as a disembodied intelligence and no single, envisionable personality is he certain of being exculpated.[33]

Weight falls on "intelligence." According to the narrator, Basini is principally corrupt, with an immorality linked to his stupidity: "The moral inferiority that was apparent in him and his stupidity both had a single origin" (69, 51★). Hence, it is as if the young Törless could not possibly be corrupt since he is so evidently not stupid.[34] Indeed, it is with this very claim to intelligence that the narrator afterwards defends Törless's taking of Basini's poison.

His tastes had become so acutely and one-sidedly focused on matters purely of the mind [*schöngeistig zugeschärft*] that, supposing he had been told a very similar story about some rake's debaucheries, it would certainly never have occurred to him to direct his indignation against the acts themselves. He would have despised such a person not for being a debauchee, but for being nothing more than that; not for his licentiousness, but for the psychological condition that made him do those things; for being stupid. (170, 112★)

Suppose, however, we cannot agree that corruption and stupidity must have the common root they allegedly have in Basini. Suppose we believe that despite Törless's intelligence, "the more or less worm-eaten hero" is defective; that as one of "such people [to whom] the things that make demands only on their moral correctitude are of the utmost indifference," he is inexcusable (169, 112★). Are we going to be persuaded that this argument is wrong by a narrator chiefly distinguished for his aesthetic intelligence?

This possibility becomes all the dimmer if we have once realized that this narrator is not "a person of aesthetic intelligence," but that the omnipresent *dissolving* character of moods appears to have done his work in "him," too, erasing in him the possibility of coincidence between a self and an actual speaking voice, figuring all his poetic speaking as a kind of impersonation masking the unlifelikeness of his narrative position.

Furthermore, even as a narrator illusorily embodied, having once called himself "I," this "detached" narrator cannot achieve immunity, as I earlier suggested; the stance he adopts is only Törless's stance vis-à-vis Basini—and improved. In keeping distance so as to guarantee a rich imagined sense of the other's inner life, he *repeats* Törless's truth, his great discovery apropos of using Basini, the truth that constitutes him. This is the truth of the superiority of the aesthetic view of persons to the moral one, the truth that says that only the detached and cognitively curious identification is productive:[35] "That kind of knowledge of human nature" is valuable as "a source of exquisite psychological enjoyment" (7, 11★). To the extent that the stance of the impersonal narrator is any more morally concerned than Törless 2's, it is only with Musil's special refinement: "From youth on I have considered aesthetics as ethics."[36] But this position is no different from that of the "dictator" Reiting: "You've only got to drop the idea that there's any relationship between us and Basini other than the pleasure we get out of what a rotten swine he is!" (63, 48★).

The problem of Musil's narrative authority in *Törless* is the same as Flaubert's in *Madame Bovary*, with a change of sign. If Flaubert's aporia is how to condemn the novelistic novelistically—how to expose, by means of a novel, the novelistic contamination of Madame Bovary's desire—Musil's aporia is how to justify an aesthetic intelligence by means of an aesthetic intelligence in practice. The narrative stance of *Törless* is sometimes dictated by science, sometimes by aesthetics ("as ethics"); it is suspended between lucid analytical modes and effects of elegance, between dictions of epistemology and expressiveness, observation and special pleading, the pursuit of founded psychological truths and moral defenses based on erotic identification.[37] In a way there is the bedazzlement of verbal intelligence in excess, and in a way too little rigor. Both are suspicious. Hence there remains at the heart of the novel, for all its intricate flights of narrative and mood, something inexcusable—in a word, scandalous—which ensures its fascination, as it has done for a century now.[38]

6

RAPTURE IN EXILE: KAFKA'S 'THE BOY WHO SANK OUT OF SIGHT'

> For he and his property are not one, but two,
> and whoever destroys the connection destroys
> him at the same time.
>
> —Franz Kafka, *Diaries* (1910)

On his own claim, Franz Kafka (1883–1924) knew an abysmal sense of exile, feeling himself at times, in words he could discover by giving them to his character K.,

so deep in a foreign place as no man before him, a foreign place in which even the air had no ingredient of the air of home, in which one must suffocate on foreignness and in whose absurd allurements one could do nothing more than go further, go further astray.[1]

If, as W. H. Auden remarked, Kafka is the Dante of our epoch—"bearing the same kind of relation to our age" as Dante did to his[2]—the identity of vehicle and tenor should not be overlooked in the exile or sense of exile that each man lived and out of which each wrote. In Kafka's first novel, *Der Verschollene* (*The Boy Who Sank Out of Sight*), Gnostic metaphors of estrangement—"homelessness, loss of orientation, 'thrownness,' exposure, vulnerability, anxiety, madness, sickness, imprisonment, alienation"[3]—are realized in the reticence of modern worldliness, the spiritual muteness of commodities in random circulation. The effect of this setting on the hero Karl Rossmann is to produce a sort of deformation of attention, a *preternatural* distraction, in the double sense of "an exceptionally absorbing . . . distraction" and a "distraction by something not quite natural, beyond the natural." Karl is fascinated by untelling objects in moments of counter-epiphany, being nonconceptual, nonmoral, and hence profoundly nonpolitical, if to be political means, at the least, to want to rescue oneself from death or humiliation at the hands of another man or woman.

For ten years, at different periods, Kafka worked on the three manuscripts that have come to be called his novels. None was ever finished, and none was published while he lived. *The Trial*, written in 1914, was published in 1925; *The Castle*, written in 1922, was published in 1926; and *The Boy Who Sank Out of Sight*, written between 1912–1914, was published in 1927. This situation might be said to give Kafka's posthumous criticism a special pertinence and responsibility: to complete or at any rate supplement the work that Kafka left behind. According to Kafka's manuscripts, the title of the last-named of these novels should be translated *The Boy Who Was Missing* or *The Boy Who Was Never Again Heard Of* or, what I think best, *The Boy Who Sank Out of Sight* (all are versions of the German word *Der Verschollene*, Kafka's preferred title for his "American novel").[4] This designator describes the fate of the novel were it not for the solicitude of Kafka's friends, editors, and readers.

During its real lifetime *The Boy Who Sank Out of Sight* could be a source of irritation to Kafka, who once referred to it as "the lowlands of writing." It is the only one of the three manuscripts that was begun in one version, subsequently destroyed, and then taken up anew in the version whose manuscript has survived. During the years of its composition,[5] Kafka often let himself be interrupted—sometimes, of course, with powerful results: on the night of November 17, 1912, he began conceiving *The Metamorphosis*, which occurred to him "during my misery in bed, oppressing me with inmost intensity."[6] But at the same time the sad refrain recurs: "my novel [is] at a standstill."[7] Immediately after composing the death-scene of the vermin Gregor Samsa, on the night of December 5, 1912, Kafka wrote to his fiancée Felice Bauer: "I hope to finish my story tomorrow and the day after tomorrow throw myself back onto the novel."[8]

The Boy Who Sank Out of Sight seems to have thwarted and obliged Kafka because of its derivative character—something that Kafka himself acknowledged. The novel is indebted to Benjamin Franklin's *Auto-*

biography, to ephemeral travel journals, and mostly to Dickens: like *David Copperfield* or *Great Expectations*, Kafka's story recounts the dismal adventures of an outcast boy. The first sentence announces that the hero, Karl Rossmann, has been packed off to America by his parents for having been raped by a housemaid who gave birth to his child. (There is already something like a gradient toward originality, or a falling off from the putative source, in this formulation of a guilt that so exorbitantly isn't one.) Nonetheless, Kafka was firm in acknowledging Dickens as his model, even though, compared with the first-person narrator of Dickens's novels, the third-person narrator of *The Boy Who Sank Out of Sight* is much less intrusive and imperial, and Kafka's novel is much more episodic—more independent in its parts. Indeed, they are less chapters than a succession of novellas having a single hero. It is precisely this margin of forgetfulness between the parts that produces its strong hermeneutic allure.

Readers persuaded by Kafka's denigration of *The Boy Who Sank Out of Sight* might conclude that only *The Trial* and *The Castle* are inspired. Still, it is possible to single out the many ways, thematically and formally, in which *The Boy Who Sank Out of Sight* is in its own fashion original, compelling, and true (even prophetically so). Moreover, in retrospect, it can also be seen as a reservoir of themes and formal devices that come vividly to the fore in the later novels.

Kafka thought the first chapter of *The Boy Who Sank Out of Sight*, which he published separately as "The Stoker," especially alive and spiritedly written. Indeed, Rilke, who once read *The Metamorphosis* aloud to his friend, the portrait painter Lou-Albert Lasard, judged it to fall short of the "rigorous coherence [*Konsequenz*]" of "The Stoker."[9] But this spiritedness is also true of much of the novel, which is full of surprises, wild humor, and audacious sexuality. Its themes are of current interest: random criminality and violence, homelessness in America, American speed, impersonality, technical know-how, information processing, melancholy, self-help, and utopianism. Within its frame of dislocation, technology, arbitrary authority, and apocalyptic rumor, its cogency continues to surface, even more forcefully than, say, that of *The Trial*, which has been, for a great many readers, *the* representative literary work of art during the period of fifty years following its publication. The difference in the reception of the two works runs along the axis dividing audiences responsive to the early modern versus the late modern

character of literature, *The Boy Who Sank Out of Sight* having a proleptically late-modern character.

The mood of *The Trial* is paranoid, its legal bureaucracy held together by acts of interpretation and writing, its violence mostly con-
cealed until the final page; and that concluding scene—a night of long
knives, swung by the arms of killers in frock coats, like "tenors"—is os-
tentatiously operatic. The mood of *The Boy Who Sank Out of Sight* is exterior: it is public, mechanical, and touched by a human quality only to
the extent that it is anxious. In its world, authority is maintained by
brute force; its violence is out in the open, suggesting a bare reminiscence of consciousness as a quality of jerky distractedness: "the din
roared, over pavement and roadway, changing its direction every minute, as if in a whirlwind, not like something produced by human beings
but like a foreign element."[10] The key word for the public life of the
America in which Karl Rossmann is trapped is "*Verkehr*"—a word
meaning traffic but also the circulation of commodities, socializing, and
sexual intercourse.[11]

The Boy Who Sank Out of Sight contains explicit junction points between Kafka's early and later work. Moments of the aestheticism that
absorbed Kafka in the years before 1912 figure alongside his growing
preoccupation with the power constellations of public life (family, busi-
ness, law court, government, "castle"). But these dimensions of aesthetic fascination and public power are not incompatibles. A generalized mood of sad searching, in public objects without aura, to redeem a
loss impossible to make good, connects *The Boy Who Sank Out of Sight*
with the later novels, as a basic tonality which, in the later work, is modified by higher tones. In *The Trial* Joseph K.'s search is more logical and
less sentimental, without Rossmann's sweetness and availability; and in
The Castle "the bitter herb" K. is tougher and shrewder than either of
the other K.'s, more determined to get what he thinks is his due. In a
journal entry for September 30, 1915, Kafka compared the heroes of
The Boy Who Sank Out of Sight and *The Trial*, noting: "Rossmann and
K., the innocent and the guilty, in the end both killed punitively without distinction, the innocent one with a gentler hand, more shoved
aside than struck down."[12] He did not compare this boy with the hero
of *The Castle*, who, although exhausted from his effort, has been neither
pushed aside nor struck down at the time the novel breaks off.

The Boy Who Sank Out of Sight anticipates formal features of the later
work as well: Kafka tries out his *style indirect libre* (free indirect discourse)

in passages where it is impossible to decide whether what is being said are the facts of the case proffered by an authoritative narrator or a reproduction of what Karl takes to be the case—hence, a flawed perception of some indeterminable state of affairs. Another narrative device, dominant in *The Castle*, also figures in *The Boy Who Sank Out of Sight*: Kafka's tactic of colligating stories told by characters within the novel. *The Boy Who Sank Out of Sight* foreshadows this technique in Therese's extended description of her mother's death. This narrative strategy also has the effect of dispersing the authority of the narrator and making the novel, to a radical degree, an affair of co-constitution between author and reader.

In such comparisons, however, something of the strangeness of *The Boy Who Sank Out of Sight* might be muffled and spirited away. Too many analogues contribute willy-nilly to the already mounting impression of its (and indeed Kafka's) familiarity. In fact the novel has for so long been more or less unconsciously cited and indeed *seen*[13] that it can seem quite settled in one's recollection until one reads it again, preferably in the "Manuscript Version" of Kafka's Collected Works (*Kafka in der Fassung der Handschrift, KKA*). There most of the novel appears as Kafka wrote it, the way it looked when it came into Max Brod's hands and before Brod chose to correct it. Other parts of it have never before been translated into English; and all these portions dispense a marvelous aura arising from the orthography of Kafka's Prague-inflected German. In this edition, Kafka is restored to his place in our imagination of exile, strangeness, and errancy: this manuscript edition is (very nearly) a textual photograph.[14]

That is one sort of benefit from rereading Kafka's early work in the new edition: another is that it supplies texts that are not found in the older *Gesammelte Schriften*. And here, I want to use one hitherto little-noticed text as a lever, and another hitherto untranslated text as an illustration of what I said is distinctive in *The Boy Who Sank Out of Sight*: a kind of rapture of distraction. In the middle of Karl Rossmann's reactions—as a rule hectic, unfocused, powerless—there surface odd moments of sensory absorption, of passionless concentration on random particulars. The rapture of distraction appears to be an extreme marker of the condition of exile.

First, as to a textual lever within Kafka: most re-readers of Kafka's posthumous works and fragments in the Manuscript Version will be surprised to find a short text at the beginning of the volume that now precedes the hero Raban's *Hochzeitsvorbereitungen auf dem Lande* (Wedding preparations in the country).[15] This text is, of all things, an exercise in formal aesthetic logic, written by Kafka in 1906 at the age of 23. It is true that these notes have been accessible earlier but in a fairly arcane place: they were originally printed with orthographical "improvements" in 1966 in *Der Prager Kreis* (The Prague circle) by Max Brod.[16] Kafka's jottings, which appear intermittently to have been conceived as a letter to Max Brod, were written in response to an article published by his friend and intellectual subaltern under the title "On Aesthetics" ("Zur Aesthetik").[17] Max Brod describes his own work as a "youthful *jeu d'esprit*" that argues that the category of "the beautiful" should be replaced by that of "the new." "The 'new apperception' or 'perception plus the internal working-through of the new impression,' a definition I borrowed from Herbart and Wundt," recalls Brod, "represented the essence of the beautiful."[18]

Brod goes on to identify the Schopenhauerian character of Kafka's response, which pits Kafka against the "Brentanist" empiricist school with which he has been wrongly identified.[19] Furthermore, in its stress on the "infiniteness and inexhaustibleness of intuitive/sensate [*anschaulich*] experience," Kafka's essay might belong in the company of his early prose piece *Description of a Struggle* and, indeed, Hofmannsthal's *Letter to Lord Chandos*.[20] Here is Kafka's text:

(a) One may not say: Only the new impression [*Vorstellung*] awakens aesthetic pleasure, but rather: every impression that does not fall into the sphere of the will awakens aesthetic pleasure. Saying this, however, means that only an impression that is new could be perceived in such a manner that the sphere of our will is not touched. Now, however, it is certain that there are new impressions that we do not evaluate aesthetically. What portion of these new impressions do we therefore evaluate aesthetically? The question remains.

(b) It would be necessary to explain [the term] "aesthetic apperception"—an expression that has not, perhaps, hitherto been introduced [into such discussions]—in greater detail or, really, in some basic way.[21] How does that feeling of pleasure arise, and in what does its peculiarity consist, in what way is it distinguished from the joy of a new discovery or of news from a foreign country or field of knowledge?

(c) The principal proof of the new view is a generally physiological—not only aesthetic—fact, and that is fatigue [*Ermüdung*].[22] Now on the one hand [the conclusion] arises from your [Max Brod's] many reservations on the concept "new" that really everything is new, for since all objects are caught in a forever changing time and illumination, and it is no different with us observers, we therefore must always encounter them at a different place. On the other hand, however, we tire ourselves out not only enjoying art but also studying and mountain climbing and eating lunch, without our being allowed to say, veal is a dish that no longer appeals to us [*keine uns entsprechende*] because today we're tired of it.

Kafka makes the point that the newness of an impression is not a sufficient condition of aesthetic judgment. That is because in one sense newness is everywhere; we never encounter the same object—even once. What object, then, is not new? That one whose newness has been taken from it. By what?

In answering the question Kafka makes his chief contribution to this discussion: he gives a rich social and existential content to Brod's abstract term "apperception" by infusing it with the modern consciousness of fatigue. Fatigue, tiredness, exhausts the newness of the object. (One could think of the permanent fatigue of exile—of Napoleon on St. Helena.)

On the other hand, fatigue is not a ground for making a negative aesthetic judgment—for example, the negative aesthetic judgment made on a lunch of veal. If there is too much newness around to allow a theory of aesthetic perception to be based on it, there is also too much fatigue around to allow a theory of nonaesthetic displeasure to be based on it. Here Kafka may be seen as opposing a view consistent with Kant's theory of aesthetic perception. For Kafka, the occasion of the specifically aesthetic judgment is *not* the purely contingent object (there are other kinds of news) nor the object that fatigue has not yet robbed of its newness. For Kant, on the other hand, it is a certain labor of concept-formation that obstructs the "pure" aesthetic reflection on its enabling condition. The work of concept-formation consumes, as it were, the raw material, a sort of nature ("*die Natur* [*des Subjekts*]"), which enables it. Objects of daily experience are grasped as everyday because the everyday is a product of fatigue—whereas the aesthetic brings enjoyment.[23]

Kafka continues:

Better, therefore: the object hovers between the aesthetic edge [*Kante*][24] and fatigue (which comes about only really from enjoyment of the time that has just preceded), hence: the object has lost its equilibrium, and in a negative sense. And yet your conclusion presses forward to a smoothing-out of this conflict, for apperception is not a state of being but rather a movement, hence it must come to a conclusion. A bit of fuss arises, in its midst this harried feeling of pleasure, but soon everything must grow quiet in its hollowed-out resting places.

Apperception could now appear to be complete: apperception appears to bring the perception into the order of experience; but the process is negative, insofar as it bears the traces of a fall into dailiness.

(d) Is there/there is a difference between aesthetic and scientific human beings.

(e) The uncertain factor remains the concept apperception. In the sense we are used to it, it is not a concept from aesthetics.[25] Perhaps it can be represented as follows. We say, I am a man with no feeling for place [*Ortsgefühl*] whatsoever, and come to Prague as to a foreign city. I want to write to you, but I don't know your address, I ask you, you tell me it, I apperceive that and don't have to ask you ever again, your address is [now] something "old" for me, this is how we apperceive science. But if I want to visit you, at every street-corner and crossing I must always keep asking, I will never be able to manage without passers-by, here an apperception is fundamentally impossible. Of course, it is possible that I get tired and go into a café, which is on the way, so as to get some rest there, and it is also possible that I give up the visit altogether: on this account, however, I still have not apperceived.

Observe that newness operates to produce fatigue.

For Kafka, there would not finally appear to be any such thing as pure "aesthetic apperception," since "*aesthetic* apperception" requires (at least) the newness of the object, but "aesthetic *apperception*" requires that it grow old. If there is to be a kind of *aesthetic* apperception, then it must carry the trace of the negative temporal fall of the object into dailiness, a conflict that may not be smoothed over. One kind of growing old of the apperceived object, its passage into "experience," is still better than the originary resistance to the perception through fatigue. But without a certain fundamental mode of live feeling—here, "the feeling for place"—there is no newness, there is only fatigue. In *The Boy Who Sank Out of Sight* Karl Rossmann can be defined essentially as the boy with a lack of feeling for place so extreme that he cannot be placed. It is suggestive here, too, to invoke Kant's principle of aesthetic judgment: "nature's formal finality for our cognitive faculties in its particular (empirical) laws [is] a principle without which understanding could not feel itself at home in nature."[26] The principle has a sort of negative aptness for Kafka's melancholy protocol.

Fatigue—especially, the fatigue of disorientation—works against the aesthetic apperception of an object. It is doubtful that for Kafka there is finally very much consolation or "acquist of true experience" in everything's growing quiet again and returning home along well-worn grooves. The fate of aesthetic apperception and, worse, of the aesthetic percipient is not to be a stay against disintegration. "The question [of aesthetic apperception] remains."

At the conclusion of his notes, Kafka turns from the problem at hand to the rhetoric of such problem-setting, mocking the kind of forensic language that Brod employs. These disjointed comments need not concern us now.[27]

For an immediate sense of the cogency for Kafka of the terms aesthetic apperception, apperception, exile, and fatigue, one could quickly consult this sentence from *The Castle*. On the texts that Barnabas delivers to K., exiled in the Castle-village, K. reflects: "They themselves continually change in value, the reflections they give rise to are endless, and precisely where one comes to a stop is determined only by chance, and so even our judgment of them is a matter of chance."[28] Tiredness is another name for the intrusion of what afterwards seems chance: it means letting in a premature end to perception.

Kafka's essay provides a frame for the kind of torn, exhausted perception-of-the-image that marks scenes of the sharpest exile in *The Boy Who Sank Out of Sight*. Here aesthetic perception cannot give way to experience: it is made to hover perpetually on the edge of fatigue.

•~•

In *The Boy Who Sank Out of Sight*, Edwin Muir once remarked, "Kafka takes us into a strange world which becomes stranger the more realistically, the more circumstantially, it is described. . . . The more visually exact he succeeds in making things, the more questionable they become; . . . they are marked by an obstinate strangeness."[29] This is the sort of claim that requires more precise demonstration.

Consider the following instances of Karl Rossmann's enraptured gazing at details, even and especially at times when it is most dangerous for him to do so, the danger consisting in his being swept away, made amorphous himself from submersion in an amorphous crowd.[30]

As Karl is leaving his Uncle Jakob's house in New York for Mr. Pollunder's country villa, driven along with Mr. Pollunder in his car, Kafka

notes that even as Karl was reporting the wild anonymous din of traffic, he "was inattentive . . . to everything except Mr. Pollunder's dark
waistcoat, across which at an angle a golden chain hung calmly."[31] As a
result of this journey, and quite possibly as a result of his failing to pay
strict attention to the words of Mr. Pollunder, Karl will be banished
forever from the home of his American protector Uncle Jakob Ben-
delmayr.

At the end of chapter 4, just after Karl, in anguish, has discovered that
he has lost his prize possession, a photograph of his parents, perhaps because one of the two rough adventurers he has picked up on his travels
has stolen it, he walks away from them, then turns and shouts up into
the darkness:

"Listen to me! If either of you still has the photograph and is willing to bring it
to me at the hotel, he can still have the trunk, and he won't—I swear—be reported to the police." No actual answer came down, only a broken-off word
could be heard, the beginning of a shout from Robinson, whose mouth evidently Delamarche immediately stopped. Karl went on waiting for a long time,
in case the men above might still change their minds. Twice, at intervals, he
shouted: "I'm still waiting!" But no sound came in reply, except that once a
stone rolled down the slope, perhaps by accident, perhaps a badly-aimed
throw.[32]

The scene fades, tinged by Karl's exhaustion, into the prolonged, faintly
harried perception of a rolling stone.

The next chapter ends:

After four o'clock in the morning a bit of calm set in, something that Karl
badly needed. He leant heavily against the banister beside his lift, slowly eating
the apple, from which, after the very first bite, a powerful fragrance streamed
out, and looked down into a lighted shaft, surrounded by the great windows
of the storerooms, behind which hanging masses of bananas were faintly
gleaming.[33]

The passage ends on a note of weariness and fined-down sensory
rapture.

Soon afterwards, Karl is seized by the Head Porter, who takes his
hand and proceeds to crush it "until it was numb."[34] While this is going
on, the narrator delivers in Karl's perspective a detailed account of the
infinitely hectic procedure of information-giving in the lobby of the
Hotel Occidental, offering this explanation of how such a report is possible: "Paying the most intent attention Karl had absorbed [*in sich aufge-*

nommen] all this in a few minutes."[35] This passage could be read as a complete apperception, if not indeed a complete aesthetic apperception; but the value of this experience is immediately contested by Kafka's diction. This tour de force of virtual apperception ends significantly: Karl makes his way out of the Hotel Occidental and on the street takes the opportunity to leap into a car beside the battered Robinson. "The car made a sharp turn into the street. It looked as if they would inevitably have an accident, but at once the all-embracing traffic flow quietly absorbed [*nahm in sich auf*] even the dead-straight movement of the car."[36] The movement accomplishing Karl's apperception of information-giving in the hotel lobby while he is being bruised by the Head Porter is impersonalized, publicly expropriated, in the same movement by which an "all-embracing" flow of human traffic absorbs the fierce directedness [*angespanntest*] of Karl's attention. But this mechanization of perception has already been forecast in the mechanical frenzy of information-giving in the lobby of the Hotel Occidental. The "vehicle"—once upon a time, the soul—of Karl's seeing belongs to the same "traffic flow" as the one he sees embrace individual exchanges of information, in the same way that the fiercely speeding individual "vehicle" in which he "escapes" is absorbed by the all-embracing automobile traffic. Benjamin's aperçu, in "The Work of Art in the Age of Mechanical Reproduction," is proved: "the distracted person can form habits. More, the ability to master certain tasks in a state of distraction proves that their solution has become a matter of habit."[37]

In this light *The Boy Who Sank Out of Sight* should be placed alongside another Benjamin essay: "On Some Motifs in Baudelaire." In Paris, capital of Amerika, the instrument of exhaustion is the shock effect: it is the great annihilator of experience or—in Kafka's word for aesthetic experience that has an end—aesthetic apperception.[38] The put-upon sensibility attaches itself in dumb rapture to any object and holds it fast. This holding fast *to anything* appears to be the precondition of being swept away. In this sense even the seemingly auratic opening of the novel fits:

As Karl Rossmann . . . sailed on the now slowing ship into New York harbor, he glimpsed the Statue of Liberty, which he'd long since sighted, as if in a sudden burst of sunlight. The arm with the sword rose up as if for the first time, and around her form the free breezes blew. "So high," he said to himself, and since he hadn't at all been thinking of leaving the ship was gradually pushed to the railing by the continually swelling crowd of porters shoving past.[39]

As a consequence, Karl will remember that he has forgotten his umbrella;[40] and as a further consequence of the search for his umbrella, he will lose, for the time being, his steamer trunk.

In *The Boy Who Sank Out of Sight* the modern aesthetic moment, unlike the classical one, is attuned by a mood of exhaustion and anxiety. The torch this Statue of Liberty holds up is a flaming sword, like the angel forbidding a return to the Eden of aesthetic apperception. As a moment of sensory indifference, following on a shock, the moment might be assimilated to Kafka's early empiricist, atomistic, aestheticist concerns. But at the close of *The Boy Who Sank Out of Sight*, in a fragment still missing from the English translation, there is a crucial, forward-looking connection to the guilty thematics of *The Trial*. The fragment is called "Brunelda's Journey."

BRUNELDA'S JOURNEY

One morning Karl pushed outside the main gate the carriage in which Brunelda was sitting. It was no longer as early as he'd hoped. They had agreed to carry out the exodus by night in order not to cause a commotion in the streets, which would have been unavoidable during the day despite the great gray shawl in which Brunelda had modestly wanted to cover herself up. But carrying her downstairs had taken too long, even with the eager assistance of the student, who was much weaker than Karl—a thing that came to light during this operation. Brunelda behaved very bravely, sighed only a little, and sought in every way possible to simplify the porters' job. Still there was no getting around their having to set her down on every fifth step to give her and themselves a breathing space. The morning was cool: a cold draft like cellar air blew through the halls, yet Karl and the student were drenched with sweat. During the breaks, in order to dry their faces, they had to use a corner of Brunelda's shawl, which she graciously handed to them. It took two hours for them to get to the bottom of the stairs, where ever since nightfall the little carriage had been waiting. It was still a bit of a job hoisting Brunelda inside, but at that point the whole operation could be judged a success, since, thanks to its high wheels, the carriage would not be hard to push. Their one remaining worry was that under Brunelda's weight the carriage could come apart at the seams. But the risk had to be taken: one couldn't bring along a spare, which the student had half-jokingly volunteered to furnish and to push. They now said goodbye to the student—indeed very warmly. Every trace of the old quarrel between him and Brunelda seemed to have disappeared; the student apologized for having offended her the time she'd been sick, but Brunelda said the incident was long forgotten and that he'd more than made up for everything. Finally, she even asked him whether he'd be so kind as to accept in remembrance of her a silver dollar, which she struggled to produce from her innumerable skirts. In light of Brunelda's famous stinginess the gift was remarkable and made the student very happy. In his delight he threw the coin high into the air but then had to look for it on the ground: Karl had to help him and finally found it beneath Brunelda's carriage. The goodbyes between Karl and the student were naturally much simpler. They just shook hands, expressing the conviction that they were sure to meet someday when at least one of them—in Karl's view, the student; in the student's view, Karl—would have achieved some great distinction, which up to this point, unfortunately, had not been the case. Then Karl cheerfully grabbed the handle of the carriage and pushed it onto the sidewalk. The student watched them as long as he could while waving a handkerchief. Karl frequently saluted him back by nodding his head; Brunelda also would have liked to turn around if only the movement hadn't been too strenuous for her. To enable her to say a last goodbye, Karl, having come to the end of the street, turned the cart in a half-circle so that Brunelda could also see the student, who took advantage of this opportunity to wave his handkerchief with redoubled ardor.

Whereupon Karl said that they could no longer afford to make even the smallest stop: the trip was long, and they had left much later than expected. In fact, they already saw a few vehicles and, though not often, people going to work. With his remark Karl had not intended to say anything more than what he actually said, but with her great tact Brunelda understood him otherwise and covered herself up completely in her gray shawl. Karl did not offer any objection; while a hand carriage covered with a gray shawl was indisputably spectacular, it was incomparably less spectacular than an uncovered Brunelda would have been. Karl proceeded very carefully: before going around a corner, he examined the street ahead of him; and whenever it seemed necessary, he even left the carriage standing and went ahead a few steps by himself. If he anticipated any kind of unpleasant encounter, he waited until the danger had passed, or else he radically changed course. But even then there was no risk of making a major detour, since he had carefully studied every possible itinerary beforehand. He did indeed run into the difficulties that he'd been afraid of, the details of which, however, could not have been anticipated. Thus in a street that rose up at a slight incline, which he could survey far and wide and which seemed to his delight to be completely empty—an advantage which he tried to make use of by pushing particularly fast—a policeman suddenly emerged from a dark corner of a house gate and asked Karl what he was transporting in a carriage so painstakingly covered. Despite his severe looks, the policeman still had to laugh on lifting the cover and catching sight of the terrified flushed face of Brunelda. "What?" he said, "I expected to find about ten sacks of potatoes in here, and instead it's a single female. Where are you going? Who are you?" Brunelda didn't dare look at the policeman and stared instead at Karl, visibly doubtful of even his ability to save her. Karl, however, had quite enough experience of the police, and the whole matter did not seem to him to be very serious. "Please, Miss," he said, "show the document that you received." "Oh, yes," said Brunelda, though the desperate way she began looking for it was really bound to arouse suspicion. "The young lady," said the policeman, with unmistakable irony, "will not find the document." "Oh, yes," Karl said calmly, "it's definitely there—she's only mislaid it." He began to look for it himself and indeed produced it from behind Brunelda's back. The policeman only glanced at it. "So that's it," he said, smiling, "that's who this young lady is. And you, my boy, are acting as the agent in charge of her delivery? Can't you find anything better to do?" Karl only shrugged: it was another instance of well-known police interference. On receiving no answer, the policeman said, "Well, have a good trip." His words were probably meant to be scornful, so Karl too left without saying goodbye. Better the scorn of the police than their attention.

Soon thereafter he had another encounter, if possible even more unpleasant. A man pushing a cart with huge milk cans accosted him, eager to discover what was in Karl's carriage under the gray shawl. It was highly unlikely that he was heading in the same direction as Karl's, but nevertheless he clung to him, however startling Karl's maneuvers. At first, he was satisfied with producing exclamations such as "That's quite a load you have there" or "You did a bad job of loading: something's about to fall out at the top." But then he asked bluntly, "What's under the cloth?" "What's it to you?" Karl said. But since that only stimulated his curiosity, Karl said finally, "Apples." The man, amazed, said, "That's a lot of apples,"[41] and never stopped repeating his comment. "That has to be the whole crop,"[42] he said at last. "Right," said Karl. But the man, whether because he did not believe Karl or else only wanted to tease him, went still further and began—even while they were moving—to reach his hand out toward the shawl as if in jest; finally, he even had the nerve to pluck at it. What Brunelda had to put up with! Out of consideration for her, Karl declined to get into a fight with the man and turned into the first open gate as if this were his final destination. "This is where I live," he said; "thanks for the company." The man, astonished, remained in front of the gate watching Karl, who calmly set about, if it had to be, pushing the carriage the whole length of the courtyard. The man could have no further doubts, but in order to vent his malice one last time, he left his cart standing, ran tiptoe after Karl, and tore at the shawl so roughly that he almost uncovered Brunelda's face. "That's so your apples can breathe," he said and ran away. Karl put up with that too, since it did finally rid him of the fellow. Then he pushed the carriage into a corner of the court, where several big, empty boxes were standing, in whose safety he meant to say a few comforting words under the shawl to Brunelda. But he had to speak to her a long time in order to convince her, since weeping badly she pleaded with him in all seriousness to spend the entire day waiting behind the boxes and only continue their trip by night. By himself Karl might not have been able to convince her how ill-advised her notion was, but when someone at the other end of the heap threw an empty box onto the ground with a noise that resounded monstrously in the empty courtyard, she was so terrified that, without venturing another word, she drew the shawl over her and was probably ecstatically happy when Karl rapidly made up his mind to leave at once.

Now, of course, the streets were much livelier, though the carriage aroused less curiosity than Karl had feared. It might have been more sensible to choose another time for the transport. If such a trip became necessary again, Karl would try to make it during the noonday pause. Without having been molested any more seriously, he finally turned into the narrow, dark street where Company Number 25 was located. The squint-eyed manager stood in front of the door with a watch in his hand. "Are you always so unpunctual?" he asked. "There were various difficulties," said Karl. "There always are," said the manager, "that's well known, but here they carry no weight. Keep that in mind!" Karl hardly paid attention anymore to speeches of this kind: everybody used his power to abuse his inferiors. Once you got used to it, it sounded no different from the steady striking of the clock. What horrified him, however, as he now pushed the carriage into the entranceway, was the dirt predominating here, which surpassed all his expectations. On closer inspection, it was not the kind of dirt you could actually touch with your hands. The pavement of the passageway was nearly swept clean, the paintwork on the walls was fairly new, the artificial palms were not all that dusty, and yet everything was greasy and repulsive, as if everything had been misused and no amount of cleanliness could ever make it good again. Whenever Karl came to a new place, he liked to imagine the improvements that could be made and the pleasure it would be to get to work immediately, without paying attention to the perhaps infinite labor involved. Here, however, he did not know what could be done. Slowly he lifted the shawl from Brunelda. "Welcome, Miss," said the manager, in mannered tones; Brunelda had no doubt made a good impression on him. As soon as she saw this, she set to work exploiting it, as Karl noted to his satisfaction, and all the anxiety of the previous hours disappeared . . . [43]

Here the fragment ends.

It ends on a note of resignation, which can seem contrived, as belonging to the history of Kafka's forced conciliatory endings. The instability of the moment is conceptually plain: Brunelda's toying with the squint-eyed Manager won't extinguish the anxiety of the previous hours for long, especially in the objective sense of "hours," whose steady "striking" we have heard, no different from the striking down of the inferior by his master. Brunelda's sexual fascination simply crooks the clock-hand differently, but it does not make the clock run counterclockwise, let alone stop it. Karl's mood is probably best understood psy-choanalytically: the gratification dispelling anxiety is a function of a burdensome female sexuality's being redirected to another man.

But what is most impressive is the instability of the penultimate moment in "the dirt predominating here, which surpassed all expecta-tions." It is real dirt, perceived at first as material dirt, and, for the ex-hausted Karl, in the presence of the threatening Manager, a typical ob-ject of distracted perception. But in this instance, of course, it is more—and worse: for "it was not the kind of dirt you could actually touch with your hands"—rather "as if everything had been misused, and no amount of cleanliness could ever make it good again."

The dirt-object opens up an abyss of unspecifiable abuse that returns the reader to the entire commodified world of *The Boy Who Sank Out of Sight*. But this object, coming at the end of the novel, is distinctive for its exemplary, dialectically enriched character. In earlier examples, a particular object provoked Karl's distracted gaze, while all around him a current of turbulent, dangerous life threatened to sweep him away. Here both dimensions are present in a single object: its phenomenal face cap-tures Karl's gaze, while at bottom it discloses an abyss. This dirt that is not ordinary dirt breaks through the mystified facade of the other, seemingly natural objects of Karl's fascination, into which he has strained to escape. The mood of the scene returns to a moment at the outset when Karl, after listening raptly to Klara's piano playing, feels "rising within him a sorrow that reached past the end of this song, seek-ing another end which it could not find."[44] The common theme is a sort of fullness of hopeless longing.

But one should not end here without pointing up another direction of Kafka's thought that flows from this juncture. It is not Kafka's sole practice to mystify this abyss of unrecoverableness: it goes too much against the grain of his materialism, his Flaubertian and proto-critical theoretical perception of melancholy as systematic. In this perspective the truer figure of the closing chapter-fragment is not the fat woman who sits on the neck of Karl Rossmann but the fat man whom Kafka saw in a drawing of Georg Grosz: the capitalist who sits on the neck of the poor.

In 1921 Gustav Janouch, a young friend, allegedly showed Kafka a drawing from a book of illustrations by Grosz. A portly man—a capital-ist—with a top hat pulled down over his eyes, is sitting, with enormous buttocks, on piled-up sacks of money from which (here the reader must rely on a general impression of Grosz's work) a swarm of tiny people, who are being crushed or suffocated, are falling off.[45] Kafka remarked: "That is the familiar view of Capital—the fat man in a top hat squatting on the money of the poor."

From the expression on Kafka's face, Janouch was moved to ask: "You mean that the picture is false?"

Kafka then made his famous reply:

It is both true and false. . . . The fat man in the top hat sits on the neck of the poor. That is correct. But the fat man is Capitalism, and that is not quite correct. The fat man oppresses the poor man within the conditions of a given system. But he is not the system itself. He is not even its master. On the contrary, the fat man is also in chains, which the picture does not show.

The picture is incomplete, concludes Kafka, "for capitalism is a system of dependent relations [*ein System von Abhängigkeiten*]," that is, "a condition both of the world *and* of the soul [*ein Zustand der Welt und der Seele*]" (my emphasis).[46]

Kafka's last thesis has been generally adopted as the research program of the Frankfurt School. At the same time it could also prove irritating. In the hinging together of these terms—the archaic term of inwardness, *the soul*, and the modern, progressive term of exteriority, the political-economic *world*—there is a unifying impulse at work that could also seem nostalgic, mystified, or otherwise unintelligible. Or it could be a merely witty effect masking unmanageable disparity. After *The Boy Who Sank Out of Sight* the terms "soul" and "world" will seem especially disjunct when one considers what the hinge between them is made of: commodities, in systematic circulation, which erase all traces of the soul from the social relations that produce them.[47]

This paradox, which surfaces as the mood of the anonymous public self coloring exile in the land of commodities, is striking even in the early work of Kafka. One finds a surprising but enlightening remark Kafka makes about a persona of himself in a diary entry called " 'You,' I said . . . ," written in 1910, about a year before he began his first lost drafts for *The Boy Who Sank Out of Sight*: "For he and his property are not one, but two, and whoever destroys the connection destroys him at the same time."[48] Note that because he and his *property* are *not* one, but *two*, whoever destroys the connection destroys him at the same time. The point appears to be that Kafka or his persona is sustained, not by

what he most resembles but by what is most unlike him; this other thing
is his property. The connection is necessarily a tension, and a negative
one: it tilts the person downward, away from his longed-for "spiritual
world." It constrains him, but it also anchors him, it holds and captivates
him. The moment identifies Kafka's horror of the daily world and his
fascinated rapture in it.

This very term "property," in its constraining and holding function,
reappears as an intralinguistic entity in an aphorism Kafka wrote many
years later:

For everything *outside the phenomenal world*, language can only be used allusively
[*andeutungsweise*], but never even approximately as a comparison, in the mode
of an analogy [*vergleichsweise*], since, corresponding as [language] does to the
phenomenal world, it is concerned only with property and its relations.[49]

Language and property are not one, but two, and whoever destroys the
connection, one might say, destroys language too. But this is the destruction that Kafka has determined to risk. "Metaphors," he wrote,

are one among many things which make me despair of writing. Writing's lack
of independence of the world, its dependence on the maid who tends the fire,
on the cat warming itself by the stove; it is even dependent on the poor human
being warming himself by the stove. All these are independent activities ruled
by their own laws; only writing is helpless, cannot live in itself, is a joke and a
despair.[50]

In his work he must pull toward something else, allusively, for he is also
part of "everything outside the phenomenal world," the domain that
has begun to be heard from again. As in Celan's lines, "es sind / noch
Lieder zu singen jenseits / der Menschen [There are / Still songs to be
sung on the far side / of mankind]." For Karl Rossmann this would be
songs in which that other sorrow could find its end, not in assuagement
but in idoneous lament.

7

HEARING HOMONYMY IN TRAKL'S "DE PROFUNDIS"

For Howie

> A strong song tows
> us, long earsick.
> Blind, we follow
> rain slant, spray flick
> to fields we do not know.
> —Basil Bunting, cited
> in Simon Goldhill,
> *Reading Greek Tragedy*

The poetry of Georg Trakl (1887–1914) has proved extraordinarily resistant to interpretation. As a result, critics, frustrated by their failure to break through to a drift of argument, have tried to circumvent this obstacle in one of two ways. The first follows from Walther Killy's study of the tangled prehistory of Trakl's poems.[1] After scrutinizing these unreadable drafts, full of arbitrary substitutions of words that hardly qualify as revisions or refinements of "works" in progress, readers conclude that Trakl's poems are semantically indeterminable. "This is not really a poetry," Killy puts it, "that asks to be understood at the level of content [*inhaltlich*]."[2] Its polysemic abundance can seem like only the reverse side of an absence of intentional meaning.[3]

Attributions of poverty and richness are exchanged easily in this sort of discussion, where the matter is opaque. For Gustav Kars, the symptoms of Trakl's schizophrenia are so disquieting that "one might well ask whether a literary or conceptual study of his work is in any sense possible," since what the critic has before him are only "the spawn of a deranged fantasy life."[4] For Heidegger, on the other hand, Trakl is the poet embarked on a journey of spiritual transfiguration who points the way to the still hidden promise of the "land of evening [*das Abend-land*]."[5] In Trakl's case, it appears, we are dealing neither with the incommensurableness of (say) Goethe's elaborate productions—of *Faust* or *Wilhelm Meister*—nor the hermetic rigor of Hölderlin nor the logical paradoxicalness of Kafka. The strangeness of Trakl's poetry lies in the impossibility of paraphrase. This opacity, of course, can just as well be called evidence of its poetic character and its genealogy derived from the late poems of Hölderlin's madness.[6]

The stress on its incoherence serves as a tireless stimulant to an apparently opposed but in fact related argument, which tries to find a formal order in Trakl's poetry despite its apparent chaos. The same indeterminacy provokes a heightened attention to the work's aesthetic dimension, beginning with sensory images that can be organized into small complexes—just barely. In this perspective, the critic isolates "poetic moments" on the strength of patterns of likeness and opposition—identifying, for example, dark and light, static and moving, rigid and trembling, "rising" and "falling" moments, movements of integration as opposed to movements of disintegration, gestures of inwardness and silence as opposed to gestures of perception and address to natural things. It can then seem telling to assign positive or negative values to the terms constituting these oppositions, in the sense, say, that "a hyacinth," an image of immortal youth, is better than "a blue deer that softly bleeds in the thorn-thicket" or "a brown tree that stands secluded there." This value-charged grid might then be fitted to stable, quasi-factual formal dimensions of the poems—the audible or perceptible order of distinctions and gradations produced by rhyme, assonance, meter, even grammar (Siegbert Prawer proposes the term "grammetrics" to cover the participation of grammar in such formal effects).[7] In this way, the vacuum of scenes, plots, persons, and wisdom sentences in Trakl's poetry is filled in by an apparently secure latticework of aesthetic, formal, even moral properties. One kind of discussion about Trakl's obscurity ends on this note of moral uplift: his poems are seen as longing for reconstruction, for a wholeness that would recover their meaning, typically, from a lost narrative telling of a fall from innocence into chaos and division.

Trakl's vision of a universe in dying shards provokes critics to take a more direct route to its lost order. From points outside the text, they reconstruct the original story on which his actual poems play compulsive, masking variations through substitution, displacement, and scission. Maire Kurrik's luminous essay and Michael Sharp's pioneering book are positive examples of this psychoanalytical criticism.[8] These writers substitute for Trakl's radical unintelligibility the concept of his madness. In this way his unintelligibility is first of all relativized; it is conceived of as but a moment, part of a *metanoia*, a movement toward abundant meaning (less toward particular meanings than toward the register of meaning, toward a symbolic order)—indeed, as a movement toward cure. Sharp evokes as a goal Trakl's "true self": after the poet has damned and killed off the factitious ego in a violent poetry, in a truthful light that the ego cannot endure, the genuine self is freed and comes alive.[9] This kind of criticism attempts to stage Trakl's poetry as moments of greater or lesser truthfulness, of greater or lesser proximity to his authentic self— what Maire Kurrik calls, in good Lacanian, the "true inner inexpressible self."[10]

This approach, however, invites criticism of the metaphysical assumptions that stage it—undiscussed ideas of authentically centered selfhood and states of mind anterior to self-consciousness, indeed, anterior to language. In fact, a Lacan-based psychoanalytical criticism of lyric poetry can seem actually to be repeating the procedures of the aesthetic criticism just described. It too takes movements of opposition, likeness, displacement, and fissuring at the order of the signifier (or, like Prawer's reading of Trakl's poem "De Profundis," at the order of grammar, of syntax) as the evident workings of an authentic self. It too considers the order of the sound/look of the signifier as a stratum anterior to conventional linguistic meaning—as a pure being-toward-perception—possessing attributes of grounded, self-identical being.

The psychoanalytic critic Sharp understandably wishes to see Trakl's work "no longer reduced to a purely linguistic dimension." If only it had been possible to commit such an error! Sharp admirably calls for an analysis that goes "deeper" than the description of the formal qualities of Trakl's verse, one that addresses "the experiential factor," in order to register there, among other signs of metanoia, the workings of ambivalence.[11] But the psychoanalytic critic's perception of ambivalence falls short of the readiness to see it informing the signifier of "experiential" ambivalence. In the same vein we can grasp the phenomenon of multiple selves: this phenomenon of fissuring, if it is to be radical enough, must extend throughout the verbal signifier.

The point of this chapter, now, is to show, especially in the case of "De Profundis," the impossibility of isolating a so-called integral stratum of the signifier en route to the recovery of a stable, coherent narrative. As a consequence, it becomes equally difficult to posit an affective, self-identical prelinguistic being—an inner ground—which could constitute the subject of cure.

·～·

The poem "De Profundis" begins:

> Es ist ein Stoppelfeld, in das ein schwarzer Regen fällt.
> Es ist ein brauner Baum, der einsam dasteht.
> Es ist ein Zischelwind, der leere Hütten umkreist.
> Wie traurig dieser Abend.
>
> There is a stubble field on which a black rain falls.
> There is a tree which, brown, stands lonely here.
> There is a hissing wind which haunts deserted huts.
> How sad this evening.[12]

A great deal of the power of the poem is stored in the line "Es ist ein Stoppelfeld, in das ein schwarzer Regen fällt." I begin by focusing on the homophony of "Stoppelfeld" and "Regen fällt." "Homophonous echo" is Prawer's term for this rhyme: he means to link it to the echolike phenomenon of the syntactic pause (marked by a comma) which occurs in the same place in the metrical structure of each of the first three lines—after the sixth syllable (which also bears the third stress): "Es ist ein Stoppelfeld" / "Es ist ein brauner Baum" / "Es ist ein Zischelwind." In Prawer's words:

The feeling of hopeless repetition which this induces is reinforced yet further by the homophonous echo "-feld/fällt" (so different from a true rhyme!) which links the end of the first main clause ("Es ist ein Stoppelfeld") to that of the first subsidiary clause ("in das ein schwarzer Regen fällt").[13]

"Hopeless repetition"? "Links" the clauses? I am not sure that these are the obviously right words.

With "Regen fällt," we deal not only with the homophonous echo of "Stoppelfeld" but with a heard homonym—"Regenfeld." In addition to meaning "rain is falling," this "word"—on the example of "Regenbach" ("brook made by rain"),[14] "Regendach" ("roof raised against the rain"), "Regenflut" ("rain flood"), "Regentag" ("rainy day"), or

"Regenwald" ("rain forest")—also means "Regenfeld" ("rainfield"),
though this, at least up through Grimm, is a neologism. Thus the line
also "reads," that is to say, sounds as if it reads, "It is a stubble field, into
which a black rainfield . . . " I literally find such a scene in a grisly, disastrous painting like Anselm Kiefer's "Maikäfer" (Cockchafer). In Hölderlin's "Der Winkel von Hardt" (The nook/corner at Hardt), "the
forest hangs down [hinunter sinket der Wald]"; in "Hälfte des Lebens"
(Half of life), "the land hangs into the lake [. . . hänget / . . . Das Land
in den See]."[15]

Now, I hasten to point out the considerable obstacle in "De Profundis" to hearing the homonym *Regenfeld*—an obstacle not only at the order of diction but at the order of syntax. For some readers, the homonymic reading will be inaudible because it is plainly offensive to grammar. For others it will come into being even though accompanied by
the murk of a grammatical mistake—but one that is only feeble and
whose net effect is to subordinate syntax to the image and thus actually
to heighten the latter's power. This kind of interference comes from the
fact that as a plain point of grammar, *Regenfeld* requires the neuter "-es"
ending after "schwarz," a little hiss of the "Zischelwind" which no silent reading is entitled simply to tack onto it. For if there is to be true
homo*nymy* (exceeding mere homo*phony*), the same word must be able
to function grammatically in different semantic registers. And so, to
produce the homonymy that I hear in it, Trakl's actual sentence would
have to be modified (in a violent, totally unacceptable way) to: "in das
ein schwarz*es* Regenfeld"; but, of course, the text says, and must say, "in
das ein schwarz*er* Regen fällt."

What I am now proposing, however, is in fact a different scene of
reading—yet one no less real, too, in which auditors are asked to hear
the following reading aloud: "Es ist ein Stoppelfeld, in das ein schwarz'
Regenfeld." This enunciation brings about the impression of genuine
homonymy—where phonically identical signifiers joined at one syn-
tactical position signify different things in good grammar. Here, where
the "z"-sound is stressed—hence "schwar*z*' Regenfeld"—the adjectival inflection "er" becomes inaudible; the stressed sibilant erases the signifier "er" that stands in the way of the homonymy, allowing it to be absorbed into the "R" of "Regenfeld." Put positively: this minute glottal
impediment makes the homophony grammatical and lends it the same
semantic power as the hiss in "schwarzes Regenfeld." In a word, the

reader's text requires "schwarzer," but the hearer's "text" may erase the
ending without doing violence to the poem. The difference between
"schwarzer Regenfeld" and "schwarz' Regenfeld" cannot be heard.
The full homonymic effect arises in the instant the hearer experiences
such phonetic irresolution. The "story" narrated in the poem is therefore not obviously—as Prawer proposes—a "hopeless repetition." For
what the proposed out-loud reading produces is also the unexpected semantic augmentation (and conflicting differentiation) of "ein schwarz'
Regenfeld": a black mud field drenched in rain—equally: a mirror of
rain—the lucent rain flashing off the black tain of the canted "field" as
so many minute, fractured, but constellated mirroring drops, entering
at a violent angle into the gutted field ("in das . . . Stoppelfeld")—or, as
Bunting writes, "rain slant, spray flick / to fields we do not know."[16]
Each of these meanings contends with the steady drizzle of the black
rain ("ein schwarzer Regen[, der] fällt"). Certainly, therefore—again
pace Prawer—we do not have, in any obvious way, a homophony that
"links" things. What arises, instead, is an effect produced by semantic
division and struggle (as the moving, drizzling rain of the "visual" reading battles for sense with the rain of the "audible" reading that coalesces
into a plane even as it comes angling into the horizontal stubble field).

Furthermore, on the strength of such phonetic puzzlement, we
could very well feel brushed by a wing of anxiety as to the arbitrariness
and insufficiency of grammar *tout court* in legislating meaning; for the
adjectival ending "-er" indicates the masculine, but, as a result of its being spoken and elided—as an effect of the stem ("schwarz'") dragged
alongside the "r" of "Regen"—it indicates the neuter. Because the
phonetic difference is inaudible, the grammar of the sentence gives no
definite instruction to the listener except: feel cognitive dissonance!

In the case of "De Profundis," we might be inclined to suppose that
Trakl will extend this moment of phonetic indetermination throughout the poem actively to produce the semantic aporias of the homonym
in a kind of effusion of homonyms.[17] This is so: we shall see this in a moment. But let us first secure the point that the first line already gives an
indication of the difficulty—perhaps, even, the undesirability—of
postulating in "De Profundis" and, by implication, in other poems of
Trakl, an integral pure order of the signifier.

This extraordinary poem continues:

Am Weiler vorbei
Sammelt die sanfte Waise noch spärliche Ähren ein.
Ihre Augen weiden rund und goldig in der Dämmerung
Und ihr Schoß harrt des himmlischen Bräutigams.

Bei der Heimkehr
Fanden die Hirten den süßen Leib
Verwest im Dornenbusch.

Ein Schatten bin ich ferne finsteren Dörfern.
Gottes Schweigen
Trank ich aus dem Brunnen des Hains.

Auf meine Stirne tritt kaltes Metall
Spinnen suchen mein Herz.
Es ist ein Licht, das in meinem Mund erlöscht.

Nachts fand ich mich auf einer Heide,
Starrend von Unrat und Staub der Sterne.
Im Haselgebüsch
Klangen wieder kristallne Engel.

Past the village pond
The gentle orphan still gathers scanty ears of corn.
Her eyes graze round and golden in the dusk
And her lap awaits the heavenly bridegroom.

Returning home
The shepherds found her sweet body
Rotting in the thorn bush.

I am a shadow far from gloomy villages.
God's silence
I drank from the grove well.

On my forehead cold metal beads.
Spiders seek my heart.
There is a light that dies in my mouth.

At night I found myself on a heath
Caked with garbage and the dust of stars.
In the hazel bushes
Crystalline angels clanged again.

This is one reader's text. The German hearer's text is more complex, more overwritten, one that secretes uncontainable nuances through evoked homonymy. One might attribute to "De Profundis" the rhetorical intention of making simple assertions, even of asserting simplicity—especially at the outset. One would do this in vain. The sharply marked, individualizing visibility of the opening is rapidly scattered in complications of rhetoric. The rhetorical disintegration of homonymic effects anticipates the theme of the disintegration of bodily substance. The myth of "De Profundis" unfolds in a mood of dwindling visual stability, a dwindling downward into the "depths" of unrepresentability and all of "De Profundis" that we shall be able to experience here. In the course of the poem the lightness of the poetic image-world coalesces into "ein Licht, das in meinem Mund erlöscht," a light extinguished in the poet's mouth. It is not haphazard that at the close the crepuscular speaker evokes the saving clangor of "*crystalline* angels."

In a famous comment Rilke wrote of Trakl:

I think that even standing up close, one still experiences these insights and outlooks as if pressed up against a glass pane: for Trakl's experience proceeds as in mirror images and fills his entire space, which, like the space in a mirror, cannot be entered.[18]

The force of the "mirror image," especially in the light of the author of this image, is not of a protected and genuine reflection but rather a distortion of nature, an uncanny or even horrific metamorphosis (one thinks of the mirror episodes in Rilke's *The Notebooks of Malte Laurids Brigge*). The ensuing discussion about Trakl's strangeness has frequently followed in this direction, taking its impetus from Rilke in order to stress the bizarre, beyond-the-looking-glass character of Trakl's images. But I am concerned to assimilate the special case of ocular distortion in Trakl to the general case of the unrepresentability of the Traklian image because of the homonymic, hence unspecifiable character of the verbal sign for his image.

What assails the reader throughout a reading of Trakl is, technically speaking, the aporia of the homonym. As a result of the peculiar intensity with which this figure posits both identity and difference, it functions in a way even more semiotically interesting than the metaphor (metaphor, on one view, being a subset of the homonym): a blind homonym. The homonym is a single signifier, an acoustic image generating opposed and disparate, radically irreconcilable concepts. In "De Profundis" the acoustical homonym "Waise" yields "orphan" but also "air, song." But what, then, is a metaphor, if not an acoustical mark to which we assign a triumphantly natural, integrating function by supposing that it fuses contrary concepts into a super-image or super-idea—and to which we're inclined to attribute, by virtue of the aura of its synthesizing power, an intrinsic harmony of likeness as between it (the signifier) and the supersignified as well. The truth, however, is otherwise: for, where a metaphor actually functions, it does so only as the effect of the least scrutinized convention. In fact we merely associate (impose a metonymy between) the verbal signifier and its alleged parent and derivative meanings. The metaphor, that privileged vehicle of meaning, is the product of an unreflected pact among language users bent on conceiving the habitual association of meanings as an intrinsic fittingness of meanings. About the homonym, that orphan sport of language or that prime music of language, no such illusions reign. Trakl creates homonymy, not metaphor, contradictory ciphers, not images fusible with meaning: as consider, now, the "sanfte Waise [the orphan and the song]," "die noch spärliche Ähren sammelt": are these "Ehren," honors, being gathered for this poem? or is, indeed, a gathering curse being described? In *Einbahnstraße*, Walter Benjamin recalls the ancient custom of the *libatio*, which survives in the warning against "gathering in abandoned ears and picking fallen grapes," for this would be to rob the earth of its due or deny one's ancestors, who confer blessings.[19]

A stubble field into which (only) a black rain falls is barren—as barren as the stubble field in Hölderlin's *Hyperion*: "Ich ziehe durch die Vergangenheit wie ein Ährenleser über die Stoppeläcker, wenn der Herr des Lands geerntet hat [I wander through the past like a gleaner of ears (of grain) over the stubble field after the lord of the land has harvested]."[20] But that stubble field "into which a black rainfield," a mirroring sheet reflecting the black heaven, enters, is bizarrely and uncontainably fertile as the prefigurer of exactly this "Regenfeld." Its agency is the heard homonym, which now extends throughout all the second stanza and thereafter. "Am Weiler vorbei": in it we can also hear "der Weihel," that part of the nun's veil which covers the forehead and which conjures the heavenly bridegroom of line 8; "der Weihler," the shrouded pond, double of the "schwarz'. . . Regenfeld." The gentle orphan "Waise" or song "Weise" takes in the scanty fruit of the stubble field. This is the fruit of heard homonymy, for note: "Ihre Augen weiden rund und goldig in der Dämmerung," her eyes graze round and golden or, round and golden, gloat in the twilight, gloaming, dusk, or dawn. Whose eyes? the orphan's or the wheat's (their eyes are golden grain), or are the eyes the song's—"Die Augen der sanften Weise"? And furthermore, is the heard homonym "Augenweiden" one substantive, one complex word?[21] Is it then the visible pleasures of the orphan that are spherical, golden, and lovely? And "ihr Schoß": is this lap already "der Schössling," the first sprout of the scanty ears, doing her . . . poor honor; or is it the archaic "Schoss," as "Zoll, Steuer, Abgabe [duty, tax, tribute]," the dowry that awaits the heavenly bridegroom? The decaying "body [Leib]" cannot be told apart from the "loaf (of bread) [Leib]" as a token of Christian union. The angelic music that has sounded "once more [wieder]" in the hazel copse may be the sounding "back [wieder]" of responsive angels.[22]

We will not be surprised to encounter in other poems of Trakl the effects produced by such strategically situated heard or real homonyms as, for example, "Lider" in "Verfallene Lider öffnen sich weinend im Haselgebüsch [Ruined lids open weeping in the hazel bushes]" (from the poem beginning "Finster blutet ein braunes Wild im Busch [darkly a brown deer bleeds in the bush]"), which yields "collapsed" but also "addicted lids" as well as "decadent songs" (compare "the rough songs of sunburnt girls [Brauner Mädchen rauhe Lieder]" in "In den Nachmittag Geflüstert [Whispered into the afternoon])"; or "Lachen," throughout Trakl's work, which yields all at once "pools," "tree-blazes," and "the laughter of many"; or, finally, "Kirchhofsschauer" in "Trompeten [Trumpets]," which yields "a rainshower in a graveyard," "a shudder evoked by a graveyard," "a shudder that runs through a graveyard," or even "the [Dionysian] observer of a graveyard."[23]

I want to emphasize that in Trakl *melos*, euphony, converges on homophony—homophony on homonymy—and homonymy disseminates the poem among contending, irreconcilable fields. It is the counterpart at the order of the signifier of "the theme of violation, introducing into Trakl's poetry dissonance and instability of key."[24] The effort to escape semantic uncertainty finds no shelter in the beautiful signifier. In Trakl euphony does not bring about harmony and synthesis. As homonymy it redistributes the chaos, which is what our (metaphorical) language is always doing anyway, although it is probably better for us to imagine that it is containing it.[25] Homonymy could sign the loss of the power to make firm distinctions, a covert feature of Trakl's desperate fascination with boundaries and borders (thus: "Pain petrified the threshold [Schmerz versteinerte die Schwelle]"), his obsession with a confinement that is always lacking, whose antonym is dissolution and decay, but this is an irritable reaching after fact and reason. Meanwhile, there is reward in a certain Dionysian ecstasy of shattering tropes—one in its own way more potent than even the infections of empathy with lived schizophrenia.[26]

8

BENJAMIN'S "AFFECTIVE UNDERSTANDING" OF HÖLDERLIN'S ODES "THE POET'S COURAGE" AND "TIMIDITY"

> The impenetrability of the relations resists every mode
> of comprehension other than that of feeling.
> —Walter Benjamin

THE POET'S COURAGE

Are not all the living related to you?
Does not the Parca herself nourish you for service?
Then just wander forth defenseless
Through life, and have no care!

Whatever happens, let everything be a blessing for you,
Be disposed toward joy! or what could then
Offend you, heart! What
Could you encounter there, whither you must go?

For, ever since the poem escaped from mortal lips
Breathing peace, benefiting in sorrow and happiness,
Our song brought joy to the hearts
Of men; so, too, were

We, the poets of the people, gladly among the living,
Where much joins together, joyful and pleasing to all,
Open to everyone; thus indeed is
Our ancestor, the sun god,

Who grants the joyful day to poor and rich,
Who in fleeting time holds us, the ephemeral ones,
Drawn erect on golden
Leading strings, like children.

His purple flood awaits him, takes him, too,
Where the hour comes—look! And the noble light
Goes, knowing of change,
With equanimity down the path.

Thus pass away then, too, when the time has come
And the spirit nowhere lacks its right; so dies
Once in the seriousness of life
Our joy, a beautiful death!

TIMIDITY

Are not many of the living known to you?
Does not your foot stride upon what is true, as upon carpets?
Therefore, my genius, only step
Naked into life, and have no care!

Whatever happens, let it all be opportune for you!
Be rhymed to joy! What could then
Offend you, heart? What
Could you encounter there, whither you must go?

For, since the heavenly ones, like men, a lonely deer,
And leads the heavenly ones themselves toward homecoming,
The poem and the chorus of princes,
According to their kinds, so, too, were

We, the tongues of the people, gladly among the living,
Where much joins together, joyous and equal to everyone,
Open to everyone; thus is indeed
Our Father, the god of heaven,

Who grants the thinking day to poor and rich,
Who, at the turning of time, holds us, who pass away in sleep,
Drawn erect on golden
Leading strings, like children.

Good, too, are we and skillful for [*or* sent to] someone to some end,
When we come, with art, and bring one
From among the heavenly beings. Yet we ourselves
Bring suitable [*or* appropriate] hands.[1]

In a youthful work of literary commentary, unpublished in his life-time,[2] Walter Benjamin examines the transformation of one ode by Hölderlin—"Dichtermut" (The Poet's Courage)—into a superior one—"Blödigkeit" (Timidity), even though the latter word has un-wonted negative connotations of bashfulness, even feebleness.[3] After a quarter-century of critical oblivion following its publication in 1955, Benjamin's essay has begun to be scrutinized despite, or perhaps pre-cisely because of, its exalted rhetoric.[4] A categorically excited language makes unsuspected use of plain images and etymological resonances, broadening them into metaphysical tokens in the daring, transgressive way that forecasts Benjamin's essay on Goethe's *Elective Affinities* ("Goe-thes Wahlverwandtschaften") of 1924.[5] Except for intermittent im-pulses from the George Circle, the rhetoric of Benjamin's essay on Höl-derlin does not appear to have a model in works he could have read in 1914.

Benjamin must have felt the task of comparing these two odes by Hölderlin to be assigned to him by the young Hölderlin-scholar Friedrich Norbert von Hellingrath in his doctoral dissertation on Höl-derlin's translations of Pindar.[6] Hellingrath wrote:

It is in relation to the poetic recastings of older odes that one can follow the de-velopment of Hölderlin's lyric power. One has only to compare "Timidity" with the first version of "The Poet's Courage" to see that each passage acquires a fullness of being only as a result of these changes.[7]

The idea of the "task" recurs throughout Benjamin's essay.

His actual work, meanwhile, would refute any view of it as a dutiful exercise in examination-answering, however conceived: in its (Kant-ian) synthetic power and metaphysical driving force, it complicates to unrecognizability distinctive tenets of the George Circle—especially any program, for example, of divinizing the poet as a creator. This cri-tique is already implicit in the valorization of the commentator in the essay on method that precedes Benjamin's detailed study of the two odes. At the same time the diction of the essay shows significant traces of the occasion that may have prompted it: it is painfully scholastic in manner and style. Gershom Scholem wrote that it was "deeply meta-physical";[8] it is also hieratic, cryptic, and high-flown, and in places writ-ten in a German whose tortuousness defies deciphering.

One of the peculiarities of Benjamin's style in this essay is the culti-vation of the passive voice to a degree unheard of even in bad academic writing.[9] This mortification of the passive—part of Benjamin's lifelong exploitation of the possibilities of subordination offered by German syntax—may be a reflex of his desire to go one better than the academic source of his "assignment."

For all its arcana, the essay raises a number of basic leading questions: What contribution does its theorizing make to a general theory of poetry? What contribution does it make to an understanding of Hölderlin? How does it figure in Benjamin's developing reflection on poetry and poetics? I shall try to address each of these questions.

The empirical history of Benjamin's manuscript is interesting, not least for the way it has justified its devaluation by readers who have found a personal obsession at the heart of Benjamin's major essays. The work was written toward the winter of 1914, the first winter of the war. In the draft of an article on Stefan George, Benjamin wrote:

In early 1914 . . . [George's] *Stern des Bundes* [the poetic cycle "The Star of the Covenant"] rose, and a few months later, the war came. . . . My friend [the poet Fritz Heinle] died. Not in battle. . . . Months followed. . . . In these months, however (which I devoted entirely to my first work of some scope—an essay on two poems of Hölderlin, which was dedicated to my friend)—the poems he was able to leave behind came to occupy the few places in my being where poems could still have a decisive effect on me [*wo noch in mir Gedichte bestimmend zu wirken vermochten*].[10]

The slim poetic legacy Benjamin speaks of refers to the work of the stricken Heinle, who committed suicide in protest against the war, though it is also teasingly difficult to decide whether it does not at the same time refer to Hölderlin's work.[11] In either case, the untimely death of a poet prompts Benjamin to read Hölderlin—and precisely his poems "The Poet's Courage" and "Timidity." For these poems aim to inspire the courage to continue in a young poet (like Benjamin!) dejected by the contemplation of the death of another poet or poetic agency. (For Hölderlin, in "The Poet's Courage," that poet appears to be Empedocles and thereafter Apollo.) The circumstances of its composition also help explain the exalted tone of Benjamin's essay, its desire to address first and last things. It is as if only an ultimately high seriousness could make a contribution suited to a world-historical time of extremity—to world war. Poetry, says Benjamin, could move him then in only a "limited" way. In wartime, especially, the civilian Benjamin could occupy himself with poetry only insofar as it revealed the most fundamental truth—indeed, a truth of affirmation.

Scholem, as I noted, described the Hölderlin essay as "deeply meta-physical." This is not wrong, but it is misleading, for its roots are poeto-logical: the essay is provoked by Hellingrath's study of Hölderlin's rela-tion to Greek poetic models—a relation chiefly involving questions of metrics and tonalities, especially as they bear on Hölderlin's turning from a nostalgia for Greek models toward a more intricately dialectical view of the history of poetics that calls for a "more severe," "more so-ber" diction. Before entrusting the manuscript to Scholem in 1915, Benjamin had mentioned to him in conversation Hellingrath's thesis on Hölderlin and Pindar, which, Benjamin said, had made an overwhelm-ing impression on him. Some of this impact is literally readable in the essay; it prompts Benjamin, for example, to devalue these lines in "The Poet's Courage": "For, ever since the poem escaped from mortal lips / Breathing peace, benefiting in sorrow and happiness, / Our song brought joy to the hearts / Of men . . . ," saying, "These words give only a feeble hint of the awe that filled Pindar—and also the late Hölderlin— before the figure of poetry" (23, *110).[12] Benjamin afterwards men-tioned his intention to have Hellingrath read the manuscript, "the ex-ternal occasion of which"—the inner one being the death of Heinle— was "the position of its theme in [Hellingrath's] thesis on the Pindar-translations."[13] But by 1917 Hellingrath, too, was dead, killed in the trenches outside Verdun. The "position" in the thesis of which Benja-min speaks might refer to Hölderlin's heightened sense of the responsi-bility of the poet in a godforsaken age.

Benjamin afterwards included the essay in the "splendid founda-tions" that he had "laid down in his twenty-second year" (the year of its composition) and in a letter to Scholem in 1930 regretted that during his lifetime he had never afterwards been able to build on those founda-tions.[14] Indeed, the essay on Hölderlin appears to want to secure the very idea of a foundation.

Benjamin stresses at the outset the novelty of devoting an "aesthetic commentary" to the modern poet Hölderlin (18, *105). The kind of commentary he envisages his work to be had traditionally been reserved for Greek tragedy. The notion of addressing with this sort of seriousness and intensity two poems by a modern writer requires a preliminary statement on method.

These poems have an essentialist dimension, to which the actual poems stand in an only more or less imperfect relation. Benjamin's task will be less to spell out these poems than to bring to light this essence, *das Gedichtete*, which translates as what in these poems is poetically rendered (or "poetized"), the essence out of which these poems are made.[15] *Das Gedichtete*, which I shall henceforth call "the poetized," is at the same time future-directed and aims at the truth that the poem renders (effects, produces) as well as the subsisting ground of which the poem is the poem or which has been made (or remade) as poem. The substantivized participial form of *das Gedichtete* contains both vectors and responds well to a principle that is simultaneously Platonic in conception as a static ground of truth and Kantian in its progressive and heuristic character.[16]

Benjamin also calls the poetized the "poetic task" and thereafter "inner form" and—relying on authority—what Goethe called *Gehalt*, perhaps "inner content."[17] The word "inner" should not be taken as a warrant of authority, as if the actual poem were only the envelope of an indwelling goal. The task is articulated in its "solution"—a solution, moreover, necessarily shot through with the failure or defeat also implied by the German word for task, *Aufgabe*—since no single poem realizes its task.[18] Nonetheless, it is the "seriousness and greatness" of the task that authorizes commentary. Hence, the modern poem is "classical" after the fact: the future-oriented thrust of the poetized guarantees its authority, whereas the authority of the classical work (the tragedy) is guaranteed in advance by a sort of historical prejudice (*Vorurteil*).[19]

It is easier to say what this poetic task or poetic precondition is not. It is not the expression of the personality or weltanschauung of the poet; neither is it the empirical "process of lyrical composition" (18, *105). The poetized, Adorno noted, in his famous essay on Hölderlin's late paratactic style, is not an affair of the poet's meaning or intention; it is not what can be thought (*das Gedachte*) but is more nearly what has been kept dark (*das Dunkle*).[20] As a polemical term, therefore, it is aimed against the Diltheyan notion of a poetry—especially a lyric poetry—of flashlike, immediately intelligible lived experience (*Erlebnis*)—though something of the categorial thrust of Dilthey's aesthetics does surge back when Benjamin writes: "In the poetized, life determines itself through the poem. . . . Life, as the ultimate unity, lies at the basis of the poetized. . . . The analysis of great works of literature will encounter [a unity] . . . as the genuine expression of life" (20, *107–8). The latter phrase is a reminiscence of Dilthey's dictum: "Poetry is suffused with the feeling that it has to provide the authentic interpretation of life it-self."[21] Where Benjamin plainly departs from Dilthey, however, is his excising of Dilthey's mediating term "experience [*Erlebnis*]," which posits an empirical subject. (Dilthey wrote: "Every individual *Erlebnis* occurs in relation to a self.")[22] Benjamin offers no account of what it might have been like for Hölderlin to become conscious of the change in the inner form of his odes, let alone any judgment on the authenticity of his experience. In Benjamin's reading of "Timidity," the poet does not function as mediator but is himself the "middle," the precondition of which is the emptying out of personality. This loss of subjective con-sciousness in the producer provokes a corresponding valorization of "commentary," which turns out to mean a good deal more than the ap-propriation of meaning by a self-subsistent reading subject. The project is nonhermeneutic. It requires of the commentator, too, a special kind of courage, a letting go, like the attention defined in Benjamin's late, witty formulation of the paradox "To have presence-of-mind means letting yourself go at the moment of danger."[23]

The aesthetic commentary does not intend to produce a facsimile of the poem, for this is never more than one possible solution to the task in-forming it.[24] What the commentary aims to reproduce—and at the same time co-produce—is the poetized, "the sphere [of the poetized] being at once the *product* and the subject of this investigation" (18, ★105; my emphasis). Benjamin's formulation prepares the way for a commen-tary that could be called, anachronistically, a *Zwiesprache*, a dialogue, between a poet and a thinker.[25]

Benjamin's claim to produce with his commentary a work not onto-logically inferior to the work he is addressing is striking. The "good" circular logic of this argument repeats the circular structure in Benja-min's account of the poetized, which preexists every poem and is at the same time constituted only as the poem's product. In a sense more figu-ratively concrete than one might have realized at first, the poetized is a "sphere."

The poetized and commentary co-constitute "that peculiar domain containing the truth of the poem," a "synthetic unity of the intellectual and perceptual orders." To this extent Benjamin's entire essay is circu-lar—and hence self-validating. The essay is true, as the poetized is true, as a result of the coherence of its parts. Consider its structure: The opening section on method concerns itself with its own procedure as a commentary and with the poetized in general. The second section, which does the main work of the essay, shows the increase in coherence in the poetized of "Timidity" over that of "The Poet's Courage." Now, the poetized in general is defined as a unity of "intellectual and perceptual world" (18, *105), a world that can be distinguished from the poem itself by its greater degree of "determinability [*Bestimmbarkeit*]" (19, *106). At the same time, however, the poetized of the particular poem "Timidity" can also be distinguished from the barely crystallized poetized of "The Poet's Courage" by the more nearly complete unity of its intellectual and perceptual order—"the precondition of [Hölderlin's late] poetry being more and more to transform the figures borrowed from a neutral 'life' into members of a mythic order" (28, *116).[26] The second poem, "Timidity," is also thus distinctive for its higher degree of determinability, which comes to light in yet another way: it allows a selective extrapolation of features from its empirical totality for the sake of articulating the rule of its "functional unity" (19, *106). This move, which Benjamin calls a "loosening up" of the poem's actual organization, is a requirement of commentary and the path to the poetized. What this analysis comes down to is the fact that Benjamin can justify his claim to constitute the poetized of "Timidity" by means of his commentary. His account of "Timidity" reads true because it coincides with the theoretical essence of poetry argued for in the methodological part of the commentary—an essence that, like that of the commentary itself, is defined as the most complete unity of the most extensive coherence. Such unity in coherence is the warrant of truth. This circularity suggests Heidegger's "elucidations" of Hölderlin, which seek to establish in Hölderlin the presence of the theme of being—if not, indeed, of the experience of being—on the grounds of the urgency of the theoretical assertion that there be such an experience.[27] But Benjamin's claim to establish the poetized in the transformation of two poems by Hölderlin is the more nearly credible one, since its urgency is sustained by its own coherence, one that it attempts to illustrate through the unity of its methodological and practical parts. As such, it exhibits the chief characteristic of the poetized—obsessive coherence.

One gets a similar result by proceeding along a parallel track: Benjamin's reading of "Timidity" can claim to be true because its outcome coincides with the essential requirement of poetry—according to Benjamin. The coherence of his own demonstration evokes the coherence of the poetized itself. The poetized of Hölderlin's ode is constituted as the truth of his own essay. This procedure is clearest toward the end, when Benjamin announces that *only at this moment of his argument* is it possible to adduce a constitutive feature of the poetized of "Timidity": "The transformation of the duality of death and poet into the unity of a dead poetic world 'saturated with danger,' is the relation in which the poetized of both poems stands. Now, for the first time, in this passage, reflection on the third and middle verse has become possible" (34, ★124). This middle verse, moreover, is not just topographically central: it is eschatologically charged, speaking of the homecoming of men and the gods. Reading this essay, you have the sense that the poetized is being constructed before your eyes.

Benjamin's essay proceeds as an ever stronger insistence on the superiority of the later version of the ode "Timidity" to the first version, "The Poet's Courage." The increase in value is immeasurable (that is, it is metaphysically large): it can only be suggested by such words as greater profundity, greater precision, and a higher degree of coherence vis-à-vis the duplicity and fragmentariness of the first version. Toward the end of the analysis the kind of value that "Timidity" possesses becomes so dependent on exalted and oxymoronic qualities (or indeed the sublation of all mere qualities, as for example in its fusion of the limited and the illimitable) that this value becomes, strictly speaking, inconceivable. Here the tonality of near-sacred revelation sounds, which would be disturbing, or at any rate would be even more disturbing, if it were not for Benjamin's Kantian proviso at the start: "The disclosure of the pure poetized, the absolute task, must remain—after all that has been said—a purely methodological, ideal goal. The pure poetized would otherwise cease to be a limit-concept: it would be life or poem" (20–21, ★108). The tendency to assert irrefrangible unity, however, as a feature of the poetized, persists; and not too many pages later Benjamin, in his enthusiasm for the superiority of "Timidity," this "fulfilled" version of poetic courage, over "The Poet's Courage," declares the superlative realized:

With respect to all individual structures—to the inner form of the verses and images—this law [of identity] will prove to be fulfilled, so as to bring about, finally, at the heart of all the poetic connections, the identity of the perceptual and intellectual forms among and with one another—the spatiotemporal interpenetration of all configurations in a spiritual quintessence, the poetized that is identical with life. (25, ★112)

This tension of writing about Hölderlin in a certain Hölderlinean mode of exaltation promoted by the George Circle while maintaining a Kantian prudence (a prudence also found par excellence in Hölderlin) characterizes Benjamin's essay throughout.[28]

Benjamin's reading of the two odes begins with a gesture tending toward what I spoke of as the self-validation of the essay. The transition from the methodological section to the particular reading occurs through a reflection on the word "Mythos"—myth. The German word, like the English, means a story, fable, or narrative about origins, gods, and heroes.[29] But here it also appears to allude to the Greek senses of *"mythos"*—"word" or "speech," things thought or said. In these senses it begins to function as what Benjamin has called the poetized; for myth, too, mediates between the orders of life and the particular work of art. "The underlying basis [of the poetized]," writes Benjamin, "is not the individual life-mood of the artist but rather a life-context determined by art. The categories in which this sphere . . . can be grasped . . . should perhaps more readily be associated with the concepts of myth." The circle of connection is then fully drawn: "The strongest [poetic achievements] . . . refer to a sphere related to the mythic: the poetized." For what is at stake here is "the inner greatness and structure of the elements (which we term, approximately, 'mythic')" (20, *107).

The single reference most useful in clarifying the uses of myth in this essay is, as Michael Jennings has pointed out, Benjamin's reading of Hölderlin's essay "On Religion." Here, Hölderlin declares that the conditions of religion require a mythic presentation, with the result that all religions are "essentially poetic [*ihrem Wesen nach poetisch*]."[30] The reference heightens one's sense of what Benjamin does and also does not owe to Hölderlin, because, in the last resort, it is only with difficulty that one can grasp myth in Benjamin's essay as "essentially poetic."

At the same time that Benjamin brings the poetized and myth into intimacy with one another (along with the aesthetic commentary itself, which, according to a certain myth of commentary, *produces* the poetized), he takes pains to ward off their identification. Note the curious but persistent qualifications: "should perhaps . . . be associated with," "related to," "approximately." Again, in this vein, "the analysis of great works of literature will encounter . . . *not* myth *but* rather a unity produced by the force of the mythic elements straining against one another" (20, *108; my emphasis). As a result, one cannot say that Benja-

min's concept of myth in this essay is positive. It need not then be ex-
cused as having been automatically received from the George Circle, for
which Benjamin at this time had a certain affinity. And it is then untrue
that it was not until four years later, in the essay "Destiny and Character," that Benjamin finally developed a theory of myth that has due respect for what in myth is negative, threatening, compulsive, for this
sense is already present in the Hölderlin essay.[31] The force of Benjamin's
distinction between mythology and myth is redoubled in the distinction between the singular "myth," which in post-Greek times is never
nakedly encountered as a unity, versus "mythic element*s*." The distinction is important enough for Benjamin to want to repeat it almost word
for word at the close of the essay. In the case of Hölderlin's "greatest creations," he writes, "the contemplation of the poetized, however, leads
not to the myth but rather . . . only to mythic connections [*Verbunden-
heiten*], which in the work of art are shaped into unique, unmythologi-
cal, and unmythic forms that cannot be better understood by us" (35,
*126). Thus, at the same time that in this essay Benjamin appears as a
great promulgator of a sort of mythic thinking in and about literature,
he is its refined critic.

Now the superiority of "Timidity" to "The Poet's Courage" is
based on the claim that its myth (at once a regulative idea and an idea of
regulation) is independent of the Greek mythological content that runs
wild through the fable of the earlier poem and disrupts its coherence.
The transformation of mythology into myth is marked by the increase
in the density of connectedness:

The mythological emerges as myth only through the extent of its coherence.
The myth is recognizable from the inner unity of god and destiny. . . . In the
first version of his poem, Hölderlin's subject is a destiny—the death of the poet.
Hölderlin praises in song the sources of the courage to die this death. This death
is the center from which the world of poetic dying was meant to arise. Existence
in that world would be the poet's courage. (22, *109)

The early poem, however, fails to convey the legitimacy and inexora-
bleness of this process. The sense of cosmos is lacking; myth leans on
mythology, the deluded fable of myth: "The sun god is the poet's ancestor, and his death is the destiny through which [the] poet's death, at first
mirrored, becomes real." The key word is "destiny." The closest one
might come to specifying the central mythic element of Hölderlin's
later poetic cosmos (and perhaps the modern myth purely and simply) is

the destiny of the poet—namely, "Life in poetry, in the unwavering poetic destiny which is the law of Hölderlin's world" (26, *113). If, at the beginning of "Timidity," the poet's active "familiarity" with many of those who are alive has a "mythic character," it is because this myth "is based on its following the course prescribed by destiny; indeed it already comprehends the fulfillment of destiny" (26, *114). The transition from "The Poet's Courage" to "Timidity" is a transition accomplished in Hölderlin's poetic career from Greece to a modernity that reflects on Greece—a modernity whose essential shape must be produced by poetry, by an "art" threatening the extinction of the empirical subject: this is the myth of modernity.

A key articulation in the argument for the superiority of "Timidity" is therefore its way of presenting poetic courage. A source of the poet's courage is his posited relation or relatedness to all those who are alive. But what sort of legitimacy has this connection? Reading "The Poet's Courage," Benjamin reads strongly so as to postpone an answer. He knows Hölderlin's "solution": the poet takes courage from the indestructible life of living beings taken as a whole, a life that comprehends him. But Benjamin finds in the early poem only the statement of a problem—one that will be differently stressed in the second version, where this mere "relation" becomes an act of knowing and "a relation of dependency . . . , an activity" (26, *114). The fact of the coherence of the living community *among itself* as it is revealed to the poet in "The Poet's Courage," and not as comprehending him, cannot be enough to inspire his courage. The poet and the community need to be bound together in a common situation (*Lage*) of truth, as only in "Timidity," where "temporal existence in infinite extension, the truth of the situation [*Lage*], binds the living to the poet" (27, *115).

Where, then, in "The Poet's Courage," according to Benjamin, do you find the autonomous power of the poet who does not need to grope for safety among alien orders, "nach Volk und Gott" (23, *109)? This source is missing from the early version and thence arises as the poetized of the later poem. In "Timidity" Hölderlin exhibits for the first time in the trajectory of the odes a fully appropriated Greek consciousness of poetry—Greek awe, the awe of Pindar. We pass from poets who are "bards" to those who are the very "tongues of the people." The doubleness of the vision of "The Poet's Courage," which produces the mere analogy between the poet and Apollo, is unified in "Timidity," where poets "bring one of the heavenly powers" with them. In "The Poet's Courage" death is "the extinguishing of the plastic, heroic essence in the indeterminate beauty of nature, not—as it is later understood to be—form in its deepest degree of union" (23, ★110). In the second poem, death means the passage from an empirical ("plastic") subject, whose sense of beauty is "natural," to the ascetic subject, for whom beauty is the law of pure relationship. Benjamin might be understood here as envisaging Hölderlin's "Hesperian turn," Hölderlin's growing investment in the principle of style he calls the "sobriety of representation," which evokes the death of an immediate sense of felt life.

Finally, the shortcoming of "the formative principle" in the first poem can be perceived even in the demotic character of its title. Benjamin asks us to hear in the expression "*Dichtermut*" ("The poet's courage" but also "the kind of courage found in poets," that is, not a universal or a genuine courage] a vulgar phrase and a vulgar idea, as in *Weibertreue*—the kind of fidelity, this phrase says, found in women, an only odd and certainly deficient sort of fidelity).[32] But in his program of exalting the later poem, Benjamin does not pay equal attention to the troublesome word *Blödigkeit*, which while unquestionably meaning "timidity," also, like *Blödheit*, suggests short-sightedness and, in certain contexts, stupidity. Even if this unsavory connotation is set aside, there is still the relativizing effect that this title exercises on the full poetic affirmation that Benjamin finds in the poem. The poem has to be seen as an answer supplied urgently and perhaps excessively to the crisis (of confidence) marked out in the title—an essay in courage rather than a statement of the fact of courage. Benjamin, I think, glides too rapidly over this difficulty in affirming the "passivity" of the timid poet as in a deeper sense the very essence of courage.

Another way of reading this crux has recently been suggested by the critic Bart Philipsen, who gives grounds for valorizing the term "timidity" from the start.[33] Philipsen studies Hölderlin's reception of Rousseau's sense of "simplicity" and "lethargy" as an exemplary self-forgetting that opens the self to another sort of being: "Nichts, d.h. Anderem."[34] Following Philipsen's lead, *Blödigkeit* would no longer mean the opposite of *Dichtermut* but would be another way of naming this courage—hence, a positive term. But since neither Hölderlin nor least of all Benjamin makes this argument explicit, I am not inclined to accept it. I see, rather, *Blödigkeit* as identifying the starting-off point of an exhortation, as that which provokes the exhortation and must be overcome. I shall return to this point.

By now, the basic "fable" of Benjamin's commentary is evident: only in the last version of his ode does Hölderlin realize "the interpenetration of individual forms of perception [that is, space and time] and their connectedness in and with that which is intellectual, as idea, destiny, and so on" (32, *122). This coherence is gained by a movement toward ascetic sobriety and concretization. Benjamin's own demonstration of this logic is most persuasive when it puts aside its relentless neo-Kantian diction of connection ("determinedness," "coherence," "order," "law," "relation," "function," "series," "unity") to address the rhetorical quiddities of the odes, such as the tropes that liken the sun's rays to the golden leading strings of children and translate the poet's "living in truth" as walking on a richly ornamented Oriental carpet. By stunning feats of induction, Benjamin finds threading throughout "Timidity" a visual and etymological network of word-roots and images for spatial relations, like Goethe's "replicated mirrorings [*wiederholte Spiegelungen*]"—turning on the Middle High German root-cluster "*lāge, leger, legen*"—a network itself threaded through by an equally intricate pattern of temporal terms, the point of which is to establish an unheard-of degree of "perceptual-intellectual," world-constituting coherence. This is a tour de force of close reading fifty years *avant la lettre*. Here is one particularly striking detail in this system of connections. The words "*geschickt* [sent *but also* skillful]" and "*schicklich* [appropriate, suitable]" engender various associations. Michael Hamburger, Hölderlin's translator, gives the background:

"Geschickt," literally "sent," also means "skillful"—so that there is an etymological connection between the artist's skill and his mission or his fitness to serve, for fitness is implied in the German word "Geschicklichkeit." Yet the nouns "Geschick" and "Schicksal" also mean fate or destiny—and again Hölderlin takes up the etymological link.[35]

Benjamin stresses the link of temporalizing and spatializing agencies in individual words: the temporal sense is evident in the process of sending, while the spatial sense comes in, in the extreme concreteness and nearness to life of "someone [whom], some way, we serve," where these living beings thus served are associated, through the extraordinary carpet-image, with "the extension of space, the outspread plane." This image is then dazzlingly modulated into a Byzantine mosaic, into which, at the center, the figure of the poet is flattened into the stones. Like forms in the mosaic radiating out from the center, the figures of Hölderlin's poetic cosmos—"those who are alive"—emanate from the poet's "passivity": "depersonalized, the people appear as if pressed in the surface around the great flat figure of its sacred poet" (28, *116). The virtual sacralization of the poet is realized through his loss of particular identity in the ontological principle of courage itself, the center of all relationship, that holds together time and space, gods and men.

It is noteworthy, if we think back to the phenomenon of homonymy in Trakl, that Benjamin's tour de force arises here from homonyms ("*geschickt*" and, earlier, "*gelegen*")—terms not stressed by Benjamin as instances of homonymy, let alone as homonymy that disperses meaning or redistributes chaos. A relentless Platonic-Kantian focus on a world of retrievable ideas overrides any semiotic suspicion as to the unreliability of the homonym. In a word, rhetorical awareness abets the discovery of philosophical truth. This is a modern position that can seem archaic in the postmodern view that considers such obstinate rhetorical figures as homonymy, found at key junctures in a text, to prohibit a priori its recuperation. In Benjamin there is no collision along the lines projected by the truth content of the poetized and the homonymic signifier; the tension of homonymy is absorbed in the metaphysical drive to recover truth.

Benjamin's profiling of the poetized of Hölderlin's second ode thus defines a direction in modern poetics that can be called counter-subjective.[36] Benjamin aims with a Kantianism of the First Critique to correct the Kantianism of the Third Critique that obliterates the truth-content of poetry in favor of another goal: of setting into play ineffable moods (*Stimmungen*) and by extension nonconceptually cognitive subjective experiences, for example, a felt harmony of the faculties, a heightened sense of bodily life.[37] On Benjamin's account, the superiority of "Timidity" to "The Poet's Courage" is its greater truth; the intensity of perceived relationship is an affair of a real series and not of intellectual faculties. Moreover—a "moreover" that means to superadd a Platonism to Kant—this truth addresses last things: it constitutes a cosmos informed by a maximum of identity, striving to overcome even the difference between gods and the human poet, between space and time, between the people and the poet's genius. This ascetic, counter-subjectivist strain (which valorizes the "coherence" of the "form [*Ge-*

stalt]" and makes the participation of a subjective consciousness only contingent vis-à-vis a superhuman courage) is also pronounced in Heidegger's later poetics and in Adorno's *Aesthetic Theory*. This tendency points to the concretization in the poem of a (phenomenologically) "transcendental" poetic project. This project, which Benjamin calls the "poetic task," possesses truth value by virtue of its identification with poetic language—with this provision: by "poetic language" one must understand the most radical and extensive capacity for relationship ("Poet and poetry in the cosmos of the poem are not differentiated. The poet is nothing but a limit with respect to life" [34–35, *125]). Here one can see Benjamin's reading accomplishing well in advance the so-called *Kehre* (turning) in Heidegger's thought to "[an]other mode of thinking that abandons subjectivity," in which "every kind of [philosophical] anthropology and all subjectivity of man as subject . . . [are] left behind."[38] Part of this poetological modernism, too, is vivid in de Man's early—and, thereafter, abandoned—assertion: "Literary criticism, in our century, has contributed to establishing this crucial distinction between an empirical and an ontological self."[39] The Benjamin essay does mean to establish, in "Timidity," something like the ontological subject in the figure of the heroic poet, the middle of a new intellectual-temporal order.[40] And not trivially for the argument of this book, the term enabling this stance is the name of an affect—courage.[41]

Within Hölderlin studies, Benjamin's essay could support the tendency of Heidegger's celebration of Hölderlin as a poet of being and not of the differences legislating the eternal separation of word and being, poet and hero, poet and god. Writing of the middle strophe of "Timidity," Benjamin alleges a literal fusion of poetic and sacred destinies in the *Einkehr*, the return to earth of the gods, enabled by the poem:[42] "It is evident . . . that in this center [the 'return (*Einkehr*)' of the gods among men] lies the origin of song . . . , that here the idea of 'art' and the idea of the 'true' arise as expressions of the underlying unity" (34, *124). The poet's existence is at once human and sacred (33, *123). In these lines, Benjamin, like Heidegger, tends to produce the Hölderlin of "*sacred* sobriety [*das heilig Nüchterne*]," with stress on "sacred." These words of Hölderlin, as Benjamin notes, had been used by Hellingrath to identify

a tendency of his later creations. They arise from the inner certainty with which those works stand in his own intellectual life, in which sobriety now is allowed, is called for, because this life is in itself sacred, standing beyond all exaltation in the sublime. (35, ★125)

Benjamin also uses the words that in this passage appear only as a citation.

It would be appropriate today, then, to worry about Benjamin's relentless tendency to find unity in "Timidity." The best place to worry from would be, as I have suggested, the character of the poem as well as the essay as an excessive, compensatory, eristic response (for Benjamin as for Hölderlin) to its antithetical starting-off point—to timidity, to shortcoming. This negativity of mood is founded in an initial godforsakenness, from whence a return of the gods, according to the myth of the poem, is conceivable.[43] Benjamin is eager to get past this negativity and does so through a certain interpretive speeding. Via his own mythic mode of "affective comprehension [*fühlendes Erfassen*]," he claims for Hölderlin the intellectual-perceptual totality that was in reality an elusive term and an eternal problem for Hölderlin's "swift conceptual grasp [*schneller Begriff*]." If we take the Fourth Maxim as a benchmark, then the poetized that Benjamin finds realized in "Timidity" is true only in another sort of mythic sense: as a consoling fiction, more nearly in the sense in which Nietzsche speaks in *Birth of Tragedy* of myth as sheltering against the experience of obliteration: "the symbolic image of the myth *saves* us from the *immediate* perception of the highest world-idea, just as thought and word save us from the uninhibited effusion of the unconscious will" (my emphasis). In Nietzsche's view, the myth introduces a separation from the immediate experience of the Dionysian, whose destructive force can typically be read from Hamlet; for, "like the Dionysian man, having once looked truly into the essence of things, [Hamlet] has *gained knowledge* ['true knowledge, an insight into the horrible truth'], and nausea inhibits action."[44] The myth Benjamin finds constructed in "Timidity" is the myth of a beneficent death, equivalent to a courageous extinction of personality for the sake of a higher speaking.[45] In fact, "myth" here could signal an ideological investment in a constructed *belief*—contrived to fend off "the horrible truth"—the belief in the good death of poetic impersonality.

On Benjamin's account one might very well want to stress that, unlike Nietzsche in *The Birth of Tragedy*, Hölderlin does not steadily intuit the "divine" totality as threatening his destruction. In *Hyperion*, for example, nature manifests itself immanently as "quietness" and "life." A more nearly beneficent version of the consuming "heavenly fire" is "the philosophical light." So, not needing Nietzsche's picture of the Dionysian—having anticipated it as the "fiery element" in its distinction from the gladsome object of intellectual intuition—Hölderlin, in "Timidity," cannot be accused of deliberately masking a terrifying insight. So the argument goes. On the other hand, it is enough to note that the term *Blödigkeit*, as "timidity," literally denotes a (Hamlet-like) inhibition— or, at the least, tarrying and hesitation. As such it answers precisely to that tarrying and hesitation which Hölderlin, in the maxim on "swift conceptual grasp," saw as an inevitable defect, being the definitive behavior of a finite intellect denied an intuition of the whole. As a totalizing interpreter of "Timidity," then, Benjamin's procedure—more absolute than Hölderlin's own wording warrants—is the same one I earlier identified as Hölderlin's procedure in the Fourth Maxim. Given the uncertainty of constituting a "divine" totality on the basis of an "organized feeling," it becomes the mark of an only mythical leap out of danger when the author, in a final formulation, elevates the poet's achievement to a hyperbolic totality of life.

At the close of his essay, Benjamin manages entirely to identify timidity with the courage of the poet: " 'Timidity' has now become the authentic stance of the poet. Since he has been transposed into the middle of life, nothing awaits him [the poet] but motionless existence, complete passivity, which is the essence of the courageous man—nothing except to surrender himself wholly to relationship [*Beziehung*]" (34, ★125). (In a Schopenhauerian-Nietzschean light, in which "relationship" answers to the fourfold root of phenomenal illusion, this will seem a dubious achievement!) No matter what the light, however, the difference between the titles of the two versions—to Benjamin's mind so unequal—needs to be preserved, especially as the source of differences that flow through both poems. The first assumes the quality of courage naively, unproblematically, while the second must fight through to it through its absence. The second poem overcomes its title dialectically while the first merely posits it as present. If, however, timidity *is* courage, then there never was anything really to fight through to.

The crucial point needs to be looked at one more time. I have been stressing the fact that the title "Blödigkeit" literally means something negative—timidity, stupidity, passivity; in a word, the opposite of courage. If the poem is read as taking its starting point from the literal sense of its title, and as having its career in the passage from this deficient hypothesis about the poet to his fulfillment (the exhortation accomplished), then it will be right to raise questions about the legitimacy of positing this good end, the speed with which the poet achieves it, the means by which it is achieved, and so forth. And then one might very well accuse Hölderlin and Benjamin of interpretive speeding. The passage to virtue occurs too swiftly.

It would not be occurring too swiftly, however, if the poem had been charged in advance by author and interpreter with an idea about how the passage to courage had to take place *because* the end was already present in the beginning. Then *Blödigkeit* would already have meant courage, would already have been only a metaphor for courage—an idea that has resonance in the special context in which Hölderlin may have understood timidity, namely, his reception of Rousseau, in whom sloth (*paresse*) and even a certain "stupidity" are the preconditions of a rapport with being.[46] Since, however, the paradoxicalness of this latter reading flies in the face of normal usage, we might consider Hölderlin's very use of the word *Blödigkeit* to mean poetic courage as itself a performance of poetic courage, a piece of the audacity that the poem, at the level of argument, only elicits. This reading would be consistent with the program Hölderlin sets forth in "Nature and Art or Saturn and Jupiter": the injustice of worldly things will be rectified to the degree that acts resemble acts of poetic speaking.

On the other hand, it is impossible to forget that the poem is structured as an exhortation, so the first reading, which takes *Blödigkeit* literally, continues to be cogent. But the insistence within it of the reading based on Rousseau's paradox allows for the work of exhortation to be achieved (indeed, to be performed) in the course of the poem both by argument and by foregone conclusion, tautologically.

I am dwelling on this instance of poetic tension because it is so arresting an example of the kind of fragility, admiration, and wonder that I have termed complex pleasure.

This sort of pleasure, then, complicates the rather univocal strain of exaltation in Benjamin's essay, which is one aspect of his procedure but not the whole story. In another important sense, Benjamin's essay adumbrates its own demythification by striving to stay short of divinizing the poetic awareness in Hölderlin's later poetry. Benjamin's citation of

Hellingrath's use of the phrase "sacredly sober" is preceded by the proviso that he, Benjamin, has actually refrained until now from employing Hölderlin's phrase to describe the tonality of the inner form of "Timidity"; he has waited until a correct understanding of this phrase could be reached. There is in this formulation, which responds well to the protocols of early phenomenologically based deconstruction, a nuance of appropriate distantiation, as there is in the fact that Benjamin leaves undecided the degree of responsibility he is willing to accept for the application of *"sacred* sobriety." Benjamin's own exegesis tends to stress the term "sobriety," to interpret potentially substantialist-sounding unities as neo-Kantian functional unities of opposing elements. Moreover, the essay stresses the thrust to unity in a poem rare in Hölderlin's canon for the directness with which it sets about suppressing doubt and difference, suppressing "timidity." Heidegger, on the other hand, finds the statement of unity in, for example, "Wie Wenn am Feiertage" (As when on a holiday), a poem that rather explicitly says the opposite of unity.[47] This difference in the degree of conformity of the exegesis to the text is important, quite apart from the interpreter's conclusion.

Furthermore, unlike Heidegger's "elucidations," nothing that Benjamin writes gives a grain of support to the blunt thesis of Hölderlin's "Hesperian turn" as envisaging an immediate poetry of *national* themes. Benjamin finds in "Timidity," despite its celebration of the "bard of the people," the presence of an unconstrainable "Orientalism," a foreignness dissolving plastic form. A reflection on Hölderlin's Orientalism—better, his "Egyptianism"—when rightly carried through, disrupts any totalizing picture of the relation of Greek and Hesperian poetics.[48] The Greek plastic principle is "transcended and balanced out" by the Oriental principle of unboundedness (34, *124); Benjamin triangulates with interminable results the polarity of Greek and Hesperian poetic principles.

A final point rather affirming a concentrated conceptual sobriety in Benjamin's own development is the fact that Benjamin's notion of the poetized as a fit object of aesthetic *commentary* answers to the goal of "critique [*Kritik*]," not commentary, as this distinction is laid out in the 1924 essay on Goethe's *Die Wahlverwandtschaften* (Elective affinities). For there, in 1924, critique—in distinction to commentary—is preoccupied with the "truth content" of a work of art, whereas "commentary" is concerned with "objective" or "material" or "concrete" content—namely, the "Sachgehalt." It is revealing of the ongoing demythologization of Benjamin's own categorial perspective that he should write of *Elective Affinities,* "The *mythic* is the real material content [*Sachgehalt*] of this book" (my emphasis).[49] We remember that the poetized, with its near-identity with the mythic, is, in the Hölderlin essay, "the peculiar domain containing the truth of the poem" (19, *105). "Myth," it thus turns out, will have an only increasingly ambivalent—read "negative"—relation to "truth content." So that in Benjamin's essay on Goethe's novel *Elective Affinities* ("Goethes Wahlverwandtschaften") that "truth" with which myth was virtually identified is finally only its seductive simulacrum: not truth at all but only the truth of natural appearance. And any other form of truth in poetry finally becomes inexpressible—becomes, quite literally, *"das Ausdruckslose."* This shift in Benjamin's thought also belongs to the pattern that rejects the attribution of divinity to the poet Hölderlin: in the *Elective Affinities* essay "Goethe is denied every sort of creativity that would allow the conclusion of his connection with the divine."[50]

• ᵔ •

It is fitting that this book on feeling should end on the note of sobriety that could be felt only on the strength of Benjamin's "feeling mode of comprehension [*fühlendes Erfassen*]." One could feel the conclusion of Benjamin's reading of Hölderlin's odes to be enacting Hölderlin's insight: "There where sobriety abandons you is the limit of your inspiration." But it is again "feeling," writes Hölderlin, that "is the best sobriety and reflection of the poet."[51] Benjamin's essay is a powerful modern exemplar of the view that poetic feeling enables a distinctive kind of disclosure.

Reference Matter

NOTES

Preface

1. From an imaginary conversation with Shakespeare: Slavoj Žižek, *For They Know Not What They Do: Enjoyment as a Political Factor* (London: Verso, 1991), 39.

2. Friedrich Nietzsche, "Der Wanderer und sein Schatten," Aphorism 109, *Menschliches, Allzumenschliches*, vol. 2 in Friedrich Nietzsche, *Werke in drei Bänden*, ed. Karl Schlechta (Munich: Hanser, 1954–56), 1:921.

3. *Conversations with Eckermann (1823–1832)* [Thursday, July 5, 1827], trans. John Oxenford (San Francisco: North Point Press, 1984), 172 (translation modified). Johan Peter Eckermann, *Gespräche mit Goethe in den letzten Jahren seines Lebens, Gedenk-Ausgabe der Werke, Briefe, und Gespräche*, ed. Ernst Beutler (Zurich: Artemis, 1948), 24:384, 257. For a witty discussion, see "Rilke and Nietzsche: With a Discourse on Thought, Belief, and Poetry," in Erich Heller, *The Disinherited Mind* (Harmondsworth, Middlesex: Penguin, 1961), 109.

4. Like Goethe in this passage, Hegel, in his *Aesthetics*, identifies poetry with the imagination, shifting the conflict between reason and imagination outside literature. Addressing "the sort and manner of [artistic] production," Hegel writes: "Nor is it a scientific production which passes over from the sensuous to abstract representations and thoughts or is active entirely in the element of pure thinking. In artistic production the spiritual and the sensuous aspects must be as one. For example, someone might propose to proceed in poetic composition by first apprehending the proposed theme as a prosaic thought and then putting it into poetical images, rhyme, and so forth, so now the image would simply be

hung on to the abstract reflections as an ornament and decoration. But such a procedure could produce only bad poetry, because in it there would be operative as *separate* activities what in artistic production has validity only as an undivided unity. This genuine mode of production constitutes the activity of artistic *imagination* [*Phantasie*]" (my italics). This text is conveniently found in *German Aesthetic and Literary Criticism: Kant, Fichte, Schelling, Schopenhauer, Hegel,* ed. David Simpson (Cambridge: Cambridge University Press, 1984), 214.

5. Jacques Derrida, *Points*, cited in Christopher Norris, *Derrida*, Modern Masters (Cambridge, Mass.: Harvard University Press, 1987), 16–17.

6. I am speaking here of literary feeling as a generalized complex pleasure: in the strict (Kantian) sense, this pleasure would have to be specified as "the sublime." For "aesthetic pleasure in beauty consists in the harmonious play of the two cognitive faculties. In the sublime it is reason and imagination qua faculty of sense which are compared and related—not through their harmony, but through their conflict." Rudolf A. Makkreel, *Imagination and Interpretation in Kant: The Hermeneutical Import of the "Critique of Judgment"* (Chicago: University of Chicago Press, 1990), 78. But the notion of harmony between faculties also supposes a factor of difference and hence of minimal tension between them.

7. "The concept of *différance* is neither simply structuralist, nor simply geneticist, such an alternative itself being an 'effect' of *différance*. I would even say . . . that it is not simply a concept." Jacques Derrida, *Positions*, ed. and trans. Alan Bass (Chicago: University of Chicago Press, 1981), 9.

8. Paul de Man, *Allegories of Reading: Figural Language in Rousseau, Nietzsche, Rilke, and Proust* (New Haven: Yale University Press, 1979), 19.

9. Paul de Man, *The Rhetoric of Romanticism* (New York: Columbia University Press, 1984), 70. Many other such instances could be adduced from his writing.

10. On the idea of this tension, see Henry Staten: "Whether language is performative or constative, or whether it oscillates undecidedly between the two, it is always a network of cathetic pathways, no matter how repressed or sublimated or cunningly disguised." In *Nietzsche's Voice* (Ithaca, N.Y.: Cornell University Press, 1990), 129.

11. Edward Said, "The Importance of Being Unfaithful to Wagner," *London Review of Books* (February 11, 1993): 12.

12. In his "anthropological" lectures dating from the early 1770s, Kant set a standard by writing: "The realm of the imagination is the proper domain of [artistic] genius because imagination is creative and . . . more apt for originality." *Anthropology from a Pragmatic Point of View,* trans. Mary J. Gregor (The Hague: Martinus Nijhoff, 1974), 93. On the role of the imagination as *an interpretive agency* in Kant's major works, see Makkreel, *Imagination and Interpretation*

in Kant. The association of poetic genius with the imagination and hence with the capacity to excite feelings is a commonplace of (English) Romantic poetics. In "Two Kinds of Poetry" (1833), for example, John Stuart Mill writes of "that person [who] is a poet": "Doubtless he is a greater poet in proportion as the fineness of his perceptions, whether of sense or of internal consciousness, furnishes him with an ampler supply of lovely images—the vigor and richness of his intellect with a greater abundance of moving thoughts. For it is through these thoughts and *images* that the *feeling* speaks" (my emphasis). *Dissertations and Discussions*, 2 vols. (London: J. W. Parker & Son, 1859), 1:89–90. On this revolution in poetics, consult M. H. Abrams's *The Mirror and the Lamp: Romantic Theory and the Critical Tradition* (Oxford: Oxford University Press, 1953), especially the pages on "Expressive Theories," 21–26.

13. The distinction between smooth conjuncture (*glatte Fügung*) and severe conjuncture (*harte Fügung*) is this: In the first instance everything depends on stopping *the word itself* from imposing itself on the reader. The effect of sensuality gradually vanishes; the word is less immediate and subordinated to the concept. The result is traditional, and the word degenerates into convention. In the second instance, everything depends on stressing the word and stamping it into the reader's consciousness, which grants the word maximum sensuality. (Friedrich Norbert von Hellingrath applied this rhetorical distinction, taken from the writings of Dionysius of Halicarnassus [fl. ca. 20 B.C.], to Hölderlin's translations of Pindar. See Hellingrath, *Hölderlin-Vermächtnis*, ed. Ludwig von Pigenot [Munich: F. Bruckmann, 1936], 23.)

14. *Letters Written in Sweden, Norway, and Denmark*, Letter XIX, in Butler, 7 vols. (London: Pickering, 1989), 6:325. Cited in David Bromwich, "Passion the Mother of Reason," *The Times Literary Supplement* (4529) January 19–25, 1990: 52. For the same sentiment, see *A Vindication of the Rights of Woman*, ed. Miriam Brody Kramnick (Penguin: Harmondsworth, Middlesex, Eng., 1982), 114. In *A Vindication*, Wollstonecraft further distinguishes between the novelistic sensibility and "that superiority of mind which leads to the creation of ideal beauty, when life, surveyed with a penetrating eye, appears a tragic-comedy, in which little can be seen to satisfy the heart without the help of fancy" (309). Suzanne K. Langer's plangent extension of Wollstonecraft's point, a century and a half later, is: "Art is the creation of forms symbolic of human feeling." *Feeling and Form* (New York: Scribners, 1953), 40. This position, inspired by Ernst Cassirer's *Philosophy of Symbolic Forms*, has great merit.

15. Gerhard Neumann, "Umkehrung und Ablenkung: Franz Kafkas 'Gleitendes Paradox,'" in *Franz Kafka, Wege der Forschung*, ed. Heinz Politzer (Darmstadt: Wissenschaftliche Buchgesellschaft, 1973), 475.

16. *The Diaries of Franz Kafka, 1910–1913*, ed. Max Brod, trans. Joseph Kresh (New York: Schocken, 1948), 291 (translation modified).

17. "Not a bent for writing, my dearest Felice, not a bent, but my entire self." Franz Kafka, *Letters to Felice*, trans. James Stern and Elizabeth Duckworth (New York: Schocken, 1973), 309.

18. "Christa T." is the thought-tormented heroine of Christa Wolf's novel, *The Quest for Christa T.*, trans. Christopher Middleton (New York: Farrar, Straus, and Giroux, 1970), 73.

19. Thomas Mann, *Doctor Faustus* (New York: Vintage, 1948), 485.

20. Compare Henry Staten: "It is in connection with the notion of self-enjoyment that we should understand Nietzsche's descriptions of will to power as 'the primitive form of affect' (WP 688) and as 'a *pathos*' (WP 635). (Notice, too, the strangeness of his calling this most essentially active of principles—a *pathos*!)." *Nietzsche's Voice*, 89 ("WP" is *The Will to Power*, trans. Walter Kaufmann and R. J. Hollingdale [New York: Vintage, 1968], 366).

21. I say "fateful," following Terry Eagleton in *The Ideology of the Aesthetic* (London: Blackwell, 1991), to acknowledge his argument as to the deludedness of the claims made by subjective feeling to power and autonomy. These claims, it is alleged, have only lately been demystified. The aesthetic might emerge only now from the disgrace of its forced conscription into a sinister ideology. This story is not persuasive.

22. From a letter to Engelmann, in Ray Monk, *Ludwig Wittgenstein: The Duty of Genius* (New York: The Free Press, 1990), 408.

23. Joachim Storck, "Arbeitsgespräche: Trakl und Rilke," in *Salzburger Trakl Symposium*, ed. Weiß and Weichselbaum (Salzburg: Otto Müller, 1978), 165.

24. Staiger's description of a procedure for genuine literary interpretation begins with a polemic against the "leading interpreters," whose alleged interpretive abilities consist in nothing more than their "doing intellectual history" and delivering old-style commentaries on only the most "difficult" texts, like Hölderlin's late hymns and Rilke's *Sonnets to Orpheus*. But "bemühen sie sich, an einem kleinen Gedicht zu begreifen, was uns ergreift [let them try to grasp what it is about a little poem that has gripped us]," then "they" rarely get beyond the most embarrassingly vague and impressionistic cant. *Kunst der Interpretation: Studien zur deutschen Literaturgeschichte* (Munich: Deutscher Taschenbuch Verlag, 1971), 8. For Staiger, it's "them" against "us."

Staiger then goes on to center genuine interpretation in the reader's feeling for the unifying style of the artwork, which guides his reading as a touchstone. This side of Staiger's understanding of hermeneutic theory comes out of Heidegger's *Being and Time*, which asserts the primacy of a *preconceptual* orientation toward the world of things and others. Interestingly, Staiger's essay includes a debate with Heidegger on Staiger's exemplary reading of Mörike's "Auf eine Lampe." (Here Heidegger provides evidence for reading the verb "scheint" in conformity with Hegel's *Aesthetics* as *lucet*, not *videtur*.) This entire matter of method achieves a peculiar consistency ever since, in the mid-1930's, Heidegger first got down to doing literary interpretation on his own—a practice that, strictly speaking, he had rejected in favor of a silent "conversation [*Zwiesprache*]" with the poem. For here he shuns "any sort of rational drawing of conclusions, justification, conceptual grasping [*alles rationale Schließen, Begründen, Begreifen*]." This point is developed in a bracing polemical essay written against Heidegger's pretension to another "method" by Klaus Weimar and Christoph Jermann, "'Zwiesprache' oder Literaturwissenschaft?: Zur Revision eines faulen Friedens," *Neue Hefte für Philosophie* 23 (1984): 145.

25. "Philosophical modes of presentation are *arguments*, and poetic modes of presentation are *performances*," Richard Kuhns, *Structures of Experience: Essays on the Affinity between Philosophy and Literature* (New York: Harper Torchbooks, 1974), 104. But Kuhns finds soon enough that he cannot abide with this binary, and on p. 106 he adds: "What holds performance together is the interpenetration of sensory and conceptual capacities." We cannot do better than talk of a dialectical field marked by a concentration of "capacities" nowhere to be found in a pure state, localizable at a site.

26. Franz Kafka, *Beschreibungen eines Kampfes und andere Schriften aus dem Nachlaß*, in *Franz Kafka, Gesammelte Werke in zwölf Bänden, nach der Kritischen Ausgabe (KKA)*, ed. Hans-Gerd Koch (Frankfurt a.M.: Fischer Taschenbuch Verlag, 1994), 5:12.

27. At the close of Chapter 2, however, I shall suggest a return, a resurgence of the contingent in Kant's aesthetic theory.

28. The Greek equivalents are assigned by Hans Robert Jauss in "Sketch of a History and Theory of Aesthetic Experience," in *Aesthetic Experience and Literary Hermeneutics*, trans. Michael Shaw (Minneapolis: University of Minnesota Press, 1982), xxviii.

29. Cf. Adorno: "The orientation on the part of the subject toward objectivity in the aesthetic mode of behavior conjoins eros and knowledge." Theodor W. Adorno, *Gesammelte Schriften*, ed. Rolf Tiedemann (Frankfurt: Suhrkamp, 1970), 7:490.

30. Von Hellingrath, *Hölderlin-Vermächtnis*, 51. See Rudolf Speth, *Wahrheit und Ästhetik: Untersuchungen zum Frühwerk Walter Benjamins* (Würzburg: Königshausen and Neumann, 1991), 12.

31. There are conspicuous omissions in this list. "Romantic irony" is one, but see Philippe Lacoue-Labarthe and Jean-Luc Nancy, *The Romantic Absolute: The Theory of Literature in German Romanticism*, trans. Philip Barnard and Cheryl Lester (Albany: SUNY, 1988). I omit the "idea-feeling," theorized by Hannah Arendt as the element of "passionate thinking," from which Dostoyevsky composed his novels, but see Donald Fanger, "Introduction," *Notes from Underground* (New York: Bantam, 1983), xxi. I have also left out most "amorous

affects," but see Alice Kuzniar: "In its day, literature was granted hegemony over the visual arts (by Lessing), history (by Schiller), philosophy (by Schelling and Hölderlin), and science (by Novalis). It is also the privileged discourse in which *the subjectivity of the bourgeois individual was forged via its amorous affects*, a process that included the carving out of a space for the exploration of same-sex desire. For it is precisely literature (including the epistle self-consciously styled as literature) in which a self-awareness is articulated around homoerotic feelings and where, notwithstanding the distancing such sublimation entails, these emotions often become the object of idealization and nostalgia." In *Outing Goethe* (Stanford: Stanford University Press, 1996), 31–32. Finally, but not finally, there is "longing [*Sehnsucht*]." Consult Paola Carletti Mayer, who writes: "What has not so far been recognized is that, in Neoplatonist mysticism, the German Romantics found a combination of these two concerns, namely, a philosophy which derived the universe from one spiritual principle, and which, by describing this as desire or divine love, accorded a central cognitive role to feeling, and thereby satisfied their emotional needs." "The Concept of Longing in German Romanticism and Neoplatonic Mysticism," an unpublished essay, Princeton University, 1995.

32. Rolf Grimminger, "Die Utopie der vernünftigen Lust. Sozialphilosophische Skizze zur Ästhetik des 18. Jahrhunderts bis zu Kant," in *Aufklärung und literarische Öffentlichkeit*," ed. Christa Bürger, Peter Bürger, and Jochen Schulte-Sasse (Frankfurt: Suhrkamp, 1980), 128.

33. For J. M. Bernstein, this tension is radical, hearkening back to, memorializing, a split between reason and sensate feeling. *The Fate of Art: Aesthetic Alienation from Kant to Derrida and Adorno* (University Park: Pennsylvania State University Press, 1992).

34. Immanuel Kant, *The Critique of Judgment*, trans. James Creed Meredith (Oxford: Clarendon, 1952), §23, 91. *Kritik der Urteilskraft*, ed. Karl Vorländer (Hamburg: Meiner, 1963), 88.

35. Richard Kuhns, writing on "Art as a Phenomenology of the Imagination," detects a dialectical procedure common to Hegel's *Phenomenology of Mind* and Wordsworth's *The Prelude*; the "initial dialectic," which in the latter work structures the "history of the poet's imagination," is the "tension of beauty and sublimity." *Structures of Experience*, 96, 101.

36. *Basic Writings of Nietzsche*, ed. and trans. Walter Kaufmann (New York: Modern Library, 1966), 56.

37. Martin Heidegger, *Gesamtausgabe*, II. Abteilung, *Vorlesungen 1923–1976*, *Nietzsche: Der Wille zur Macht als Kunst* (Frankfurt: Klostermann, 1985), 62–63.

38. Robert Musil, *Young Törless*, trans. Eithne Wilkins and Ernst Kaiser (New York: Pantheon, 1955), 63.

39. Walter Benjamin, "Zwei Gedichte von Friedrich Hölderlin. 'Dichtermut'—'Blödigkeit,'" *Gesammelte Schriften*, ed. Rolf Tiedemann and Hermann

Schweppenhaüser (Frankfurt a.M.: Suhrkamp, 1972), 2(1): 117. "Two Poems by Friedrich Hölderlin: 'The Poet's Courage' and 'Timidity,'" trans. Stanley Corngold, ed. Marcus Bullock and Michael Jennings, *Selected Writings*, ed. Michael Jennings (Cambridge, Mass.: Harvard University Press, 1996), 1:29.

40. The injunction is Paul de Man's in "Reading and History," in *The Resistance to Theory* (Minneapolis: University of Minnesota Press, 1986), esp. 64, and "Phenomenality and Materiality in Kant," in *Hermeneutics: Questions and Prospects*, ed. Gary Shapiro and Anthony Sica (Amherst: University of Massachusetts Press, 1984), esp. 137–38. Geoffrey Galt Harpham brilliantly queries the sense of this injunction in "Aesthetics and Modernity," in *Aesthetics and Ideology*, ed. George Levine (New Brunswick: Rutgers University Press, 1994), 124–49.

41. Cf. endnote 20.

42. Musil, *Young Törless*, 169.

Introduction

1. Honoré de Balzac, *Père Goriot*, trans. Henry Reed (New York: Signet, 1962), 115. The words are spoken by the character Rastignac.

2. As a condition of the ever-moot possibility of attributing truth-value to the "disclosure" of the aesthetic, Terry Eagleton proposes a consonance of the terms "particularity" and "mode of cognition" in aesthetic discourse (see Terry Eagleton, *The Ideology of the Aesthetic* [Oxford: Blackwell, 1990], 2). But what is here proposed as a unity might better be represented from the start as the locus of the dispute that will mark aesthetic theorizing henceforward and, indeed, define it. Right on the face of it, "particularity," concreteness, would seem to rule out any sort of cognition that could rise above the particular—that *must*, as cognition, rise above it. Hence the first thing of importance is to qualify the kind, position, and value of such cognition that is in the ordinary sense nonconceptualizable, or what J. M. Bernstein calls knowledge different from "truth-only cognition" (*The Fate of Art: Aesthetic Alienation from Kant to Derrida and Adorno* [University Park: Pennsylvania State University Press, 1992], 2). It is exactly the struggle to provide this qualification that characterizes aesthetics throughout.

In the matter of such "consonance," however, Eagleton is a realist and appears to see this aesthetic unity as actually becoming the case in eighteenth-century Germany and, hence, the condition for the inscription of autocratic law on the unresisting heart. But why this process of subjection should be abetted by the cultivation of aesthetic consciousness through literature—leaving aside a literature explicitly recommending obedience—is hardly self-evident. There were feelings before there were literary feelings, the kinds of feeling that literature produces.

In *The Fate of Art*, J. M. Bernstein argues that this different sort of cognizing pleasure, in Kant and hence for a long tradition, is "memorial": it is the memorial of an original cognizing pleasure that is no longer accessible (17), as in Benjamin the sensory leisure of the *flâneur* is the memorial of the composure once enjoyed by every man of the crowd. It is hard to see, though, how this alienated view could fit Kant's characterization of the principle of aesthetic judgment—"nature's formal finality for our cognitive faculties in its particular (empirical) laws"—as "a principle without which understanding could not feel itself at home in nature." Immanuel Kant, *The Critique of Judgment*, trans. James Creed Meredith (Oxford: Clarendon, 1964), 35.

3. On the question of whether it isn't futile, given the scathing polemics of the likes of I. A. Richards and John Dewey dating from the late 1920's, to go on considering aesthetic feeling as distinct from ordinary experience, it is bemusing to note Richards and Dewey also affirming, in almost the same words, the distinctiveness of the aesthetic. Richards writes that "while admitting that such experiences [as aesthetic experiences] can be distinguished, I shall be at pains to show that they are closely similar to many other experiences, that they differ chiefly in the connections between their constituents, and that they are only a further development, a finer organization of ordinary experience, and not in the least a new and different kind of thing." *Principles of Literary Criticism* (New York: Harcourt, Brace, 1928), 16. But what does it mean to hold that an (aesthetic) experience is "distinguishable" from ordinary experience but not in any way a "different kind of thing" from it? For Dewey, too, who deplores the putative "remission" of art to a "separate realm," works of art remain "refined and intensified forms of experience." *Art as Experience* (New York: Minton, Balch, 1934), 3. But who, after Nietzsche's *Will to Power*, will not be ready to take very seriously the point at which an increase in *quantum* becomes a *quale*?

4. In a letter to John Taylor at the time of writing *Endymion*, Keats proposed the figure of the "Pleasure Thermometer" as one "of the greatest [intellectual] Service to me," for "it set before me at once the gradations of happiness." *The Letters of John Keats, 1814–1821*, 2 vols., ed. Hyder Edward Rollins (Cambridge, Mass.: Harvard University Press, 1958), 1:218.

5. Martin Heidegger, *Being and Time*, trans. John Macquarrie and Edward Robinson (New York: Harper and Row, 1962), 205. For further discussion, see my *The Fate of the Self: German Writers and French Theory* (Durham, N.C.: Duke University Press, 1994), 197–218.

6. John Passmore, *Serious Art: A Study of the Concept in All the Major Arts* (London: Duckworth, 1991), 123.

7. Dewey, *Art as Experience*, 10.

8. Passmore, *Serious Art*, 279, 280.

9. Franz Kafka, letter to Max Brod (July 5, 1922), *The Metamorphosis by Franz Kafka*, Norton Critical Edition, ed. Stanley Corngold (New York: Norton, 1996), 73.

10. Cited without a source in Laurence Lerner, "Emotion," *The New Princeton Encyclopedia of Poetry and Poetics*, ed. Alex Preminger and T. V. F. Brogan (Princeton: Princeton University Press, 1993), 328.

11. Richards, *Principles of Literary Criticism*, 112.

12. See Philip Rieff, *The Feeling Intellect*, ed. Jonathan B. Imber (Chicago: University of Chicago Press, 1990).

13. Breitinger shifts aesthetic judgment, in the words of Wolfgang Preisendenz, into "the medium of a subjective mirroring and refraction of empirical reality." "Mimesis und Poiesis in der deutschen Dichtungstheorie des 18. Jahrhunderts," in *Rezeption und Produktion zwischen 1570 und 1730, Festschrift für Günther Weydt zum 65. Geburtstag*, ed. Wolfdietrich Rasch, u.a. (Bern and Munich: Francke, 1972), 546.

14. See Steven Connor, "Aesthetics, Pleasure, and Value," in *The Politics of Pleasure: Aesthetics and Cultural Theory*, ed. Stephen Regan (Buckingham, U.K.: Open University Press, 1992), 203–20. Connor argues the necessity of "resisting the reductive binarity of pleasure or value" as models inadequate to all recent critical thought on the matter (204). It would follow that models of purely congruent or purely contingent relations of feeling and disclosure in literary experience are hapless.

15. Heidegger, *Being and Time*, 186.

16. Ibid., 181.

17. The best-known articulation of the aesthetic ideology is Paul de Man's, in "Aesthetic Formalization: Kleist's *Über das Marionettentheater*," *The Rhetoric of Romanticism* (New York: Columbia University Press, 1984), 264: "The 'state' that is being advocated [in Schiller's *Letters on the Aesthetic Education*] is not just a state of mind or of soul, but a principle of political value and authority that has its own claims on the shape and the limits of our freedom. It would lose all interest if this were not the case. For it is as a political force that the aesthetic still concerns us as one of the most powerful ideological drives to act upon the reality of history." For a critical view of de Man's reading of the figure of the dance in Schiller's *Letters* as a model of "restrictive [political] coercion" (265), see Stanley Corngold, "Potential Violence in Paul de Man," a review-article of *Paul de Man: Deconstruction and the Critique of Aesthetic Ideology* by Christopher Norris, *Critical Review* 3 (1989): 117–37.

18. J. M. Bernstein's *The Fate of Art* builds on Habermas's high valuation of the way that Kant's critical project constitutes intellectual modernity. Bernstein writes: "The categorial divisions of reason represented by the three *Critiques* inscribes a theory of modernity through its provision of a categorial understanding of the differences between what have come to be called the language games of knowing, right action and moral worth, and art and aesthetics" (5). The motor, in turn, of Terry Eagleton's discussion of eighteenth-century aesthetics in *The Ideology of the Aesthetic* is his substitution of the term *middle-class* for

the middle-faculty—the aesthetic—in Kant's articulation. Eagleton's effort to ground the end of the aesthetic ideology in something more materially powerful than "language games" is interesting—and witty—but can it do any work? For Eagleton what counts in Kant's new subject matter called "aesthetics" is less its "logical grammar" (Bernstein, 66) than its ideological code.

19. Tobin Siebers writes: "Plato called art irrational and banned it from his republic. Kant calls art irrational and says that we must have more of it or never establish a culture of moral feeling." "Kant and the Politics of Beauty," *Philosophy and Literature* 22.1 (1998): 38.

20. For example, Moses Mendelssohn's *Briefe über die Empfindungen* (1755, 1771) "argues elegantly," writes Victor Lange, "that the aesthetic experience, although located in the 'dark' area between rational and sensual perception, offers in 'Empfindung' a specific mode of knowledge." *The Classical Age of German Literature, 1740–1815* (New York: Holmes and Meier, 1982), 17. The notion of "disinterested pleasure" central to Kant's account is already present in Mendelssohn's *Morgenstunden, oder Vorlesungen über das Daseyn Gottes* (1785).

21. Immanuel Kant, *Sämmtliche Werke*, ed. Karl Rosenkranz and Friedrich Wilhelm Schubert (Leipzig: Voss, 1842), 11:240.

22. "Le sentiment de l'existence, depouillé de toute autre affection," Jean-Jacques Rousseau, *Les rêveries du promeneur solitaire, Oeuvres Complètes* (Paris: Gallimard, 1959), 1:1047.

23. G. E. Lessing, *Hamburgische Dramaturgie*, ed. Otto Mann (Stuttgart: Alfred Kröner Verlag, 1978), 17. *Hamburg Dramaturgy*, trans. Helen Zimmern (New York: Dover, 1962), 14 (trans. rev.).

24. *Beyond Good and Evil*, in *Basic Writings of Nietzsche*, trans. and ed. Walter Kaufmann (New York: The Modern Library, 1968), 290.

25. This is literally so, since "every genius is a born critic" (ibid., 254), which is to say that moral genius has an affinity for articulation. Lessing could not fail to see this—if Nietzsche is right: "It might be said of Euripides," wrote Nietzsche, "as of Lessing, that his extraordinary fund of *critical* talent, if it did not create, at least constantly stimulated his productive *artistic* impulse." *The Birth of Tragedy*, in *Basic Writings of Nietzsche*, 80.

26. Strictly speaking, *h*eautonomously.

27. Friedrich Schiller, "Über Witz und Scharfsinn," apropos of Bürger's poems in *Sämtliche Werke*, Säkular-Ausgabe, ed. Eduard von der Hellen (Stuttgart: n.d.), 16:227. Cited in "From the Recreation of Scholars to the Labor of the Concept," by Friedrich Kittler, in *Reading After Foucault: Institutions, Disciplines, and Technologies of the Self in Germany, 1750–1830*, ed. Robert S. Leventhal (Detroit: Wayne State University Press, 1994), 69.

28. "The separation of subject and object is both real and illusory. True, because in the cognitive realm it serves to express the real separation, the dichot-

omy of the human condition, a coercive development. False, because the re-sulting separation must not be hypostatized, not magically transformed into an invariant." Theodor W. Adorno, "Subject and Object," *The Essential Frankfurt School Reader*, ed. Andrew Arato and Eike Gebhart (New York: Urizen Books, 1978), 499.

29. Fulke Greville, *Mustapha*, in *Poems and Dramas of Fulke Greville, First Lord Brooke*, ed. Geoffrey Bullough (Edinburgh: Oliver and Boyd, 1939), 2:136.

30. See Paul de Man's "Autobiography as De-Facement," in *Rhetoric of Romanticism*, which gives autobiography a rhetorical universality of sorts: "Autobiography is . . . a figure of reading or of understanding that occurs, to some degree, in all texts. . . . Any book with a readable title page is, to some extent, autobiographical" (70). This is far from being an innocent state of affairs since "autobiography veils a defacement of the mind of which it is itself the cause" (81).

31. Consult the many publications of Manfred Frank.

32. Cf. Gerhard Kurz, *Mittelbarkeit und Vereinigung: Zum Verhältnis von Poesie, Reflexion, und Revolution bei Hölderlin* (Stuttgart: Metzler, 1975), 71.

33. Friedrich Hölderlin, *Sämtliche Werke*, ed. Friedrich Beißner (Stuttgart: Kohlhammer, 1943–72), 2:64–65.

34. Friedrich Hölderlin, "Allgemeiner Grund" [to the Empedocles-drama], *Sämtliche Werke, "Frankfurter Ausgabe"* (Frankfurt: Roter Stern, 1979), 13:870.

35. Ibid., 4:226. This earlier definition of the relation of feeling or intuition to tragedy stems from Hölderlin's essay "On the Different Forms of Poetic Composition" (1799). The fact that it profiles the master term "intellectual intuition [*intellektuelle Anschauung*]" reveals Hölderlin's indebtedness to a prevailing discourse. The term was coined by Kant and thereafter redefined by Fichte, Schelling, and Schiller to include a more pronouncedly sensate element. Klaus-Rüdiger Wohrmann remarks suggestively that the later expression " 'feeling of totality [*Totalempfindung*]' is Hölderlin's self-conscious testimony to the individuality of his interpretation of intellectual intuition," a term that he never again uses after the essay of 1799. *Hölderlins Wille zur Tragödie* (Munich: Fink, 1967), 72.

36. Hölderlin, *Sämtliche Werke, "Frankfurter Ausgabe,"* 13:868.

37. Terry Eagleton, *The Ideology of the Aesthetic* (Oxford: Blackwell, 1990), 9. Cf. further Michael Jennings: "Random, esoterically charged allegorical images, in their similarity to the denatured things of this world, reflect a history that has itself become increasingly analogous to the natural and capitalistic production of shattered, fetish objects." " 'Eine gewaltige Erschütterung des Tradieren': Walter Benjamin's Political Recuperation of Franz Kafka," in *Fictions of*

Culture: Essays in Honor of Walter Sokel, ed. Stephen Taubeneck (Las Vegas: Peter Lang, 1991), 204.

38. Marie Henri Beyle [Stendhal], *The Charterhouse of Parma*, trans. C. K. Scott-Moncrieff (New York: New American Library, 1987), 338.

39. Lord Byron, *Don Juan* (I:ccxiv), ed. Leslie A. Marchand (Boston: Houghton-Mifflin, 1958), 57.

40. Ralph Waldo Emerson, "The Poet," *Selected Essays*, ed. Lazar Ziff (Harmondsworth, Middlesex: Penguin, 1987), 274.

41. Herman Melville, *Billy Budd and Other Stories* (Harmondsworth, Middlesex: Penguin, 1986), 327–28.

42. Consult the excellent work by John Neubauer, *The Fin-de-Siècle Culture of Adolescence* (New Haven: Yale University Press, 1992).

43. Robert Musil, *Young Törless*, trans. Eithne Wilkins and Ernst Kaiser (New York: Pantheon, 1955), 210–11. For more on this explanatory model of the circle, see Chapter 2, "What Is Radical in Kant's 'Critique of Aesthetic Judgment'?," and also Chapter 5, "Telling Sadism in Musil's *Young Törless*."

44. "The splendid 'naivete' of the earlier Greeks, which . . . must be conceived as the blossom of the Apollinian culture springing from a dark abyss, as the victory which the Hellenic will, through its mirroring of beauty, obtains over suffering and the wisdom of suffering." Nietzsche, *Basic Writings*, 109.

45. Steven Aschheim has it right. Citing Nietzsche's autobiographical remark from "Why I Write Such Good Books," in *Ecce Homo*, *Basic Writings*, 265, he comments: "Nietzsche's determinedly shifting narrative point of view clearly facilitated varied appropriations." *The Nietzsche Legacy in Germany: 1890–1990* (Berkeley: University of California Press, 1992), 8.

46. Roland Barthes, *The Grain of the Voice: Interviews 1962–1980*, trans. Linda Coverdale (New York: Hill and Wang, 1985), 331.

47. Bernstein, *The Fate of Art*, 9.

48. Walter Benjamin, "Zwei Gedichte von Friedrich Hölderlin. 'Dichtermut'—'Blödigkeit,'" *Gesammelte Schriften*, ed. Rolf Tiedemann and Hermann Schweppenhäuser (Frankfurt a.M.: Suhrkamp, 1972), 2(1): 111. "Two Poems by Friedrich Hölderlin: 'The Poet's Courage' and 'Timidity,'" trans. Stanley Corngold, ed. Marcus Bullock and Michael Jennings, *Selected Writings*, ed. Michael Jennings (Cambridge, Mass.: Harvard University Press, 1996), 1:24.

49. A vivid example of this sort of slippage is found in Kant's *Dissertation* of 1770: "In the *Dissertation* coordination is a convertible concept for 'form.' The form of the sensuous world is cognized through intuition, but the law of intuition is that of coordination. Nonetheless, Kant also speaks of a form of the *rational world* [*Verstandeswelt*]. Whence the contradiction that form and coordination are at first taken as moments of any nonsensuous order whatsoever, whereas it emerges later that coordination applies only to the sensuous world." Alfred

Baeumler, *Das Irrationalitätsproblem in der Ästhetik und Logik des 18. Jahrhunderts bis zur Kritik der Urteilskraft* (Darmstadt: Wissenschaftliche Buchgesellschaft, 1975 [1923]), 320.

50. "Zur Aesthetik" (On aesthetics), in *Gegenwart* 69, 8 (Feb. 24, 1906), 118.

51. Guido Morpurgo-Tagliabue, *L'Esthétique contemporaine* (Milan: Marzorati, 1960), 597.

52. Friedrich Nietzsche, *Morgenröte*, in *Werke in Drei Bänden*, ed. Karl Schlechta (Munich: Hanser, 1954), 1:1095.

53. Heidegger, *Holzwege* (Frankfurt: Vittorio Klostermann, 1980), 263. A distinctive source of this tendency is A. W. Schlegel's definition, in his *Dramatic Lectures*, of "organic" versus "mechanical" form, the latter being "essentially additive, imposed from without, and therefore quite possibly arbitrary." The opposite is organic form, "generated from within, coexistent with the material, complete only when the object itself is complete, working its way just as natural forms do." See Frederick Garber, "Form," *The New Princeton Encyclopedia of Poetry and Poetics*, ed. Alex Preminger and T. V. F. Brogan (Princeton: Princeton University Press, 1993), 421. Via Coleridge, who repeats Schlegel's distinction in his *Lectures on Shakespeare*, the distinction operates practically as a regulative principle in subsequent English poetics.

54. "Every work of art endeavors to show us life and things as they are in reality, but these cannot be grasped directly by everyone through the mist of objective and subjective contingencies. Art takes away this mist . . . Its object is to facilitate knowledge of the Ideas of the world in the Platonic sense." Arthur Schopenhauer, *The World as Will and Representation*, trans. E. F. J. Payne (New York: Dover, 1966), 2:407–8.

55. Nietzsche, *The Birth of Tragedy*, in *Basic Writings*, 34, 36.

56. Ibid., 60.

57. Benjamin, "Goethe's Elective Affinities," in *Selected Writings*, trans. Corngold, ed. Bullock and Jennings, 1:340.

58. The lapsed Husserl-student Johannes Pfeiffer wrote this phrase in *Umgang mit Dichtung: Eine Einführung in das Verständnis des Dichterischen* (Leipzig: Felix Meiner, 1936), 29.

59. George Santayana, *The Sense of Beauty*, cited in *Perspectives in Aesthetics: Plato to Camus*, ed. Peyton E. Richter (Indianapolis: Bobbs-Merrill, 1979), 334.

60. "In the aesthetic fact, expressive activity is not added to the fact of the impressions, but the latter are formed and elaborated by it. . . . The aesthetic fact, therefore, is form, and form alone." Benedetto Croce, *Aesthetic as Science of Expression and General Linguistic*, trans. Douglas Ainslie (London: Macmillan, 1922), 5. For Oscar Wilde, "The real artist is he who proceeds, not from feeling to form, but from form to thought and passion." *The Critic as Artist—Part II*, in *Oscar Wilde*, The Oxford Authors, ed. Isobel Murray (Oxford: Oxford University Press, 1989), 289.

61. Rudolf Speth, *Wahrheit und Ästhetik: Untersuchungen zum Frühwerk Walter Benjamins* (Würzburg: Königshausen and Neumann, 1991), 54.

62. See Eric Santner, *Friedrich Hölderlin: Narrative Vigilance and the Poetic Imagination* (New Brunswick: Rutgers University Press, 1986).

63. *On the Genealogy of Morals*, in *Basic Writings of Nietzsche*, 516, 513.

64. Bernstein, *The Fate of Art*, 13.

65. Walter Benjamin, "The Work of Art in the Age of Mechanical Reproduction," *Illuminations*, trans. Harry Zohn (New York: Harcourt, Brace and World, 1968), 244. Cf. Hannah Arendt's similar judgment on the purpose of Nazism. In 1945, she wrote: "Nazism owes nothing to any part of the Western tradition, be it German or not, Catholic or Protestant, Christian, Greek or Roman. . . . On the contrary, Nazism is actually the breakdown of all German and European traditions, the good as well as the bad," i.e., nihilism in action, "basing itself on the intoxication of destruction as an actual experience, dreaming the stupid dream of producing the void." Hannah Arendt, "Approaches to the German Problem," *Partisan Review* 12, 1 (Winter 1945): 81–83. Cited in Steven Aschheim, *Culture and Catastrophe: German and Jewish Confrontations with National Socialism and Other Crises* (New York: Macmillan, 1997), 112.

66. Hans-Georg Gadamer, *Truth and Method*, trans. William Glen-Doepel (London: Sheed and Ward, 1979), 10–39.

67. Bernstein, *The Fate of Art*, 8. That strain of aesthetic modernism is exactly the itinerary this book takes from Chapter 4 to Chapter 8, a line of thought flowing from Nietzsche through Benjamin.

68. Terry Eagleton is ingenious in undertaking such political connections but, elegant as they are, they can seem wayward. On page 9 of *The Ideology of the Aesthetic*, for example, we see him strongly suggesting that the idea of subjective autonomy is first inspired in Enlightenment aestheticians by their reflection on the commodity—the purposeless artifact, detached from all human ends. But on page 14, the impulse to authentic speculation would seem to be impelled by the need to furnish autocratic princes with the means to rule more incisively over the sentient somatic life of their subjects; bourgeois aesthetic thought answers their call.

69. *On German Architecture. Von Deutscher Baukunst*: "Und läßt diese Bildnerey aus den willkürlichsten Formen bestehen, sie wird ohne Gestaltsverhältniß zusammenstimmen, denn Eine Empfindung schuf sie zum karackteristischen Ganzen." *Der junge Goethe*, neue bearbeitete Ausgabe in fünf Bänden, ed. Marina Fischer-Lamberg (Berlin: Walter de Gruyter, 1966) 3:106. John Lyon discusses this passage in his Princeton University doctoral dissertation *The Wounded Body* (1996).

70. Edward Said, *Beginnings* (New York: Basic Books, 1975), 157.

71. Tilottoma Rajan astutely perceives one such major obstacle in the way of telling the story I do tell in Chapter 4 about Nietzsche's lost mood. See her Introduction to *Studies in Romanticism* 29 (Spring 1990): 5–6.

72. The phrase is mine. It is based on the question that Socrates puts to Phaedrus in the dialogue of this name: "Can we discern another kind of discourse [namely, speech], *a legitimate brother* of this one [namely, the discourse of 'written words']?" I stress, of course, the literal meaning of "legitimacy." See Plato, *Phaedrus*, trans. with Introduction and Notes by Alexander Nehamas and Paul Woodruff (Indianapolis: Hackett, 1995), 80–81, and, further, Stanley Corngold, "Nietzsche, Kafka, and Literary Paternity," *Nietzsche and Jewish Culture*, ed. Jacob Golomb (London and New York: Routledge, 1996), 137–57.

73. Gerald Bruns, *Heidegger's Estrangements: Language, Truth and Poetry in the Later Writings* (New Haven: Yale University Press, 1989), 15.

74. Johann Wolfgang von Goethe, *Elective Affinities*, trans. Judith Ryan, *Collected Works* (Princeton: Princeton University Press, 1995), 11:147.

75. Fyodor Dostoevsky, *Notes from Underground*, in *Three Short Novels of Dostoevsky*, ed. Avrahm Yarmolinsky, trans. Constance Garnett (New York: Doubleday, 1960), 258.

76. Ibid., 294.

77. *Sentimental Education*, trans. Robert Baldick (Harmondsworth, Middlesex: Penguin, 1964), 22.

78. "Edouard's Journal," *The Counterfeiters*, cited in *Existentialism*, ed. Robert C. Solomon (New York: Random House, 1974), 171.

79. Baudrillard, *Forget Foucault* (1977), cited in Geoff Waite, *Nietzsche's Corps(e)* (Durham: Duke University Press, 1996), 124.

80. If the "language" of the imagination is more nearly poetry, a poetry rich in figures of condensation and displacement, then it is fitting that the overdetermined language of bodily symptoms should become its text.

81. "Es ist mir dann, als bestünde mein Körper aus lauter Chiffern, die mir alles aufschließen. Oder als könnten wir in ein neues, ahnungsvolles Verhältnis zum ganzen Dasein treten, wenn wir anfingen, mit dem Herzen zu denken." Hugo von Hofmannsthal, *Ein Brief*, in *Erzählungen; Erfundene Gespräche und Briefe; Reisen, Gesammelte Werke in zehn Einzelbänden* (Frankfurt a.M.: Fischer Taschenbuch, 1979), 469.

82. Gillian Rose, *Love's Work: A Reckoning with Life* (New York: Schocken, 1995), 143.

83. Immanuel Kant, *The Critique of Judgment*, trans. James Creed Meredith (Oxford: Clarendon, 1952), §23, 91. *Kritik der Urteilskraft*, ed. Karl Vorländer (Hamburg: Meiner, 1963), 88.

84. A formulation I owe to Slavoj Žižek.

85. Gilles Deleuze, *Kant's Critical Philosophy: The Doctrine of the Faculties*

[1963], trans. Hugh Tomlinson and Barbara Habberjam (Minneapolis: University of Minnesota Press, 1990), 51; emphasis added.

86. Brian Tayan, an unpublished essay, Princeton University, 1995. The citation is from Thomas Mann, *Doctor Faustus*, trans. H. T. Lowe-Porter (New York: Vintage, 1948), 61.

87. In this connection it is interesting to consider Broch's hero-reflector Bertrand: "Well, the most persistent things in us are, let us say, our so-called feelings. We carry an indestructible fund of conservatism about with us. I mean our feelings, or rather conventions of feelings, for actually they aren't living feelings, but atavisms."

"So you consider that conservative principles are atavistic?"

"Oh, sometimes, but not always. However, I wasn't really thinking of them. What I meant was that our feelings always lag half-a-century or a full century behind our actual lives. One's feelings are always less human than the society one lives in. Just consider that a Lessing or a Voltaire accepted without question the fact that in their time men were still broken on the wheel—a thing that to us with our feelings is unimaginable." Hermann Broch, *The Sleepwalkers, Part One: The Romantic (1888)* (San Francisco: North Point Press, 1985), 52.

88. Benjamin, "Goethe's Elective Affinities," *Selected Writings*, ed. Jennings, 1:353.

89. Walter Benjamin, "Two Poems of Friedrich Hölderlin," *Selected Writings*, ed. Jennings, 1:34.

90. Consider Goethe's aperçu: "In the morning we are shrewdest, but also most anxious; for even anxiety is a species of shrewdness, though only a passive one." *Conversations with Eckermann (1823–1832)* [Monday, August 16, 1824], trans. John Oxenford (San Francisco: North Point Press, 1984), 57.

91. Tobin Siebers puts this succinctly: "Aesthetics is about the imagination of self and other and other selves by the self, and about the pleasure and pain felt by the self in the process. It is affective, and we have yet to find a way of describing emotions in other than an individual register because emotions cannot be represented without the presence of a particular body." *On the Aesthetic Ideology*, forthcoming.

92. Nietzsche, *Morgenröte*, 1095.

93. Charles Sanders Peirce, *The Collected Papers of Charles Sanders Peirce*, 8 vols., vol. 1–6, ed. Charles Harshorne and Paul Weiss (Cambridge, Mass.: Harvard University Press, 1931–35), 6:173. Cited in Terrance King, "Mimesis, Binary Opposition, and Peirce's Triadic Realism," in *Mimesis, Semiosis and Power. Mimesis in Contemporary Theory: An Interdisciplinary Approach*, ed. Ronald Bogue (Philadelphia and Amsterdam: John Benjamins, 1991), 69.

94. The phrase is Nietzsche's, to describe the "Greek concept of culture— . . . as a new and improved/transfigured *physis* [einer neuen und verbesserten Physis]." In "Vom Nutzen und Nachteil der Historie für das Leben," *Unzeit-*

gemäße Betrachtungen ("On the Use and Disadvantage of History for Life," *Thoughts out of Season*), *Werke*, 1:285. It becomes a leading theme in Walter Kaufmann's reading of Nietzsche in *Nietzsche—Philosopher, Psychologist, Anti-Christ* (Cleveland and New York: World, 1963), 134–37.

95. Cf. Franz Kafka, *The Diaries of Franz Kafka, 1910–1913*, ed. Max Brod, trans. Joseph Kresh (New York: Schocken, 1948), 28.

96. See my *Franz Kafka: The Necessity of Form* (Ithaca, N.Y.: Cornell, 1988), 4–5.

97. Only in a weak sense are moods aimed at objects. See Paul Schröder, *Stimmungen und Verstimmungen* (Leipzig: Barth, 1930), 10. Felix Krüger perceives in feeling the "striving to produce a rounding of 'contour,' to bring about regularity or order, to supplement an absence . . . , in a word, to experience everything as a closed and—to the greatest possible extent—sustainable unity." "Das Wesen der Gefühle. Entwurf einer systematischen Theorie," in Felix Krüger, *Über das Gefühl. Zwei Aufsätze* (Darmstadt: Wissenschaftliche Buchgesellschaft, 1967), 55. The key word in Krüger is "striving," which does not imply success but opens up an object (feeling) to an analysis of all the ways it fails to arrive at its end. The recurring argument of my own book is that many authors thematize differently the goal of this striving and the various ways it comes to grief or does not end. Stephan Strasser makes a further, useful distinction between "felt intentional acts (of perception, evaluation, actuation) and the non-intentional (pre-intentional) felt interiority of one's own basic dispositions. . . . In both cases feeling plays a role that is 'totality-producing,' binding, 'embedding.'" Krüger would say—more correctly, in my view—that this role is one that feeling "strives" to play. Strasser continues: "But, in the first case, it functions as a rebinding of the intentional directedness-toward-the-world back to the center of one's own being. In the other case, it functions as the intimate experience of that center itself." *Phenomenology of Feeling* (Pittsburgh: Duquesne University Press, 1977), 97. These formulations belong to a phenomenological tradition that owes much to Heidegger's *Being and Time*. But such phrases as "closed . . . unity" (Krüger) and "intimate experience of that center itself" (Strasser) are hardly adequate to Heidegger's own grasp of the matter. The latter sense of feeling is in play only when feeling is grasped as mood, as when Heidegger writes: "In 'poetic discourse' the communication of the existential possibilities of one's state of mind [mood] can become an aim in itself, and this amounts to a disclosing of existence." *Being and Time*, trans. John Macquarrie and Edward Robinson (New York: Harper and Row, 1962), 205. On Heidegger, see further my *The Fate of the Self: German Writers and French Theory* (Durham, N.C., Duke University Press, 1994), 197–218. Again, I stress that one can—and should—acknowledge distinctions concerning aims (in Krüger and Strasser) without buying into their casual evocations of center and closure.

98. Theodor Adorno, *Ästhetische Theorie* (Frankfurt: Suhrkamp, 1970), 27.

Hans Robert Jauss, "Sketch of a History and Theory of Aesthetic Experience," in *Aesthetic Experience and Literary Hermeneutics*, trans. Michael Shaw (Minneapolis: University of Minnesota Press, 1982), 28.

99. Eagleton, *Ideology of the Aesthetic*, 21.

100. From a work in progress on the pertinence of Hegel's aesthetics, provisionally entitled *Literature in the Age of Technology*.

101. Bernstein, *The Fate of Art*, 12.

102. David Bromwich, *Politics by Other Means: Higher Education and Group Thinking* (New Haven: Yale University Press, 1992).

103. Nietzsche, "Über Stimmungen," *Werke*, 3:113. See Chapter 4.

Proem

1. The following text—Friedrich Hölderlin's "Natur und Kunst oder Saturn und Jupiter"—can be found in his *Sämtliche Werke* (Frankfurt: Roter Stern, 1979), 5:793–94.

NATUR UND KUNST ODER SATURN UND JUPITER

Du waltest hoch am Tag' und es blühet dein
    Gesez, du hältst die Waage, Saturnus Sohn!
        Und theilst die Loos' und ruhest froh im
            Ruhm der unsterblichen Herrscherkünste.

Doch in den Abgrund, sagen die Sänger sich,
    Habst du den heil'gen Vater, den eignen, einst
        Verwiesen und es jammre drunten,
            Da, wo die Wilden vor dir mit Recht sind,

Schuldlos der Gott der goldenen Zeit schon längst:
    Einst mühelos, und größer, wie du, wenn schon
        Er kein Gebot aussprach und ihn der
            Sterblichen keiner mit Nahmen nannte.

Herab denn! oder schäme des Danks dich nicht!
    Und willst du bleiben, diene dem Aelteren
        Und gönn' es ihm, daß ihn vor Allen,
            Göttern und Menschen, der Sänger nenne!

Denn, wie aus dem Gewölke dein Bliz, so kommt
    Von ihm, was dein ist, siehe! so zeugt von ihm,
        Was du gebeutst, und aus Saturnus
            Frieden ist jegliche Macht erwachsen.

Und hab' ich erst am Herzen Lebendiges
    Gefühlt und dämmert, was du gestaltest,

Und war in ihrer Wiege mir in
Wonne die wechselnde Zeit entschlummert:

Dann kenn' ich dich, Kronion! dann hör ich dich,
Den weisen Meister, welcher, wie wir, ein Sohn
Der Zeit, Geseze giebt, und, was die
Heilige Dämmerung birgt, verkündet.

"Kronion" means "the son of Kronos," i.e., of Saturn. Thus Jupiter is at once the godly son of Saturn but also, like mortals, the son of time (Chrónos).

2. In a suggestive essay on this ode, Glenn Most warns against a too swift identification of Jupiter with art and Saturn with nature, for this is to make a flat equivalence of things that cannot be equated, of mythological and allegorical figures. The poem cannot be understood "in terms of a polar dichotomy of the two mythical figures Saturn and Jupiter, or of principles unambiguously allied with them" ("The Bait of Falsehood: Studies in the Rhetorical Strategy of Poetic Truth in the Romantic Period," doctoral dissertation, Department of Comparative Literature, Yale University, 1980, 251).

3. Cf. W. G. Kudszus, who writes: "It has become customary to confuse the impossible with the undoable. Yet in the order of poetry, that which is impossible can be closely linked with the deed." In *Poetic Process* (Lincoln and London: University of Nebraska Press, 1995), 5.

4. The Alcaic, which expresses movement, contrasts with the stoniness of the Asclepiadic. See Wolfgang Binder, "Hölderlins Odenstrophe," in *Über Hölderlin*, ed. Jochen Schmidt (Frankfurt a.M.: Insel, 1970), 9–10, and Rudolf Speth, *Wahrheit und Ästhetik: Untersuchungen zum Frühwerk Walter Benjamins* (Würzburg: Königshausen and Neumann, 1991), 51.

5. It acquires for many readers through its date stamp an unsavory rhetorical proximity to *Kirche, Kinder, Küche.*

6. See Chapter 8.

7. "Parca" is the goddess of Fate or Destiny, one of the three Parcae or sisters.

8. Walter Benjamin, "Zwei Gedichte von Friedrich Hölderlin. 'Dichtermut'—'Blödigkeit,'" *Gesammelte Schriften*, ed. Rolf Tiedemann and Hermann Schweppenhaüser (Frankfurt a.M.: Suhrkamp, 1972), 2(1): 114. "Two Poems by Friedrich Hölderlin: 'The Poet's Courage' and 'Timidity,'" trans. Stanley Corngold, ed. Marcus Bullock, *Selected Writings*, ed. Michael Jennings (Cambridge, Mass.: Harvard University Press, 1996), 1:26.

9. Michel de Certeau, "The Institution of Rot," in *Psychosis and Sexual Identity: Toward a Post-Analytic View of the Schreber Case*, ed. David Alliston et al. (Albany: SUNY Press, 1988), 91. De Certeau's opposition of the word "signification" to "meaning"—a variation on the opposition imagination/reason, rhetoric/logic, performance/argument—makes good sense. It's instructive, here, to attend to the dictionary definition of "signify." *The Random House Dictionary*

of the English Language gives as the first meaning: "to make known by sign, speech, or action," a definition that attractively mingles categories of semiosis, voice, and performance—none of which points univocally to the certain production of meaning and profiles, instead, the modality of the medium. For what, finally, is the sense of a "sign" *or* "speech" *or* "action"? In what way could "speech," say, *fail* to "sign" or to "act"? "Signification" is thus evidently an affair of profiling the process by which meaning might be produced as an activity of embodied signs inviting hermeneutic involvement without closure. To "signify" a concept could mean to undo or suspend the production of a concept by tarrying on the process by which it is produced.

Chapter 1

1. For an eloquent discussion of the Hölderlin quote in the epigraph above ("Vergleichen ist schön"), see Eric Santner, *Friedrich Hölderlin, Narrative Vigilance and the Poetic Imagination* (New Brunswick, N.J.: Rutgers University Press, 1986). Also see my *The Fate of the Self: German Writers and French Theory* (Durham, N.C.: Duke University Press, 1991), 26.

The following epigraph, originally "Ein Mensch kann durch lauter Gleichmachen so leicht dahin kommen, daß er das Unähnliche vergisset, wie auch die Revolution beweiset," is cited in Timothy Chamberlain, "Rigidity and Movement: Metaphoric Concepts in Jean Paul's Political, Emotional and Aesthetic Perspective," doctoral dissertation, Princeton University, 1987, 308–9.

2. As, once before, according to Nietzsche, "optimistic" (Socratic) dialectic had driven music out of tragedy "with the scourge of its syllogisms." *The Birth of Tragedy*, in *Basic Writings of Nietzsche*, ed. and trans. Walter Kaufmann (New York: The Modern Library, 1968), 92.

3. "Urtheilskraft ist das Specifische des sogenannten Mutterwitzes." Immanuel Kant, *Werke*, ed. G. Hartenstein (Leipzig, 1838), 2:155. Cited under "Mutterwitz" in Grimm's *Deutsches Wörterbuch* (Leipzig: Hirzel, 1885), 6:2830.

4. Paul Böckmann, "Das Formprinzip des Witzes bei Lessing (1932/33)," in *Gotthold Ephraim Lessing, Wege der Forschung*, ed. Gerhard Bauer and Sibylle Bauer (Darmstadt: Wissenschaftliche Buchgesellschaft, 1968), 532.

5. Immanuel Kant, *The Critique of Judgment*, trans. James Creed Meredith (Oxford: Clarendon, 1952). References to particular passages of this work will be indicated in the body of the essay by arabic numerals in parentheses. Italic numerals following refer to source passages in Immanuel Kant, *Kritik der Urteilskraft* (Hamburg: Meiner, 1974).

6. See Karl Vorländer, "Einleitung des Herausgebers," in Kant, *Kritik der Urteilskraft*, xii.

7. On the Romantic resurgence of wit as an aesthetic category, see John

Neubauer, *Symbolismus und Symbolische Logik* (Munich: Fink, 1978) and Philippe Lacoue-Labarthe and Jean-Luc Nancy, *The Literary Absolute*, trans. Philip Barnard and Cheryl Lester (Albany: SUNY Press, 1988), especially 52–55.

8. Lessing's apothegm continues, "And in his left the unique, ever-live striving for truth, albeit with the addition that I should always and eternally err, and he said to me, 'Choose!'—I should humbly clasp his left hand, saying: 'Father, give! Pure truth is after all for thee alone!' " This celebrated passage from Lessing is found at the end of his *Duplik* of 1778, where, in Nietzsche's words, "Lessing dared to announce that he cared more for the search after truth than for truth itself." *Birth of Tragedy, Basic Writings*, 95.

9. Hans Blumenberg, *Der Prozess der theoretischen Neugierde* (Frankfurt a.M.: Suhrkamp, 1984), 235–36.

10. Bernd Schoeller, *Gelächter und Spannung: Studien zur Struktur des heiteren Dramas* (Zurich: Atlantis, 1971), 34. Schoeller's definition owes much to Jean Paul.

11. "Erkläre sich der Herr [Templar] . . . / . . . Ob der Herr sich das / Nur bloß so dichtet, . . . / Denn ist der vorgetragene Fall . . . / Ein Spiel des Witzes: so verlohnt es sich / Der Mühe nicht, im Ernst ihn durchzudenken" (Act IV, Scene 2). It could seem that the cogency of this discussion is spoiled by its conflating two meanings of "wit"—the older sense of "cleverness based on the perception of similarity" and the more nearly modern sense of "facility in making amusing ripostes." But the question is resolved by Lessing when he remarks, apropos of Greek comedy, "It would be foolish to imagine that wit for the Greeks—even the Greeks—was not funny." *Lessings Werke*, ed. Julius Petersen and Waldemar Olshausen (Berlin: Deutsches Verlagshaus Bong, n.d.), (14): 192. Additional citations from this edition are indicated by PO, volume number in parenthesis, and page number. The figure of the "*Spiel des Witzes* [play of wit]" as meaning a merely pejorative exercise of reason has a long half-life, extending right up into Heidegger's notorious Rector's Address (Rektoratsrede), viz., "For 'Geist' is neither empty ingenuity nor the irresponsible play of wit nor the boundless bustle of rationalistic analysis, least of all the world spirit; *Geist* is originarily attuned, knowing resoluteness toward the essence of being." Martin Heidegger, *Die Selbstbehauptung der deutschen Universität* (The self-assertion of the German university) (Frankfurt: Klostermann, 1983), 14. A comparably negative distinction is found in Kafka's analysis of Karl Kraus's scandalous pamphlet *Literatur oder Man wird doch da sehn. Eine magische Operette* on Jews writing in German, which Kafka divides into three parts: (1) truth, (2) pitiable wretchedness, and (3) "mere wit [*nur Witz*]." Kafka, *Briefe, 1902–1924*, ed. Max Brod (Frankfurt a.M.: Fischer, 1958), 336.

12. "Sie sagten mir: es denken anders Götter / Denn Sterbliche. Was Ernst den Einen dünk', / Es dünke Scherz den andern. Götterernst / Sei Geist und

Tugend, aber Spiel vor ihnen sei / Die lange Zeit der vielgeschäfftgen Menschen." Friedrich Hölderlin, *Sämtliche Werke, Kritische Textausgabe,* ed. D. E. Sattler (Darmstadt: Luchterhand, 1986), 12:240.

13. Gotthold Ephraim Lessing, *Hamburg Dramaturgy,* trans. Helen Zimmern (New York: Dover, 1962), 83 (translation modified). *Hamburgische Dramaturgie,* ed. Otto Mann (Stuttgart: Alfred Kröner Verlag, 1978), 120–21. Subsequent page references to the English translation are indicated in the body of the book by arabic numerals; italic numerals following refer to pages in the German edition. For a discussion of the eighteenth century's hunt for contingencies (*Zufälligkeiten*), with a view to driving them out of representations or analyses of life, see Reinhart Koselleck, "Der Zufall als Motivationsrest in der Geschichtsschreibung," in *Vergangene Zukunft. Zur Semantik Geschichtlicher Zeiten* (Frankfurt a.M.: Suhrkamp, 1979), 158–75.

14. Walter Benjamin, "Zwei Gedichte von Friedrich Hölderlin. 'Dichtermut'—'Blödigkeit,'" *Gesammelte Schriften,* ed. Rolf Tiedemann and Hermann Schweppenhaüser (Frankfurt a.M.: Suhrkamp, 1972), 2(1): 107. "Two Poems by Friedrich Hölderlin: 'The Poet's Courage' and 'Timidity,'" trans. Stanley Corngold, ed. Marcus Bullock and Michael Jennings, *Selected Writings,* ed. Michael Jennings (Cambridge, Mass.: Harvard University Press, 1996), 1:20.

15. Böckmann, "Das Formprinzip des Witzes," 530.

16. Ibid., 183 ff. The exact place where Böckmann locates the collapse of the hegemony of wit is the controversy about "heart" and "conviction [*Gesinnung*]" in Lessing's early play *Der Freigeist.* According to Böckmann's construction of an Enlightenment "postulate," wit needs an unambiguous transparency of language in order to function. But the surmise in *Der Freigeist* that witty language may in fact be opaque implies that only a language of the heart could be expressive of what matters—namely, the heart—that is to say, passionate conviction or the conviction of passion.

17. "Two Poems by Friedrich Hölderlin," ed. Bullock and Jennings, 20.

18. Apart from the question of whether in the *Hamburg Dramaturgy* Lessing authorizes a later eighteenth-century valorization of the affective life, another question poses itself: Whether such a heightening of affect implies liberation in any sense. It would seem to, in one way, in producing a heightened sense of subjective autonomy, of an irreducible, unreachable place in the mind—"the heart"; but in another sense, which Eagleton explores—as does Stendhal in *The Charterhouse of Parma*—the heart is the tender medium that the law inscribes and so creates unheard-of possibilities of subjection. In *The Ideology of the Aesthetic,* Terry Eagleton writes that "The aesthetic signifies a creative turn to the sensuous body, as well as an inscribing of that body with a subtly oppressive law" (London: Blackwell, 1990), 9. In *The Charterhouse of Parma* Stendhal writes: "Absolute power has this advantage, that it sanctifies everything in the eyes of

the public." Marie Henri Beyle [Stendhal], *The Charterhouse of Parma*, trans. by C. K. Scott-Moncrieff (New York: New American Library, 1987), 107. This power finds in the feeling of virtue a supple medium for inscribing its authority. It engenders in subjects the belief that it is sublime to obey the rules and that such sublimity is the source of justification. There is a rhetoric to create the illusion that converts into virtue the desire to avoid imprisonment. Eagleton's point would be that this language finds support in the language of literature—whose fertile irrationalism devours critique. As Beatrice Wehrli notes: "Discursive language, which Reason puts to use, has never had things easy. Critical theory cannot satisfy the claim to emancipate language from opaque compulsions; its critique of ideology comes under the suspicion of ideology; and it appears that the idea of Enlightenment once again falls into discredit and the language of reason—hardly rehabilitated—must give way to irrationalistic enterprises. Methods of knowledge acquisition which insist not on dialogue but on the ultimate ineffability of experience gain influence, and the self-annihilation of reason is misunderstood as the critique of reason." *Kommunikative Wahrheitsfindung. Zur Funktion der Sprache in Lessings Dramen* (Tübingen: Niemeyer, 1983), 1.

19. Georg Lukács, *Die Zerstörung der Vernunft*, *Werke*, 9:52. Cited in Leo Kofler, *Zur Geschichte der bürgerlichen Gesellschaft*, 7th ed. (Darmstadt and Neuwied: Luchterhand, 1979), 305.

20. Böckmann, "Das Formprinzip des Witzes," 536.

21. Lessing, *Hamburg Dramaturgy*, 83.

22. The artistic practice of the genius, according to Lessing, answers better to Valéry's modern conception of the writer as scientist, as an artist of calculation. In him "everything that he thought, felt, dreamed, will have to be passed through a sieve, weighed, purified, brought into *form*, and as strongly as possible condensed—poetized: he is a sober scientist, almost a mathematician." Cited without source in "Creative Construction" ("Schöpferische Konstruktion"), a radio address by Gerhart Baumann, Freiburg, April 13, 1986.

23. Michel Foucault, *The Order of Things: An Archaeology of the Human Sciences*, a translation of *Les Mots et les choses* (New York: Atheneum, 1971), 54. References to particular passages of this work are indicated in the body of the essay by numbers in parentheses.

24. PO, 23:180. The connection between wit and antithesis—antithesis being a transparent modification of *similitudo*—was a familiar one to Lessing from his correspondence with Nicolai and Mendelssohn. In his treatise on tragedy Nicolai accused French tragedians of craving to be witty everywhere and always, "hence the huge crowd of antitheses or oppositions which so often appear in their tragedies." Cited in Böckmann, "Das Formprinzip des Witzes," 178.

25. "The more wit the less true genius." "Abhandlung von dem weinerlichen oder rührenden Lustspiele," PO, 12:138.

26. "Das Theater des Herrn Diderot," PO, 11:284.

27. "Von Johann Dryden," PO, 12:379.

28. This distinction is made apropros of Aristophanes in the "Abhandlung von dem weinerlichen oder rührenden Lustspiele," PO, 12:125.

29. Cf. the discussion of "genuine [*ungekünstelter*] wit" in the "Seventh Piece" of the *Hamburg Dramaturgy*.

30. Newspaper article dated February 26, 1751, PO, 9:78.

31. "Vierundsechzigstes Stück," *Berlinische Priviligirte Zeitung*, May 29, 1755, PO, 9:405.

32. "Gescheitheit." Newspaper article, May 23, 1754, PO, 9:328.

33. "Das Neueste aus dem Reiche des Witzes," April 1751, PO, 8:31, also, "Auszug aus dem Schauspieler," PO, 12:224.

34. "Rettung des Cochläus," PO, 20:161. See also the discussion of "false wit," PO, 12:224 ff.

35. "Schließt Gründe aus." *Literaturbriefe*, PO, 4:235.

36. Lessing's review of Naumann's *Heldengedicht*, in which wit is connected with a "poetic spirit," constitutes an exception. PO, 9:212.

37. "Rettungen des Horaz," PO, 14:91.

38. "Das Neueste aus dem Reich des Witzes," May 1751, PO, 8:39.

39. *Zerstreute Bemerkungen über das Epigramm* . . . : "Furthermore, I know of no example where Martial mixed true wit and false wit in the very same epigram. He very often shows true wit, even when the object is very small, very ludicrous, very contemptible. But he never shows false wit in connection with a serious, dignified, great object. On such an occasion he can be just as serious, just as dignified, just as great, and only that is the true touchstone of the man of wit." PO, 14:156.

40. John Locke, *An Essay Concerning Human Understanding*, Everyman's Library, book 2, chap. 11 (London: Dent, 1961), 1:123.

41. Locke's point about the inferior moral and cognitive value of wit vis-à-vis judgment is picked up by many German aestheticians—by Gottsched, for example, who, in the second "Hauptstück" of the First Part of the *Versuch einer kritischen Dichtkunst* (Essay in the criticism of poetry) (1730) writes: "As necessary as philosophy is to the poet, so too must his power of judgment be strong. It would be of no help to be witty and ingenious if wit were out of place or not at all the right kind. A too ardent imagination makes a poet absurd, if the fire of fantasy is not cooled by sound reason. Not all inspirations are equally beautiful, equally well-founded, equally natural and probable. Judgment must decide the matter." "Von dem Charakter eines Poeten," in *Gottscheds Lebens- und Kunstreform, Deutsche Literatur, Reihe Aufklärung* (Leipzig: Reclam, 1935), 3:28.

42. Laurence Sterne, *The Life and Opinions of Tristram Shandy, Gentleman* (New York: The Modern Library, 1950), 198.

43. Ibid., 27. Cf. Lichtenberg: "Suddenly to alight on very remote things and thereupon show that a connection indeed existed between them: this is one of Yorick's tricks." In Heft B8 Anh., ca. 1770. Georg Christoph Lichtenberg, *Aphorismen*, Insel Taschenbuch, ed. Kurt Batt (Baden-Baden: Nomos, 1976), 49.

44. Ibid., 21.

45. Henri Fluchère, *Laurence Sterne, de l'homme à l'oeuvre* (Paris: Gallimard, 1961), 287.

46. Sterne, *Tristram Shandy*, 199.

47. Nietzsche reckoned Sterne as his favorite author.

48. "Geistige Elektrizität . . . feste Körper nötig sind." Novalis, *Schriften*, ed. F. Schlegel and L. Tieck (Berlin, 1802), 3:67. Cited under the entry "Witz" in Grimm's *Deutsches Wörterbuch* (Leipzig: Hirzel, 1960), 14/2:874.

49. Paul Mog, *Ratio und Gefühlskultur: Studien zu Psychogenese und Literatur im 18. Jahrhundert* (Tübingen: Niemeyer, 1976), 99.

50. This thesis is spelled out, especially in the chapter on "The Expressivist Turn," by Charles Taylor, in *Sources of the Self: The Making of the Modern Identity* (Cambridge, Mass.: Harvard University Press, 1989).

51. This is the action of Nietzsche's "pack of blond beasts of prey . . . , the most involuntary, unconscious artists there are." *On the Genealogy of Morals, Basic Writings of Nietzsche*, 522–23.

52. In *Der junge Gelehrte*, for example, the rhetoric of an argument attacking the vision structured as a *similitudo* makes extensive use of the *similitudo*, so that precisely the figure under attack brilliantly threads through the demonstration but in this way puts its own argument into question.

53. "Aus der beständigen Durchkreuzung solcher Fäden von ganz verschiednen Farben entstehet denn eine Kontextur, die in der Kunst eben das ist, was die Weberei Changeant nennt; ein Stoff, von dem man nicht sagen kann, ob er blau oder rot, grün oder gelb ist; der beides ist, der von dieser Seite so, von der andern anders erscheinet; ein Spielwerk der Mode, ein Gaukelputz für Kinder.

"Nun urteile man, ob der große Corneille seinen Stoff mehr als ein Genie oder als ein witziger Kopf bearbeitet habe. Es bedarf zu dieser Beurteilung weiter nichts, als die Anwendung eines Satzes, den niemand in Zweifel zieht: das Genie liebt Einfalt; der Witz Verwicklung."

54. *Anthropology from a Pragmatic Point of View*, trans. Mary J. Gregor (The Hague: Martinus Nijhoff, 1974), 89 (translation modified). "Der Witz paart (assimiliert) heterogene Vorstellungen, die oft nach dem Gesetze der Einbildungskraft (der Assoziation) weit auseinander liegen, und ist ein eigentümliches Verähnlichungsvermögen, welches dem Verstande (als dem Vermögen der Erkenntnis des Allgemeinen), so fern er die Gegenstände unter Gattungen

bringt, angehört." Immanuel Kant, *Anthropologie in pragmatischer Hinsicht*, in *Werke in Sechs Bänden*, ed. Wilhelm Weischedel (Darmstadt: Wissenschaftliche Buchgesellschaft, 1966), 6:537–38.

55. Jean Paul, *Werke* (Munich: Hanser, 1963), 5:173. Friedrich Theodor Vischer, *Aesthetik* (Leipzig, 1846), 1:422. Both Paul and Vischer are cited in Sigmund Freud, "Der Witz und seine Beziehung zum Unbewußten," *Freud-Studienausgabe* (Frankfurt a.M.: Fischer, 1970), 4:15. Sigmund Freud, "Wit and Its Relation to the Unconscious," in *The Basic Writings of Sigmund Freud*, trans. and ed. A. A. Brill (New York: The Modern Library, 1938), 634–35.

56. Kant, *Anthropologie in pragmatischer Hinsicht*, 6:424.

57. "Die deutsche Ästhetik." Wilhelm Dilthey, *Die Einbildungskraft des Dichters: Bausteine für eine Poetik, Gesammelte Schriften*, ed. Georg Misch (Göttingen: Vandenhoeck and Ruprecht, 1957), 6:119.

58. Rolf Grimminger, "Die Utopie der vernünftigen Lust. Sozialphilosophische Skizze zur Ästhetik des 18. Jahrhunderts bis zu Kant," in *Aufklärung und literarische Öffentlichkeit*," ed. Christa Bürger, Peter Bürger, and Jochen Schulte-Sasse (Frankfurt a.M.: Suhrkamp, 1980), 128–30.

59. This critique applies *mutatis mutandis* to Terry Eagleton, whose *Ideology of the Aesthetic* is brilliant in "offering parallels" (20) between aesthetic and political features, viz. "the lawfulness without a law," which Kant attributes to aesthetic form and the "authority which is not an authority" found in Rousseau's *Social Contract*. But it is exactly the impetus of the eighteenth-century critique of wit to expose the meretriciousness of (such) brilliant correspondences, however difficult the attempt to do so without falling back needily upon a rhetoric of correspondences.

60. This assertion is supported by Walter Biemel's general argument in *Die Bedeutung von Kants Begründung der Ästhetik für die Philosophie der Kunst* (Cologne: Kölner-Universitäts-Verlag, 1959). According to Hans-Georg Gadamer in *Truth and Method*, trans. William Glen-Doepel (London: Sheed and Ward, 1979), the *Critique of Aesthetic Judgment* "does not seek to be a philosophy of art," being little concerned with the essence of the work of art in its difference from nature (41). No sooner has Gadamer said this, however, than he grants the legitimacy of moving beyond Kant's point of departure in the aesthetic judgment to the ontological question. After citing Rudolf Odebrecht's *Form und Geist: Der Aufstieg des dialektischen Gedankens in Kants Ästhetik* (Berlin: Junker und Dünnhaupt, 1930), Gadamer writes: "This dimension of the question [of the mode of existence of the thing judged to be aesthetic (and hence the whole order of questions bearing on the relation of the beautiful of nature to the beautiful of art)] is necessarily opened up when the standpoint of taste is thought through—and this involves going beyond it" (46). Translation modified with reference to Hans-Georg Gadamer, *Wahrheit und Methode* (Tübingen: J. C. B. Mohr, 1965),

46. Hans Graubner decisively identifies a dimension of ontological questioning in Kant's reflections on genius in the *Critique of Aesthetic Judgment*. In the course of distinguishing between its two key components—Kant's aesthetics of taste and his aesthetics of genius—Graubner concludes that the latter "leads directly to an ontology of the autonomous work of art." " 'Mittelbarkeit' und 'Lebensgefühl' in Kants 'Kritik der Urteilskraft': Zur kommunikativen Bedeutung des Ästhetischen," in *Urszenen: Literaturwissenschaft als Diskursanalyse und Diskurskritik*, ed. Friedrich A. Kittler and Horst Turk (Frankfurt a.M.: Suhrkamp, 1977), 53. Note, however, that Kant's discussion of aesthetic reception in the first sections of the Third Critique already projects features of an ontology of the work of art as fiction.

61. Böckmann also speaks of a "peculiar enmeshing of approaches" in Lessing's dramas. He is referring to the survival in Lessing of a "Formideal des Witzes" long after Lessing had in principle rejected it on grounds of its superficiality and externality vis-à-vis the "innere Form des Dramas," i.e., a logic of causal enchainment and an ethic of feeling ("Das Formprinzip," 536). I am concerned with showing how even in Lessing's discussion of the inner form of drama a similar opposition persists between ideas of the natural and the artificial.

62. In *Beyond Good and Evil*, Nietzsche refers to a new Romantic age of German theologian-philosophers as unable to distinguish between "finding [*finden*]" and "inventing [*erfinden*]" (*Basic Writings*, 208). Lessing, however, is rather direct about making this distinction. In this connection see further the chapter "Von der 'inneren Wahrscheinlichkeit' der Poesie" as well as the discussion of Lessing's "Abhandlung über die Fabel" in Otto Haßelbeck, *Illusion und Fiktion* (Munich: Fink, 1979), 144–51 ff.

63. Nicholas Boyle, in his biography of Goethe, defines this new "matrix of eighteenth-century German aesthetics" as a nexus of "notions that literature, the visual arts, and music have something in common which sets them apart from mere technical crafts, that their products are self-contained little worlds in something like the way in which the great world, the universe, is self-contained, that these products can no more be judged by standards (for example, moral standards) external to them than can the universe, and that their producers are thus analogous to the producer of the universe Himself and so are rightly called creators." *Goethe—The Poet and the Age*, vol. 1, *The Poetry of Desire* (Oxford: Oxford University Press, 1992), 498.

64. Gerhard Kurz sees Lessing's gesture of attributing to art this power of abstraction as marking his "leavetaking from the principle of mimesis." *Mittelbarkeit und Vereinigung: Zum Verhältnis von Poesie, Reflexion, und Revolution bei Hölderlin* (Stuttgart: Metzler, 1975), 79. On the other hand, Kurz's account of this artistic abstraction in Lessing leaves one sort of mimetic grounding intact, viz.

"everything that we in Nature abstract from an object [art] . . . *truly* abstracts and gives us this object . . . in as *pure* and as succinct a form as the sentiment, which it is supposed to arouse, allows." "Seventh Piece," 171, 276–77 (my emphasis).

65. On the replacement in the eighteenth century of an ideal of mimesis by a notion of autonomous poetic production (a movement related to the movement of radical fictionalization I have been discussing but not the same thing), see Wolfgang Preisendanz, "Mimesis und Poiesis in der deutschen Dichtungstheorie des 18. Jahrhunderts," in *Rezeption und Produktion zwischen 1570 und 1730, Festschrift für Günther Weydt zum 65. Geburtstag,* ed. Wolfdietrich Rasch u.a. (Bern and Munich: Francke, 1972), 537–52; and Hans Peter Herrmann, *Naturnachahmung und Einbildungskraft* (Bad Homburg: Gehlen, 1970).

66. *Die Bedeutung von Kants Begründung der Ästhetik für die Philosophie der Kunst* (Cologne: Kölner-Universitäts-Verlag, 1959), 145.

67. This aspect of the Kantian aesthetic judgment had a decisive effect on the entire history of post-Kantian aesthetics; it gives to aesthetic experience the dominant tonality of quietude. Nietzsche railed against the passivity and asceticism—in a word, the weakness—celebrated in Kant's aesthetics, though in doing so he was no doubt reading Kant through Schopenhauerian spectacles.

68. In the sense only of "the imagination's free conformity to law" and having an only subjective validity, as "subjective agreement" between imagination and understanding. See Rudolf A. Makkreel, *Imagination and Interpretation in Kant: The Hermeneutical Import of the Critique of Judgment* (Chicago: University of Chicago Press, 1990), 46–47.

69. Gerhard Kurz, *Traum-Schrecken. Kafkas literarische Existenzanalyse* (Stuttgart: J. B. Metzlersche Verlagsbuchhandlung, 1980), 2.

70. In Kant "aesthetics becomes an analogy of a philosophy of history." Dietrich Naumann, *Literaturtheorie und Geschichtsphilosophie. Teil I: Aufklärung, Romantik, Idealismus* (Stuttgart: Metzler, 1979), 35.

71. The project of thinking past correspondence, past *adequatio,* is nourished by the fundamental intuition of a fracturing of a universal world order. This amounts to a proof *ordo inverso* of Baeumler's point, found in the Afterword to *Das Irrationalitätsproblem in der Ästhetik und Logik des 18. Jahrhunderts bis zur Kritik der Urteilskraft* (Darmstadt: Wissenschaftliche Buchgesellschaft, 1975): "Metaphoric discourse is universal, it brings to light the secret unity of all things. Those apparently academic discussions about the discovery of 'affinities [*Ähnlichkeiten*]'—i.e. of unknown relations between things, events and expressions—contain nothing less than an allusion to the world-view of the analogy" (354).

72. As a result, the principle of similarity informing wit can be seen as having fallen away from its ground; it can be seen as derivative, secondary, and its "cognitive" results as rootless.

73. On the "sliding paradox," see Gerhard Neumann, "Umkehrung und Ablenkung: Franz Kafkas 'Gleitendes Paradox,'" *Franz Kafka, Wege der Forschung*, ed. Heinz Politzer (Darmstadt: Wissenschaftliche Buchgesellschaft, 1973). For "*vergleichsweise/andeutungsweise*" see Franz Kafka, *Hochzeitsvorbereitungen auf dem Lande und andere Prosa aus dem Nachlass*, ed. Max Brod (Frankfurt a.m.: Fischer, 1953), 92; *Dearest Father*, trans. Ernest Kaiser and Eithne Wilkins (New York: Schocken, 1954), 40. "Metaphern . . . [die ihn] am Schrieben verzweifeln [lassen] (December 6, 1921)," in Franz Kafka, *Tagebücher in der Fassung der Handschrift*, ed. Hans-Gerd Koch, Michael Müller, and Malcolm Pasley (Frankfurt a.m.: S. Fischer, 1990), 875; *The Diaries of Franz Kafka, 1914–1923*, ed. Max Brod, trans. Martin Greenberg (with the assistance of Hannah Arendt) (New York: Schocken, 1949), 200–201. "Sicher ist mein Widerwillen gegen Antithesen," *Tagebücher*, 259; *The Diaries of Franz Kafka, 1910–1913*, ed. Max Brod, trans. Joseph Kresh (New York: Schocken, 1948), 157. Kafka once remarked with a witty intention that he was "as lonely as . . ." but could not finish the analogy except to say "as lonely as Franz Kafka." Cf. *Diaries, 1914–1923*, 11.

74. Benjamin's enchanting demonstration in *One-Way Street* of why books are *like* prostitutes is made without a single use of the word "like." From the standpoint of the genius of wit *he* is a one-way street. Walter Benjamin, *Kleine Prosa, Baudelaire Übertragungen*, in *Gesammelte Schriften*, ed. Tilman Rexroth, Suhrkamp-Taschenbuch Wissenschaft 934 (Frankfurt a.m.: Suhrkamp, 1972), IV:1:111.

75. It is interesting to compare Goethe: "Every existing thing is an analogy of everything that exists. Therefore, existence always seems to us to be at once separated and connected. If one takes the analogy too far, everything collapses into identity. If one fails to heed the analogy, everything becomes infinitely dispersed. In both cases [the power of] observation stagnates: on the one hand as ultralively, on the other hand as deadened." Johann Wolfgang von Goethe, *Wilhelm Meisters Wanderjahre*, in *Werke* (Zurich: Artemis, 1949), 8:323. And here is how such an observation surfaces in the rhetoric of our time. In a review of Willard Van Orman Quine's *The Time of My Life: An Autobiography*, Anthony Quinton praises Quine as "a most elegant, perceptive, and entertaining writer, combining a poetic alertness to remote likenesses with his philosophically professional nose for distinctions." It would indeed be the case that one who knew how to "combine" a flair for likeness with one for distinction would "inaugurate a new . . . Golden Age of . . . Philosophy" in America or indeed in any country. *The New Republic* 193 (Sept. 30, 1985): 41.

76. An ideologically demystified aesthetics would put a stop to that "colonization of [sensation by] reason," which in its beginnings, on Eagleton's account, Baumgartens's *Aesthetica* (1750) aimed to accomplish (15).

77. For Hölderlin, "the national" means "the element differentiated in it-

self"—a free place where differences thrive—valued as the indispensable element through which the "ideal whole" can, so to speak, become conscious of itself. The aesthetic state is characterized by the opportunities it offers to consciousness.

78. If wit is a factor productive of unity, it also and at the same time unsettles the unity and coherence of discursive argumentation. For example, it unsettles the unity of Lessing's "Thirtieth Piece" of the *Hamburg Dramaturgy*, which aims to establish intuitively an ontological or empirically verifiable difference between wit and genius.

79. Hans-Georg Gadamer, "Interview," *Sprache und Literatur in Wissenschaft und Unterricht* (1986), 17(57): 98.

80. Richard Rorty, *Contingency, Irony, and Solidarity* (Cambridge: Cambridge University Press, 1989).

81. Paul de Man, "Crisis and Criticism," in *Blindness and Insight: Essays in the Rhetoric of Contemporary Criticism*, 2nd ed. rev. (Minneapolis: University of Minnesota Press, 1983), 17.

82. "Form and Intent in the American New Criticism," in ibid., 34–35.

Chapter 2

1. "The Critique of Aesthetic Judgment" is the first part of Kant's *The Critique of Judgment*, trans. James Creed Meredith (Oxford: Clarendon, 1952). Page numbers from this edition will be given in text. The discussion of aesthetic judgment throughout this entire chapter is oriented to the aesthetic judgment of the *beautiful* (and not the sublime).

2. Many commentaries on the Third Critique operate outside the most obviously appropriate constraints: that the text is a text of unification, a bridge text between the First and Second Critiques.

3. This is an argument on Kant's part that means to divide and demote pleasure.

4. Walter Benjamin, "Zwei Gedichte von Friedrich Hölderlin. 'Dichtermut'—'Blödigkeit,'" *Gesammelte Schriften*, ed. Rolf Tiedemann and Hermann Schweppenhaüser (Frankfurt a.M.: Suhrkamp, 1972), 2(1): 119. "Two Poems by Friedrich Hölderlin: 'The Poet's Courage' and 'Timidity,'" trans. Stanley Corngold, ed. Marcus Bullock and Michael Jennings, *Selected Writings*, ed. Michael Jennings (Cambridge, Mass.: Harvard University Press, 1996), 1:30.

5. *Die Bedeutung von Kants Begründung der Ästhetik für die Philosophie der Kunst* (Cologne: Kölner-Universitäts-Verlag, 1959), 44.

6. Ibid., 45.

7. Ibid., 47.

8. At this juncture Henry Staten poses the question: "But if the mediation is

the reflection on universality, doesn't this *secure* disinterestedness?" This question cannot really be answered until the entire cluster of enabling questions it provokes is answered first, though these are not questions specifically raised by Kant. Thus, can one speak of disinterested mediation? Does not all mediation, involving the action of an intentional consciousness, introduce the factor of interest as what is at stake in the mediation? And even if the aim of the mediation is to secure disinterestedness, one must ask about the interests of disinterestedness. Why would disinterestedness be interested in securing itself? The question is posed with exemplary force by Nietzsche in *Beyond Good and Evil.* Addressing the wonder felt by "the average man" at the things that interest and attract "choosier and more refined tastes," inspiring in them a devotion which the average man terms "*désintéressé*," Nietzsche writes: "There have been philosophers who have known how to lend to this popular wonder a seductive and mystical-transcendent expression (—perhaps because they did not know the higher nature from experience?)—instead of positing the naked truth, which is surely not hard to come by, that the 'disinterested' action is an *exceedingly* interesting and interested action." *Basic Writings of Nietzsche,* trans. and ed. Walter Kaufmann (New York: The Modern Library, 1968), 338. A full discussion of these questions takes us outside the aims proposed by this chapter, but consult J. M. Bernstein, *The Fate of Art: Aesthetic Alienation from Kant to Derrida and Adorno* (University Park: University of Pennsylvania Press, 1992), 27.

9. Paul Guyer, *Kant and the Claims of Taste* (Cambridge, Mass.: Harvard University Press, 1979).

10. Ibid., 158.

11. This account, as Henry Staten has noted, is really an elaboration of the "mediated immediateness" of the pleasure of which Biemel speaks.

12. Ibid., 159.

13. "What Kant . . . suggests is that the universally communicable nature of the pleasure in question must not be merely a matter of its generating conditions. Rather the latter [this communicable nature] must . . . enter more intimately into the very identity of the pleasure." "A New Look at Kant's Aesthetic Judgment," *Essays in Kant's Aesthetics,* ed. Ted Cohen and Paul Guyer (Chicago: University of Chicago Press, 1982), 106.

14. Guyer, *Kant and the Claims of Taste,* 159.

15. Martin Heidegger, *Being and Time,* trans. John Macquarrie and Edward Robinson (New York: Harper and Row, 1962), 177.

16. For a lucid distinction between concepts of play as power and play as pleasure, see Mihai Spariosu, *Dionysus Reborn: Play and the Aesthetic Dimension in Modern Philosophical and Scientific Discourse* (Ithaca, N.Y.: Cornell University Press, 1989).

17. This text of Lessing is found in the Seventieth Letter of the *Hamburg Dramaturgy*, to which I referred in Chapter 1. Like Kant, Lessing also regards the work of art not "as the product of an individual being, but of a general Nature." Lessing, *Gesammelte Werke*, 10 vols., ed. P. Rilla (Berlin-Ost: Aufbau, 1954–58), 6:187.

18. Nietzsche, *Beyond Good and Evil*, in *Basic Writings*, 199.

19. Franz Kafka, *Dearest Father*, trans. Ernst Kaiser and Eithne Wilkins (New York: Schocken, 1954), 86.

20. Rudolf A. Makkreel, *Imagination and Interpretation in Kant: The Hermeneutical Import of the "Critique of Judgment"* (Chicago: University of Chicago Press, 1990), 2.

21. Rainer Nägele, "Peter Szondi: Text, Geschichte und das kritische Subjekt," *Uneßbarer Schrift gleich: Text, Geschichte und Subjektivität in Hölderlins Dichtung* (Stuttgart: Metzler, 1985), 6.

22. Bernstein, *The Fate of Art*, 23.

Chapter 3

1. *Conversations with Eckermann (1823–1832)* [Thursday, July 5, 1827], trans. John Oxenford (San Francisco: North Point Press, 1984), 172 (translation modified).

2. Otto Pöggeler, "Hölderlin and Celan: Homburg in ihrer Lyrik," *Bad Homburger Hölderlin-Vorträge (1988/89)* (Bad Homburg: Stadt Bad Homburg v.d. Höhe in cooperation with the Hölderlin-Gesellschaft, 1989), 65.

3. Pierre Bertaux, *Friedrich Hölderlin* (Frankfurt a.M.: Suhrkamp Taschenbuch Verlag, 1981), 382.

4. Hölderlin discusses his plans for *Iduna* in a letter to Neuffer dated June 4, 1799. Friedrich Hölderlin, *Sämtliche Werke*, ed. Friedrich Beißner (Stuttgart: Kohlhammer, 1961), 6:324.

5. In his *Remarks* to his translation of *Oedipus*, Hölderlin alludes without false modesty to the failure of his age to assure its poets a "bourgeois existence." Friedrich Hölderlin, *Sämtliche Werke, "Frankfurter Ausgabe"* (Frankfurt a.M.: Roter Stern, 1979), 16:25. All quotations from Hölderlin are taken from this edition whenever possible and are given in the text by volume and page number. Where quotations are not available from the Frankfurt edition, they are identified in the Notes as *Sämtliche Werke*, indicating the "Große Stuttgarter Ausgabe" of Friedrich Beißner (see note 6).

6. They are called *Maxims* by D. E. Sattler, the editor of the as yet incomplete Frankfurt edition of Hölderlin's works, who comments, informatively: "The *Maxims*, which were jotted down in two goes, are immediately followed by the pencilled draft of Achilles II, . . . which presumably dates from early 1799. The aphoristic form is probably stimulated by Novalis's *Blüthenstaub* (*Pollen*) and

Friedrich Schlegel's *Fragmente* in the first two *Athenaeum* articles (May and July 1798): Hölderlin had already tried it out in an entry he wrote in an album for Daniel Andreas Manskopf (June 1798). The themes of the Fourth Maxim recur in the Seventh Maxim. Further comments on the difficulty of living with common things and on artists and art are found in the letter to Neuffer of November 12, 1798. A remark toward the end could point to the Maxims: 'and so that you fully understand my brooding, I want to tell you that for several days I have got stuck in my work [on the Empedocles project]: at such moments I always fall into arguing [*Räsonnirien*]'" (14:51).

7. Cited phrases are from Terrance King, "Mimesis, Binary Opposition, and Peirce's Triadic Realism," in *Mimesis, Semiosis and Power. Mimesis in Contemporary Theory: An Interdisciplinary Approach*, ed. Ronald Bogue (Philadelphia and Amsterdam: John Benjamins, 1991), 69.

8. See Introduction to this book. Pierre Bertaux astutely links the unpoetic moment of the manifold grasped by swift conceptual comprehension with the "caesura" that Hölderlin, in his *Remarks on Antigone*, calls "the boldest" moment of the tragedy, "the way that in the middle, time turns about" (*Hölderlin*, 397). In his essay "Goethe's *Elective Affinities*," Walter Benjamin makes the caesura crucial to his notion of the "expressionless" of art: it is the moment "in which, along with harmony, every expression simultaneously comes to a standstill, in order to give free reign to an expressionless power inside all artistic media. . . . Indeed, one could not characterize this rhythm any more aptly than by asserting that something beyond the poet interrupts the language of poetry." Benjamin, *Selected Writings*, ed. Jennings, 1: 341.

9. "Ja, es ziemet sich ihr [der Nacht] Kränze zu weihn und Gesang, / Weil den Irrenden sie geheiliget ist und den Todten, / Selber aber besteht, ewig, in freiestem Geist./ Aber sie muß uns auch, daß in der zaudernden Weile / Daß im Finstern für uns einiges Haltbare sei."

10. "Es ist wohl nicht nötig, zu erinnern, daß derlei Äußerungen als bloße Phänomene des menschlichen Gemütes von Rechts wegen niemand skandalisieren sollten" (11:589).

11. See Bernhard Böschenstein's account of the theoretical basis of Hölderlin's unfinished drama *Empedocles*: "It is an internally multiply differentiated model of reconciliation, in which every contradiction asserts its necessary place in space and time: thus, the great movements of Empedocles, this critic of society and of his age, . . . enter into the rigorous service of historical necessity." Bernhard Böschenstein, "Das neuzeitliche Ich in Hölderlins *Tod des Empedokles*," in *Das neuzeitliche Ich in der Literatur des 18. und 20. Jahrhunderts: zur Dialektik der Moderne: ein internationales Symposion*, ed. U. Fülleborn and M. Engel (Munich: Fink, 1988), 164.

12. See Hölderlin's letter to Neuffer dated June 4, 1799, in which Hölderlin mentions the names of the writers and works he means to include in *Iduna*:

"The other essays will contain (1) characteristic features from the life of ancient and modern writers, the circumstances in which they developed, especially the peculiar artistic character of each. Thus, on Homer, Sappho, Aeschylus, Sophocles, Horace, Rousseau (as the author of the *Héloïse*)" *Sämtliche Werke*, 6:324.

13. Hölderlin could not have read this line in Goethe's *Faust*, since in all likelihood it was composed during the period 1800–1801.

14. Gerhard Kurz, *Mittelbarkeit und Vereinigung: zum Verhältnis von Poesie, Reflexion und Revolution bei Hölderlin* (Stuttgart: Metzler, 1975), 80. Kurz's study is an invaluable source of information on the connections of Hölderlin's political, philosophical, and poetic thought.

15. "und zeichnetest / Du nicht der Zukunft große Linien / Vor mir, so wie des Künstlers sichrer Blik / Ein fehlend Glied zum ganzen Bilde reiht" (13:710).

16. Max Kommerell, in *Hölderlin-Aufsätze*, puts "Hölderlin" more positively, as pure "opening."

17. *Sämtliche Werke*, 6:249.

18. Ibid., 6:289.

19. Ibid., 6:290.

20. "Wisst! Apoll ist der Gott der Zeitungsschreiber geworden / Und sein Mann ist, wer ihm treulich das Factum erzählt" (6:83).

21. *Sämtliche Werke*, 6:36. See the commentary of Eric Santner in *Friedrich Hölderlin, Hyperion and Selected Poems*, ed. Eric L. Santner (New York: Continuum, 1990), xxxiv.

22. Jacques Lacan, writing on the Schreber case in *La Psychanalyse* (1958), IV:44–45. Cited in Laplanche, *Hölderlin et la question du père* (Paris: Presses Universitaires de France, 1961), 46.

23. Friedrich Hölderlin, *Sämtliche Werke* (Stuttgart: Kohlhammer, 1961) 6:339.

24. For example, his readiness on one occasion of philosophical dispute to murder his best friend Sinclair. Cf. Bertaux, *Hölderlin*, 487.

25. Consult Geoff Waite, *Nietzsche/Hölderlin: A Critical Revaluation*, doctoral dissertation, Princeton University, 1978, for a rich historical account of their reception as interinvolved thinkers.

26. *Basic Writings of Nietzsche*, trans. and ed. Walter Kaufmann (New York: The Modern Library, 1966), 522–23.

27. My phrase.

28. Friedrich Schiller, *On the Aesthetic Education of Man in a Series of Letters*, ed. and trans. Elizabeth M. Wilkinson and L. A. Willoughby (Oxford: Clarendon, 1967), 19.

29. Cited in Adolf Beck, *Hölderlin—Chronik seines Lebens* (Frankfurt a.M.: Insel, 1975), 74. Pierre Bertaux defines the motive for the founding of *Iduna*— and, hence, by implication the meaning of the Fourth Maxim—as a political

one, however repressed. After the failure of Hölderlin's hopes for the establishment of a Swabian Republic, he would have undertaken in his journal "to contribute to the aesthetic education of freedom-loving Germans, who, then, perhaps, at a much later date, would found a republic 'in Hölderlin's name'" (*Hölderlin*, 570).

30. "Remarks on 'Antigone,'" in *Friedrich Hölderlin, Essays and Letters on Theory*, trans. and ed. Thomas Pfau (Albany: SUNY Press, 1988), 113.

31. Cast this way, as a type of hyperconsciousness, one will understand "swift conceptual grasp" as "narrative vigilance" (Eric Santner) or "sovereignty of consciousness" (Lawrence Ryan). According to Ryan, this hyperconsciousness, which the hero Hyperion, for one, realizes at the end of the novel *Hyperion*, achieves a "subordination of all particular moments in the development of temporal existence by an overarching comprehensive process." *Hölderlins "Hyperion." Exzentrische Bahn und Dichterberuf* (Stuttgart: Metzler, 1965), 176. Santner sees Hölderlin as relaxing this desideratum at the end of his poetic career to allow the distinct particular to emerge in its *quidditas*. Eric L. Santner, *Friedrich Hölderlin: Narrative Vigilance and the Poetic Imagination* (New Brunswick: Rutgers University Press, 1986).

32. Henry Staten asks: "Isn't it just in the nature of light that it is 'self-illuminating'? It *is* illumination, therefore at once illuminating and illuminated."

33. Compare Heidegger, in *Unterwegs zur Sprache* (En route to language): "When thinking tries to pursue the poetic word, it turns out that the word, the saying, has no being [*das Wort, das Sagen, hat kein Sein*]." Quite consistent with Heidegger's understanding of him, Nietzsche here appears to have little patience with such poverty. The difference between the mythic immediacy of Nietzsche's grasp (here) and Hölderlin's mediated grasp is striking. Consider, further, Hölderlin in the more or less contemporaneous work *On the Operations of the Poetic Spirit*: "What is harmoniously opposed in the poetic spirit is felt as opposed in a unified manner as inseparable *and is invented as something felt* [emphasis added]. This sense is truly poetic character, neither genius nor art, but poetic individuality, and it alone is given the identity of enthusiasm" (*Friedrich Hölderlin, Essays and Letters on Theory*, trans. and ed. Pfau, 71).

34. A passage from Nietzsche's *Thus Spoke Zarathustra*, which interests Nietzsche enough for him to quote it at length again in his *Ecce Homo*, is richly suggestive in conjunction with Hölderlin's maxim, as well as with Nietzsche's parable of the "blond beast." The passage conveys a depoliticized but still instinctual myth of organization, hence one more nearly like Hölderlin's swift conceptual grasp, but it also evokes a source insight from which a political vision could readily arise: Nietzsche's myth of *inspiration*, viz.: "Has anyone at the end of the nineteenth century a clear idea of what poets of strong ages have called *inspiration*? If not, I will describe it.—If one had the slightest residue of supersti-

tion left in one's system, one could hardly reject altogether the idea that one is merely incarnation, merely mouthpiece, merely a medium of overpowering forces. The concept of revelation—in the sense that suddenly, with indescribable certainty and subtlety, something becomes *visible*, audible, something that shakes one to the last depths and throws one down—that merely describes the facts. One hears, one does not seek; one accepts, one does not ask who gives; like lightning, a thought flashes up, without necessity, without hesitation regarding its form—I never had any choice.

"A rapture . . . , a depth of happiness in which even what is most painful and gloomy does not seem something opposite but rather conditioned, provoked, a *necessary* color in such a superabundance of light; an instinct for rhythmic relations that arches over wide spaces of forms—length, the need for a rhythm with wide arches, is almost the measure of the force of inspiration, a kind of compensation for its pressure and tension.

"Everything happens involuntarily in the highest degree but as in a gale of freedom, of absoluteness, of power, of divinity." Note the "superabundance of light," note "an instinct for rhythmic relations." *Basic Writings of Nietzsche*, 756–57.

35. "Eben darum verläugnet der tragische Dichter, weil er die tiefste Innigkeit ausdrükt, seine Person, seine Subjectivität ganz . . . ; er trägt sie in fremde Personalität . . . über."

36. It breaks off for Hölderlin's reader. A page of the essay is missing because it was lost by chance or because Hölderlin could not write it.

37. Again, these lines from Goethe's *Faust* were written between 1800 and 1801, shortly after Hölderlin's own.

38. We find in Wilhelm Dilthey—author of some of the first major studies of Hölderlin—a remarkably analogous depreciation of the "deed," which is "one-sided," as opposed to the act of imaginative interpretation. Typically, Dilthey elides the tragic dimension of this loss of priority. See "Dilthey's Poetics of Force," in my *The Fate of the Self* (Durham: Duke University Press, 1994), 62 ff.

39. Compare Chapter 8.

40. "Der *freie* Gebrauch des *Eigenen* das schwerste ist." *Sämtliche Werke*, 6:426.

41. Peter Szondi's essay "Überwindung des Klassizismus: Der Brief an Böhlendorff vom 4. Dezember 1801" makes the point that Hölderlin's differentiation of the origins of modern Western art—namely, Junoian sobriety—from Greek art—"heavenly fire" and "sacred pathos"—represents a departure from the single universal productive principle of "The Perspective from Which We Have to View Antiquity." This is the departure that we have been following through the *Foundation* to *Empedocles*. Peter Szondi, *Hölderlin-Studien: Mit einem Traktat über philologische Erkenntnis* (Frankfurt a.M.: Insel, 1967), 89.

42. "Sonst konnt' ich jauchzen über eine neue Wahrheit, eine bessere Ansicht deß, das über uns und um uns ist, jezt fürcht' ich, daß es mir nicht geh' am Ende, wie dem alten Tantalus, dem mehr von Göttern ward, als er verdauen konnte." I have consulted the excellent translation of some of Hölderlin's letters by Christopher Middleton in *The Poet's Vocation: Selections from Letters of Hölderlin, Rimbaud, and Hart Crane*, trans. and ed. William Buford and Christopher Middleton (Austin: University of Texas Press, 1967), especially 26–31.

43. The two figures are connected in Hölderlin's mind. In the first version of *Der Tod des Empedokles* (The death of Empedocles), Empedocles addresses a "phantom" (*Schattenbild*) of himself as "poor Tantalus" (13:706).

44. "Aber ich thue, was ich kann, so gut ichs kann, und denke, wenn ich sehe, wie ich auf meinem Wege auch dahin muß wie die andern, daß es gottlos ist und rasend, einen Weg zu suchen, der vor allem Anfall sicher wäre. . . . Ich bin jezt voll Abschieds. . . . Es hat mich bittre Thränen gekostet, da ich mich entschloß, mein Vaterland noch jezt zu verlassen, vielleicht auf immer." *Sämtliche Werke*, 6:428.

45. Gerhard Kurz sees this pattern as characteristic of the figure of Empedocles: "In that Empedocles, through the violent oppositions of his time, is torn from its 'midpoint' (4:159) and loses himself in endless 'suffering' (4:268) in the aorgic, in unconsciousness, ripped into the 'eccentric sphere of the dead' (5:197), he becomes 'in himself' insignificant, ineffectual." Kurz, *Mittelbarkeit und Vereinigung*, 200. Numbers in parentheses refer to volume and page of Hölderlin, *Sämtliche Werke*.

46. In the words of Pierre Bertaux, "It is striking that from 1799 on the word 'freedom' disappears completely from Hölderlin's lexicon, with one single, bitter-sounding exception. Let man test everything, he writes, 'und verstehe die Freiheit, aufzubrechen, wohin er will [and understand the freedom to set off whither he will].' The one freedom [*Freiheit*] remaining is that of suicide [*Freitod*]" (*Hölderlin*, 571).

47. *Sämtliche Werke*, 6:433. From the undated draft of a letter to Böhlendorff, which the editor Friedrich Beißner believes was composed in fall 1802, no later than November. The complete sentence reads, in Christopher Middleton's translation, "Storm, not only in its full power, but precisely as a power and a shape, among the heavenly forms, light in its operations, shaping forms, natively and as a principle and mode of destiny, so that something should be holy for us, . . . and the philosophical light around my window, is now my joy" (*The Poet's Vocation*, 30–31).

48. "Besondere Methode des Denkens. Gefühlsmäßig durchdrungen. Alles fühlt sich als Gedanke, selbst im Unbestimmtesten [July 21, 1913]." *Tagebücher in der Fassung der Handschrift*, ed. Hans-Gerd Koch, Michael Müller, and Malcolm Pasley (Frankfurt a.M.: S. Fischer, 1990), 568. *The Diaries of Franz Kafka, 1910–1913*, ed. Max Brod, trans. Joseph Kresh (New York: Schocken, 1948), 291

(translation modified). Compare the words of the novelist Christa Wolf: "My thinking is more darkly mixed with sensation, curious." *The Quest for Christa T.*, trans. Christopher Middleton (New York: Farrar, Straus, and Giroux, 1970), 73.

49. "Das Gefühl ist aber wohl die beste Nüchternheit und Besinnung des Dichters, wenn es richtig und warm und klar und kräftig ist." *Sämtliche Werke*, 4:233.

50. *Hyperion*, SA III:155.

51. Immanuel Kant, *The Critique of Judgment*, trans. James Creed Meredith (Oxford: Clarendon, 1952), 119.

Chapter 4

1. *Die Bedeutung von Kants Begründung der Ästhetik für die Philosophie der Kunst* (Cologne: Kölner-Universitäts-Verlag, 1959), 145. This lucid and informative work is worth consulting today.

2. In an early (unpublished) essay on two poems of Hölderlin (1914), Walter Benjamin described "courage" as a sort of mood—as "the feeling for life of the man who surrenders himself to danger, so that in his death it expands into a danger to the world and at the same time overcomes." "Two Poems by Friedrich Hölderlin: 'The Poet's Courage' and 'Timidity,'" trans. Stanley Corngold, ed. Marcus Bullock and Michael Jennings, *Selected Writings*, ed. Michael Jennings (Cambridge, Mass.: Harvard University Press, 1996), 1:33. In *Wahrheit und Ästhetik: Untersuchungen zum Frühwerk Walter Benjamins* (Würzburg: Königshausen and Neumann, 1991), Rudolf Speth discusses the "existential dimension of Benjamin's concept of courage"—more particularly, its revelation of "the disclosive character of the affects" (50).

3. As Mihai Spariosu writes, "Kant and German idealism in general unwittingly initiate the long, uneven, and by no means irreversible process of restoring mimesis-play to its high, pre-Platonic, cultural status. This process culminates in Nietzsche and is carried on in the twentieth century in the thought of Heidegger and Fink in Germany. . . . From a suppressed epistemological prop of philosophy (controlled and regulated by mimesis-imitation), mimesis-play turns once more into an indispensable cognitive tool, a fundamental way of understanding the world of Becoming." *Dionysus Reborn: Play and the Aesthetic Dimension in Modern Philosophical and Scientific Discourse* (Ithaca, N.Y.: Cornell University Press, 1989), 20. A corollary of the German Romantic and Idealist project aiming to authorize a prerational conception of play is the valorization of Mood. (The English word "mood" is a Wordsworthian word par excellence.) Both projects include especially what Thomas Mann called "Romanticism's self-transcendence in Nietzsche."

4. In *Nietzsches Werke: Kritische Gesamtausgabe (Briefe)*, ed. Giorgio Colli and

Mazzino Montinari (Berlin: De Gruyter, 1982), I, 1:363 (henceforth indicated in text as *KGB* plus volume and page number). The translation is mine, as are all other translations, unless otherwise indicated.

5. "O komm! in den Tiefen der Gebirgswelt wird das Geheimnis unseres Herzens ruhn . . ."; "Ich trauerte. . . . Sie war die Botin der Freude, diese Trauer." This collage from Friedrich Hölderlin, *Sämtliche Werke* (Stuttgart: Insel, 1961), 616, 554.

6. "Meinen innigsten Dank für diesen lieben, ausführlichen, und interessanten Brief aus Tegernsee; fürwahr, du hast eine wunderschöne Reise gemacht und werdet nun, indem ich dies schreibe, glücklich wieder heimgekehrt sein. Vielleicht hast du auch schon meinen Brief vom 3 August gelesen, vielleicht auch sind deine Stimmungen ähnliche, wie ich damals am Ende der Ferien hatte" (*KGB* I, 1:170–71).

7. Probably the edition of 1847 published by Schwab. See Geoff Waite, *Nietzsche/Hölderlin: A Critical Reevaluation*, doctoral dissertation, Princeton University, 1978, 197. Forthcoming as *A Politics of Appropriation: Nietzsche/Hölderlin* (Durham: Duke University Press).

8. "Ferienende. / Nürnberg. Schmerz ist. . . . / Ustaj. / Sendung. / Buchbinder. / Hölderlin. / Was habt ihr morgen? / Stiftungsfest versäumt. / Schreibt bald" (*KGB* I, 1:166).

9. Nietzsche's early acquaintance with Hölderlin, who was his "favorite poet," had a major impact on his intellectual development. The direction of Nietzsche's relation to Romantic poetry is basically defined by his devoted study and imitation of Hölderlin, whom he thereafter repudiates and derides. This thesis is elaborated in the valuable study by Geoff Waite. Cf. note 7.

10. *Friedrich Nietzsche: Werke in drei Bänden*, ed. Karl Schlechta (Munich: Hanser, 1954–1956), 3:113–15. Quotations from this edition will henceforth be given in the text by volume and page numbers. The translation first appeared in my "Nietzsche's Moods," *Studies in Romanticism* 29 (Spring 1990): 69–71. I have made a few revisions in the light of Graham Parkes's felicitous version in *Journal of Nietzsche Studies* 2 (Autumn 1991): 5–11. Oddly enough, Parkes reverses the sense of Nietzsche's rather important sentence on the will, which is full of proleptic force. Nietzsche writes, "Alles, was die Seele nicht reflektieren *kann*, trifft sie nicht; da es aber in der Macht des Willens steht, die Seele reflektieren zu lassen oder nicht, trifft die Seele nur das, was sie will" (Schlecta, III: 114). Parkes translates: "Anything the soul *cannot* reflect simply does not touch it; but since it does not [sic] lie within the power of the will to make the soul reflect or not, the soul is touched only by what it wants" (7). Quite the reverse is true for the young Nietzsche: it *does* lie within the power of the will to make the soul reflect.

11. This essay has since been unmasked as a plagiarism. See Waite, "Nietzsche/Hölderlin," 199–214.

12. This work is now available in an excellent translation: *Unfashionable Observations*, in *The Complete Works of Friedrich Nietzsche*, vol. 2, trans. Richard T. Gray (Stanford: Stanford University Press, 1995).

13. Martin Heidegger, *Being and Time*, trans. John Macquarrie and Edward Robinson (New York: Harper and Row, 1962), 205.

14. Cf. Walter Benjamin in *One-Way Street* (*Einbahnstraße*): "If that teaching is true that says that feeling [*Empfindung*] does not nest in the head, that we feel a window, a cloud, a tree not in the brain but rather at the place where we see them, then, we are also outside/beside ourselves in our glance at the beloved." In *Kleine Prosa, Baudelaire Übertragungen*, in *Gesammelte Schriften*, Suhrkamp-Taschenbuch Wissenschaft 934, ed. Tilman Rexroth (Frankfurt a.M.: Suhrkamp, 1972), IV:1:91.

15. For an account of the *impersonal* character of Mood according to Rousseau, see my *The Fate of the Self* (Durham: Duke University Press, 1994), 208.

16. This metaphor has had a long life. Cf. Hermann Broch's "The Romantic (1888)": "But now his [Joachim's] thoughts jostled each other like the people in the crowd round about him." In *The Sleepwalkers*, trans. Willa and Edwin Muir (San Francisco: North Point Press, 1985), 49.

17. The difference between the event of thought and the event of what thought means to be about is elegantly elaborated in Valéry's "The Evening with Monsieur Teste," in *Paul Valéry: An Anthology*, ed. James Lawler (Princeton: Princeton University Press, 1977), 6.

18. Michel Foucault, "What Is an Author?" in *Textual Strategies*, ed. Josué Harari (Ithaca, N.Y.: Cornell University Press, 1979), 142.

19. Leo Spitzer, *Classical and Christian Ideas of World Harmony: Prologomena to an Interpretation of the Word "Stimmung"* (Baltimore: Johns Hopkins University Press, 1963).

20. See "Self and Subject in Nietzsche During the Axial Period," in Corngold, *The Fate of the Self*, 96–128.

21. Gaston Bachelard, *L'air et les onges*, in *On Poetic Imagination and Reverie: Selections from the Works of Gaston Bachelard*, trans. Colette Gaudin (Indianapolis: Bobbs-Merrill, 1971), 42.

22. *Basic Writings of Nietzsche*, ed. and trans. Walter Kaufmann (New York: The Modern Library, 1966), 43. I have put brackets around the word "romantic" since it is added on by the translator. Henceforward, citations from this work are given as *BW* followed by page number.

23. In composing his major work on poetics, *Die dichterische Einbildungskraft: Bausteine für eine Poetik* (1887), Dilthey also gave prominence to this citation. This repetition could well be an event in his long-standing rivalry with Nietzsche. See J. Kamerbeek, "Dilthey Versus Nietzsche," *Studia Philosophica, Jahrbuch der schweizerischen philosophischen Gesellschaft* 10 (1950): 52–84.

24. Philippe Lacoue-Labarthe, *Typography: Mimesis, Philosophy, Politics,* ed. Christopher Fynsk (Cambridge, Mass.: Harvard University Press, 1992), 186. Lacoue-Labarthe's perception of this analogy needs to be complicated by the fact that Nietzsche also attaches a characteristic (though nonmusical) mood to the Apollinian.

25. Nietzsche's disclaimer this early in *The Birth of Tragedy* as to assertions of unmediated identity between music (as a mode of representation) and the will (as a type of subject) go some distance toward disarming the accusation that the work is confused on this point. See Paul de Man's deconstruction of *Birth of Tragedy* in "Genesis and Genealogy (Nietzsche)," *Allegories of Reading: Figural Language in Rousseau, Nietzsche, Rilke, and Proust* (New Haven: Yale University Press, 1979), 79–102. De Man's essay concludes that "the will is discredited as a self," but this point is plain throughout Nietzsche's text in Nietzsche's critique of Schopenhauer. See, too, Maudemarie Clark, "Deconstructing *The Birth of Tragedy,*" *International Studies in Philosophy* 19, 2 (1987): 67–75.

26. If, at the outset of Section 21, Nietzsche invokes, as an exception, "the mood befitting contemplation" (*BW* 124), it is also an exception that proves the rule: For even the Apollinian must strive for the condition of music—as it must follow from the fact that it is the weaker art-impulse, "forced [in tragedy] into service by the Dionysian," which, "compared to the Apollinian, [is] the eternal and original artistic power" (*BW* 131).

27. This passage forms an extraordinarily important cross-reference with Nietzsche's celebration of inspiration in *Thus Spoke Zarathustra* and *Ecce Homo.* The latter passage reads: "The involuntariness of image and metaphor is strangest of all: one no longer has any notion of what is an image or a metaphor: everything offers itself as the nearest, most obvious, simplest expression. It actually seems, to allude to something Zarathustra says, as if the things themselves approached and offered themselves as metaphors. ('Here all things come caressingly to your discourse and flatter you; for they want to ride on your back. On every metaphor you ride to every truth. . . . Here the words and word-shrines of all being open up before you; here all being wishes to become word, all becoming wishes to learn from you how to speak')." *BW,* 756–57; *The Portable Nietzsche,* 295–96. These passages bring three central figures into crucial proximity: Zarathustra, Nietzsche the poet, and the crowd swaying to Dionysian moods in Attica. The condition of poetic existence is Dionysian.

28. In addition to the Dionysian and the Apollinian, the Socratic mode, too, figures in the so-called *Philosophenbuch* as a mood—as a certain lightness of being. Nietzsche writes: "Art treats appearance as appearance; its aim is precisely *not* to deceive, it is therefore true." The translation is by Paul de Man, who adds: "But the truth of appearance, unlike the truth of being, is not a threat or a passion that could be described in terms similar to those used in *The Birth of Tragedy*

to evoke the Dionysian pathos of truth. It can therefore be said that it stands above pleasure and pain, in the ordinary sense of these terms. The artist, who is truthful in his recognition of illusion and of life for what they are, thus gains a special kind of affective freedom, a euphoria which is that of a *joyful* wisdom or of the Homeric *Heiterkeit* and that differs entirely from the pleasure principle tied to libido and desire." Paul de Man, *Allegories of Reading: Figural Language in Rousseau, Nietzsche, Rilke, and Proust* (New Haven: Yale University Press, 1979), 113–14. In describing the mood that Nietzsche attaches to Socratic insight, however, it is wrong to distinguish it from the Dionysian as a thing ontologically "higher" rather than as a thing of the same kind (a thing already very high) yet of a different type—*a different mood.*

29. "Über Stimmungen," *Werke*, 3:113. See Chapter 4.

30. Friedrich Nietzsche, in *The Portable Nietzsche*, ed. and trans. Walter Kaufmann (New York: Viking, 1954), 519–20.

31. Here and throughout Nietzsche is a master thinker of resentment; no powerful affect occurs except within a psychodialectical field securing its reaction; no infliction of cruelty goes unavenged though that reaction may go underground as resentment; no infliction of (Dionysian) ecstasy goes unavenged though that reaction may leak up as melancholy.

32. *Perspectives in Aesthetics: Plato to Camus*, ed. Peynton E. Richter (Indianapolis: Bobbs-Merrill, 1979), 348.

33. Nietzsche, *Unfashionable Observations*, 115 (translation modified). Additional citations from this work will appear in parenthesis in this text. On the connection between mood and irony in Nietzsche, see my *The Fate of the Self*, 115.

34. Lacoue-Labarthe's intuition of a fundamental link between musical moods and "the autobiographical gesture" plays suggestively here. *Typography*, 151.

35. *On the Genealogy of Morals*, in *Basic Writings*, Third Essay, section 4, 537.

36. Friedrich Nietzsche, *Gesammelte Werke* IX (Munich: Musarion, 1921), 391. Henceforth cited as Musarion in the text.

37. Friedrich Nietzsche, *The Will to Power*, ed. Walter Kaufmann, trans. Walter Kaufmann and R. J. Hollingdale (New York: Vintage, 1967), 225.

38. Nietzsche writes in *Beyond Good and Evil*: "The will is not only a complex of sensation and thinking, but it is above all an *affect*, and specifically the affect of the command" (*BW* 215). In *The Will to Power* he writes: "The will to power specializes as will to nourishment, to property, to tools, to servants (those who obey) and masters: the body as an example.— . . . There is absolutely no other kind of causality than that of will upon will. . . . Thinking, feeling, willing in all living beings. What is pleasure but: an excitation of the feeling of power by an obstacle (even more strongly by rhythmic obstacles and resistances)—so it swells up. Thus all pleasure includes pain—," etc. (347).

39. Ibid.

40. Sigmund Freud, *The Interpretation of Dreams*, trans. and ed. James Strachey (New York: Avon, 1970), 525.

41. Alphonso Lingis, "The Will to Power," *The New Nietzsche: Contemporary Styles of Interpretation*, ed. David B. Allison (New York: Dell, 1977), 50–51.

42. *The Will to Power*, 366.

43. *Nietzsches Werke: Kritische Gesamtaufgabe*, ed. Giorgio Colli and Mazzino Montinari (Berlin: De Gruyter, 1967), VIII:2:190.

44. *The Will to Power*, 347.

45. Gilles Deleuze, "Active and Reactive," *The New Nietzsche*, 95.

46. Friedrich Nietzsche, *The Portable Nietzsche*, ed. and trans. Walter Kaufmann (New York: Viking, 1954), 519–20.

47. "The animal functions are, as a matter of principle, a million times more important than all our beautiful moods and heights of consiousness: the latter are a surplus, except when they have to serve as tools of those animal functions. The entire *conscious* life, the spirit along with the soul, the heart, goodness, and virtue—in whose service do they labor?" etc. *The Will to Power*, 355.

Chapter 5

This essay was written in honor of Dorrit Cohn.

1. The novel I am dealing with is *Young Törless*, an English translation of Robert Musil's *Die Verwirrungen des Zöglings Törleß*, trans. Eithne Wilkins and Ernst Kaiser (New York: Pantheon, 1955). I have decided to base my interpretive essay on the English version of Musil's novel, checking for accuracy every sentence and not just the ones quoted. Taking the English-language version as my basic text is, I believe, a more coherent procedure than writing about the German original and then presenting my results as if they were formed around illustrative sentences torn out of the Wilkins and Kaiser translation.

2. Musil wrote apropos of *Törless* that "the reality [the subject matter] depicted is always only an excuse [*Vorwand*]." *Tagebücher, Aphorismen, Essays und Reden*, ed. Adolf Frisé (Reinbeck bei Hamburg: Rowohlt, 1955), 808. There would have been more truth, I think, in the statement, "In *Törless* the mode of depiction is the excuse."

3. Musil, *Young Törless*, 132. Henceforth, all English-language quotations are taken from this version, and page numbers are given in parentheses in the chapter. For the reader's convenience, I add onto these page numbers corresponding page numbers (with asterisks) from *Die Verwirrungen des Zöglings Törleß* (Hamburg: Rowohlt Taschenbuch Verlag, 1959). The quote above is found on 88*.

4. No wonder, since "Basini is in fact introduced into the structure of the novel as deputy and precursor of Törless." Stefan Howald, *Ästhetizismus und äs-*

thetische Ideologiekritik: Untersuchungen zum Romanwerk Robert Musils (Munich: Fink, 1984), 46.

5. More is involved, of course, than an abstract sense of difference. As Martin Swales points out, "In mimetic terms we have a narrator who is clearly, and securely, in possession of the outcome of the tale. . . . And this superior knowledge is allowed to inform the narrative performance at every turn." Swales, "Narrator and Hero: Observations on Robert Musil's *Törless*," in *Musil in Focus: Papers from a Centenary Symposium*, ed. Lothar Huber and John J. White (London: Institute of Germanic Studies, University of London, 1982), 2.

6. Eric Miller, "Fictional Representation: A Philosophical Study," doctoral diss., Princeton University, 1992, 308.

7. For example, if a part of Thomas Mann's *Joseph* tetralogy is narrated from the explicit standpoint of an angel, it is still not unreasonable to think of this fictive narrator as representing "aspects" of Thomas Mann's "personality."

8. Musil was inclined to deny the literal, autobiographical truth of the scenes and events in *Young Törless*. He said that he had been willing, for one thing, in 1901 "to make a gift of the plot" to a few "Naturalistic" writers he knew (*Tagebücher*, 803). Peter Henninger stresses how, for Musil, *Young Törless* did not constitute a deeply autobiographical, a deeply private enterprise. A year and a half after writing it, Musil began a second autobiographical novel, which he elaborated for years, bringing to this project matters that allegedly touched him more intimately than the theme of *Törless*. Henninger, *Der Buchstabe und der Geist: Unbewußte Determinierung im Schreiben Robert Musils* (Frankfurt a.M., Bern, Cirencester, U.K.: Lang, 1980), 145. The bisexual behavior described in *Young Törless*, wrote Musil, was hardly crucial: other forms of sexual pathology—"sadism, masochism, fetishism," for example—would have served as well (*Tagebücher*, 723). (It is bemusing to think of Musil *opposing* sadism and masochism to the kinds of sexual exploitation described in *Törless*.) See, further, notes 12 and 28.

9. The German word for the kind of school Törless is attending is "Konvikt," normally, an Austrian Roman Catholic boarding school.

10. Hannah Hickman, *Robert Musil and the Culture of Vienna* (La Salle, Ill.: Open Court, 1984), 28.

11. The back cover of *Young Törless* simply and audaciously describes this novel as "set in a military boarding school" and illustrates the cover with a drawing by Dagmar Frinta of a cadet holding a large boot in his gloved hand. The German-language Rowohlt edition, which has sold around a million copies, also shows on the cover a cadet wearing a shako. These are presumptions, very likely dictated by publicists' considerations—namely, the desire to make intuitively evident the "militaristic" or "fascistic" bearing of the novel's per-

sons and events as precursors of "today's dictators *in nucleo*" (Musil, *Tagebücher*, 441).

12. Volker Schlöndorff's film *Der junge Törleß* (1966) depicts the students at W. as cadets, though they do not wear shakos; and in an interview, he described the venue as a "military academy [*Kadettenanstalt*]," adding, however, that he had never conceived of his project as a faithful film adaptation. Robert Fischer and Joe Hembus, *Der neue deutsche Film, 1960–1980* (Munich: Goldmann, 1981), 29.

What was Musil's view on the fidelity of the novel to his experience? What he said could justify opposite positions. In a later biographical draft he declared that of the various motives inspiring his work, the confessional never played a role: he was not concerned "to analyze, portray, put to the test, or defend [himself] or confess, ask for absolution, repent, or plead for pardon. And yet, many people saw my first book as a confessional." On the other hand, he is supposed to have said to Klaus Pinkus: "I never invented a single word in *Törless*." See Karl Corino, "Törless Ignotus: Zu den biographischen Hintergründen von Robert Musils Roman 'Die Verwirrungen des Zöglings Törleß,'" *Text + Kritik* 21/22 (1972): 61. It is noteworthy that in his late autobiographical drafts Musil dwells on the military paraphernalia at the school where he was educated—pike and regimentals and dress boots—but there is hardly a trace of such things in Törless's school at "W."

13. Musil, *Tagebücher*, 776.

14. Friedrich Nietzsche, *Werke in drei Bänden*, ed. Karl Schlechta (Munich: Hanser, 1954–56), 1:1090.

15. Lars W. Freij has written a valuable monograph entitled *Türlosigkeit— Robert Musils "Törleß" in Mikroanalysen mit Ausblicken auf andere Texte des Dichters* (Stockholm: Almqvist and Wiksell), 1972. Compare, further, Kafka's journal entry for October 21, 1921: "All is imaginary—family, office, friends, the street, all imaginary, far away or close at hand, woman the closest. The truth, however, is only this, that you are beating your head against the wall of a windowless and doorless [*türlose*] cell." *The Diaries of Franz Kafka, 1914–1923*, trans. Martin Greenberg (New York: Schocken, 1949), 197. Translation modified in light of Franz Kafka, *Tagebücher, Band 3: 1914–1923*, in *Franz Kafka, Gesammelte Werke in zwölf Bänden, nach der Kritischen Ausgabe (KKA)*, ed. Hans-Gerd Koch (Frankfurt a.M.: Fischer Taschenbuch Verlag, 1994), 11:192.

16. The passage reads: "For the object of this longing, the image of his parents, actually ceased to have any place in it at all: *I* mean that certain plastic, physical memory of a loved person which is not merely remembrance but something speaking to all the senses and preserved in all the senses, so that one cannot do anything without feeling the other person silent and invisible at one's side" (4, 9*) (my emphasis). The identification of the first-person speaker was,

to my knowledge, first made by Burton Pike in *Robert Musil: An Introduction to His Work* (Ithaca, N.Y.: Cornell University Press, 1961), 45. In *Crisis and Continuity in Modern German Fiction: Ten Essays* (Ithaca, N.Y.: Cornell University Press, 1969), Henry Hatfield notes: "At one point, apparently inadvertently, the narrator calls himself 'I' " (181). Martin Swales discusses this point: "If Törless's development . . . can be seen . . . as an assimilation to the narrative perspective, then this explains why the narrative voice is . . . so insistently in the foreground. . . . The urgency of narrative entry here has to do with the constant intimation that . . . the making of this fiction is the only adequate medium for conveying the import of Törless's experiences" ("Narrator and Hero," 8). This analysis is surely correct, but the narrative structure can also be a reminiscence of the opening, also in a school, of *Madame Bovary*. There too the first-person narrative pronoun promptly disappears.

17. In "Narrator and Hero," Swales develops the view that the narrative perspective may be regarded as a projection of the sensibility of the emergent Törless, stressing, too, its apologetic character. It is true that the perspectives of both Törless 1 and Törless 2 appear to fuse. Dorrit Cohn notes the effect of the abundance of similes in Musil's psycho-narrative: They "seem to induce a fusion between the narrating and the figural consciousness by blurring the line that separates them." In *Transparent Minds: Narrative Modes for Presenting Consciousness in Fiction* (Princeton: Princeton University Press, 1978), 43.

18. See Stanley Corngold, *The Fate of the Self: German Writers and French Theory* (New York: Columbia University Press, 1986), 161–79. In "Without a Key: The Narrative Structure of *Das Schloss*," *The Germanic Review* 66, 3 (Summer 1991), 132–40, Eric Miller affirms the extraordinary paucity of telling information conveyed by breaks in Kafka's narrative perspective in *The Castle*.

19. The first critic known to me to have grasped *Young Törless* as a type of *Künstlerroman*—a novel portraying the unfolding of a young artist—is Theodore Ziolkowski, in "James Joyces Epiphanie und die Überwindung der empirischen Welt in der modernen deutsche Prosa," *Deutsche Vierteljahrsschrift* 35 (1961): 594–616.

20. Swales, in "Narrator and Hero," also cites Törless's newfound metaphorical powers as he defends himself before the school investigators: "These words and these figures of speech, which were far beyond what was appropriate to Törless's age, flowed easily and naturally from his lips in the state of vast excitement he was in, in this moment of almost poetic inspiration" (212).

21. From the chapter "La morale des mystiques," in Maeterlinck, *Le Trésor des humbles* (1898). For a detailed discussion of this passage, see Elisabeth Stopp, "Musil's 'Törless': Content and Form," *Modern Language Review* 63 (1968): 110.

22. Pike, *Robert Musil*, 43.

23. Törless declares to Beineberg that his intellectual life is a fraud (24).

24. Dorrit Cohn discusses the category "witness biography" in her study of "Freud's Case Histories and the Question of Fictionality," in *Telling Facts: History and Narration in Psychoanalysis*, ed. Joseph H. Smith and Humphrey Morris (Baltimore: Johns Hopkins University Press, 1992), 21–47.

25. Stephen R. L. Clark, "Aware if Alive" (a review of *The Explicit Animal* by Raymond Tallis), *The Times Literary Supplement* (August 6, 1993): 28. Clark thinks that Jaynes's account begs the question.

26. Wilhelm Dilthey, *Gesammelte Schriften* (Leipzig: Teubner; Göttingen: Vandenhoeck and Ruprecht, 1914–77), 7:206. Indeed, it might be possible to characterize the general project of turn-of-the-century Austrian literature as a basic complication of the arc leading from inwardness (the motive) to the expression—a complication, especially, of representation and the syntax of representation. In Hofmannthal's Lord Chandos letter, the arc breaks down entirely. In a story found in Kafka's diary, a kind of dramatized dialogue that begins "'You,' I said . . . ," the relationship of motive to expression is distinctively deficient. See Stanley Corngold, *Franz Kafka: The Necessity of Form* (Ithaca, N.Y.: Cornell University Press, 1988), 14.

27. Oscar Wilde, too, "depreciated action in favor of imagination because it was 'a thing incomplete in its essence, because limited by accident, and ignorant of its direction, being always at variance with its aim.'" Cited in Geoffrey Hartman, "Looking Back on Paul de Man" in *Reading de Man Reading*, ed. Lindsay Waters and Wlad Godzich (Minneapolis: University of Minnesota Press, 1989), 21.

28. That Törless's moods will strike readers as occasions for powerful revelations emerges partly from the cognitive importance attached to that category by phenomenological and existentialist writers. Many readers will read *Törless* in the perspectives, for example, of Heidegger's remarkable discussion of moods in *Being and Time* (1927) and *What Is Metaphysics?* (1929). A passage in *Being and Time* from the discussion of *Befindlichkeiten* (approximately, "ways of being in the world") defines Heidegger's stance: "The possibilities of disclosure which belong to cognition reach far too short a way compared with the primordial disclosure belonging to moods, in which Dasein is brought before its Being as 'there.' . . . From the existential-ontological point of view, there is not the slightest justification for minimizing what is 'evident' in states-of-mind, by measuring it against the apodictic certainty of a theoretical cognition of something which is purely present-at-hand. However, the phenomena are no less falsified when they are banished to the sanctuary of the irrational." Martin Heidegger, *Being and Time*, trans. John Macquarrie and Edward Robinson (New York: Harper and Row, 1962), 173–75. For Heidegger, the powers of mood to disclose exceed the theoretical knowledge of objects present at hand.

In *Törless*, moods figure as the noetic correlatives of what are called symbols.

Symbolic knowledge means felt saturation by the appropriate mood. At the outset of the novel the symbol of parallel railroad tracks conjures, for example, a correlative mood of isolation, of being lost. In his journals, thinking about *Törless*, Musil profiled the crucial constitutive power of moods: "It isn't stated that these things had this or that mood, but they have it. The attitude was in me" (Musil, *Tagebücher*, 132).

29. "Themes"—passivity, sexuality; "rhetorical features"—obsessive images, for example, poison.

30. Compare the phenomenon that Hölderlin described as a feature of Empedocles' torn subjectivity: "he distinguishes more, thinks more, compares more, forms more, organizes more, and is more organized *when he is less self-possessed (bei sich selber) and in so far as he is less conscious of himself.*" See Chapter 3.

31. See Henninger, *Der Buchstabe*, 115.

32. According to criteria recently proposed in discussion by Dominick LaCapra, *Törless* here becomes a work eminently and legitimately deconstructible. Indeed *Törless* is the very model of the self-deconstructing text. The novel sets about excluding the *scapegoat figure* (Basini) from the human community on the strength of his difference only to show subliminally—on the basis of poison and passivity—that the pillar of the community (Törless) and Basini are one and the same.

33. Corino, in *"Törleß Ignotus,"* acknowledges the risk of inculpation very pointedly. In his view, *Törless* is an autobiographical novel. Presumably unaware of the research by Ernst Kaiser reported in Stopp ("Musil's 'Törless,'" 98), Corino identified the originals of Reiting, Beineberg, and Basini, whose names Musil only very slightly altered. And Corino demystifies Musil's claim to have had nothing real and personal in mind with the plot of *Young Törless* on the grounds that to have done otherwise would have been to expose himself to juridical charges of character defamation or worse (62).

34. "For as though independently of himself, Törless's intellect lashed out, inexorably, at the sensitive young prince" (8, 12*).

35. Howald, in *Ästhetizismus*, notes the "narrator's unequivocal identification with Törless's instrumental stance" in the following passage: "It would be entirely wrong to believe that Basini had aroused in Törless a desire that was—however fleetingly and perplexedly—a thoroughgoing and real one. True, something like passion had been aroused in him, but 'love' was quite certainly only a casual, haphazard term for it, and the boy Basini himself was no more than a substitute, a provisional object of this longing. For although Törless did debase himself with him, his desire was never satisfied by him; on the contrary, it went on growing out beyond Basini, growing out into some new and aimless craving" (165).

36. Musil, *Tagebücher*, 429.

37. Howald's chapter on *Törless* in *Ästhetizismus* correctly puts pressure on the "integrity" of the narrator. Howald is alert to the major strain of special pleading throughout the novel—Musil's way of "solving" the problem of the expressiveness of inner experience by describing the actual resolutions of it made by his hero, even though he "conceives of his hero in strictly dichotomous terms of aesthetic sensibility and rational judgment" (32). Howald notes, for example, that the immature and retrograde character of Törless's "sensuality" is made into a mark of special distinction vis-à-vis the others. Törless has a "depth" that the others do not have. He is superior to his group by virtue of his "refined psychological interest in Basini and the aesthetic pleasure he draws from it" (47). The narrator profiles the aesthetic pleasure arising from the shattering of that human subject caught up in conventional values opposed to sensuality (37); certainly consciousness of the other human subject instrumental in the shattering is repressed (39). On the other hand, this destruction is incorporated as a fact into the narrator's general argument on necessary although transitional phases of moral development. Therefore, "if aestheticism neutralizes the social-critical force of immoralism and thus in the end works toward a morality of social conformism," aestheticism also appears to subserve an argument for genuine moral development (40). This is an important and unmastered contradiction.

38. I want to profile once again my conclusion as to the status of the narrator of *Young Törless*. "His" position is best situated outside two extreme positions, both of which I discard: they are the model of identity between the perspective of the author Musil and that of young Törless; and the model of radical disjunction between the author and his character—a disjunction so absolute that it is alleged also to include the radical disjunction between the author and the narrator.

The first model of identity is proposed, for example, by Gert Mattenklott, who writes, "It can be shown that the author has no superiority of knowledge over his hero. . . . Törless's aesthetic mode of perception is not only the theme of a novel about an artist; it actually *determines* the novel's own perspective." Gert Mattenklott, "Der 'subjektive Faktor' in Musils 'Törleß,' " *Robert Musil, Wege der Forschung*, vol. 588, ed. Renate von Heydebrand (Darmstadt: Wissenschaftliche Buchgesellschaft, 1982), 258, 275 (my emphasis).

This argument is clearly indefensible, because it discounts the novel's many moments of enacted disjunction. The narrator knows the direction of Törless's perplexities, as Törless himself does not, and generalizes them in a theory of necessary development. In many important places the narrator's stance is mediated by the perspective of the grown-up Törless—congruent but not identical with his own and harder and cleverer than young Törless's.

As a corrective to Mattenklott, one is inclined to suggest that even the "authorial" narrator of this novel is a fiction constructed by the author. This extreme position is implied in Eckhard Heftrich's account of Törless at work on his autobiography:

"Törless had bought himself a copy-book and now carefully set out his pen and ink. Then, after some hesitation, he wrote on the first page: De natura hominum. The Latin title was, he thought, the philosophic subject's due. Then he drew a large artistic curlicue round the title and leaned back in his chair to wait until it dried" (131, 88★). Eckhard Heftrich notes, "This is characteristically the only scene in the book in which the author *has his narrator become entirely ironic,*" in *Musil—Eine Einführung* (Munich and Zurich: Artemis, 1986), 36 (my emphasis).

But the implications of this theory are unacceptable, for they put an impassable divide between the empirical author Musil and his narrator. It becomes impossible to say a single certain thing by way of explanation, motivation, and intent about Musil's relation to his novel as a whole. If the narrative is itself a consciously fictive construction, then Musil can be holding it up for our incredulity, too, as only the kind of narrative told by the kind of narrator whose diction and opinions are no better than they are. It is interesting that exponents of this formalist principle (of the fictive authorial narrator) are determined to dignify its product as literature and never to denigrate it as a fabrication, evasion, or contrivance; yet by the latter assumption, which cannot be refuted, the twenty-two-year-old Musil could also have constructed this telling of the tale as an example of perfectly sculptured error. *In fact* he could have told it infinitely better or with an entirely different bearing. . . . One can see that this assumption is so instrumentally fruitless as to be false.

I therefore conclude that Musil constructs a heterogenous narrative position out of a bundle of paradoxical motives, of which one is much the strongest. The narrator must speak on his behalf, with intimate knowledge of a special episode—a knowledge that could only have been obtained from personal involvement in that experience and one, therefore, that could only have been in the main experienced by Musil. Yet this intimate knowledge must not involve the risk of legal or any other sort of inculpation.

I would therefore be prepared to accept Howald's interchangeable use of the terms "Musil" and "narrator" (Howald, *Ästhetizismus*, 22–80) except for the fact that this occludes the whole complex of distancing gestures at work in *Törless*—products of the built-in injunction that no reader take the narrator to be Musil. I have argued that the best approximate model for the narrator is a "friend"—of Törless's—and insofar as "Törless" is the alias of a real person, a "friend" of Musil's. This "friend" speaks on behalf of Musil but deflects censure to himself. The author displaces the narrative position from an identifiable position of real speaking, disguising the speaker beyond recovery but in his manner of doing so *becomes* Musil. For the relation of the empirical author to his narrator, Michael Jennings suggests the phrase "tormented complicity."

Chapter 6

1. This is the language of the experience Kafka attributes to "K.," the hero of his last novel. Franz Kafka, *Das Schloß*, in *Franz Kafka, Gesammelte Werke in zwölf Bänden, nach der Kritischen Ausgabe* (*KKA*), ed. Hans-Gerd Koch (Frankfurt a.m.: Fischer Taschenbuch Verlag, 1994), 4:55. K. belongs to the type of the modern German epic hero who, from the standpoint of the local inhabitant, "gives one the feeling that he came from a country where nobody else lived." The latter phrase describes Adrian Leverkühn, the artist-hero of Thomas Mann's *Doctor Faustus* (New York: Vintage, 1948), 411.

2. "Had one to name the author who comes nearest to bearing the same kind of relation to our age as Dante, Shakespeare, and Goethe bore to theirs, Kafka is the first one would think of." W. H. Auden, "The Wandering Jew," *The New Republic* (Feb. 10, 1941): 185–86. Cited in "Introduction," by Angel Flores and Homer Swander, *Franz Kafka Today*, ed. Angel Flores and Homer Swander (Madison: University of Wisconsin Press, 1964), 1.

3. Gerhard Kurz, *Traum-Schrecken. Kafkas literarische Existenzanalyse* (Stuttgart: Metzler, 1980), 150.

4. Other possibilities—*The Man Who Disappeared, Lost Without Trace*—have been proposed by the late Roy Pascal in his splendid essay on Kafka in *The German Novel* (London: Methuen, 1965), 318.

5. Kafka began writing a version of his "America novel" in late 1911 and then broke it off in August 1912; this version has not survived. The text we have arose in fall 1912; Kafka wrote on it off and on until October 1914.

6. *Briefe an Felice*, ed. Erich Heller and Jürgen Born (Frankfurt a.M.: Fischer, 1967), 101–2.

7. Ibid., 105.

8. Ibid., 160.

9. Lou-Albert Lasard, *Wege mit Rilke* (Frankfurt a.M.: Fischer, 1952), 43.

10. Franz Kafka, *America*, trans. Edwin Muir and Willa Muir (London: Routledge, 1938), 52. Translation modified.

11. To the best of my knowledge Gayatri Chakravorty Spivak was the first to identify the idea of "commerce," "the flow of commodities," in Kafka's word *Verkehr*. "In Kafka's code," she writes, "the word translated as 'traffic,' (*Verkehr*), is also the word for 'commerce,' and it is the word that is used everywhere in all the literature of political economy (including, most significantly, Marx) in German." "Discussion [following my paper "Consternation: The Anthropological Moment in Literature"], in *Literature and Anthropology*, ed. Jonathan Hall

and Ackbar Abbas (Hong Kong: Hong Kong University Press, 1986), 192. Mark Anderson has richly developed this meaning and others in "Kafka in America: Notes on a Travelling Narrative," in *Kafka's Clothes: Ornament and Aestheticism in the Habsburg Fin de Siècle* (Oxford: Clarendon Press, 1992), 98–122.

12. Franz Kafka, *Tagebücher 1914–1923*, in *Franz Kafka, Gesammelte Werke in zwölf Bänden, nach der Kritischen Ausgabe (KKA)*, 3:101.

13. As is the case in the very interesting movie version *Klassenverhältnisse* by Daniele Huillet and Jean Marie Straub.

14. When I wrote these lines, I had not yet read Roland Reuss's acerbic critique of the *KKA* for the deviations from Kafka's manuscripts that have found their way into the Manuscript Edition. To the extent that these changes conform to a pattern, they can be summed up as follows: the *KKA* does not indicate in its apparatus where Kafka's crossed-out "mistakes" are located on the line; it adds periods when there are none in the manuscripts, adds quotation marks to form pairs of such marks when one is missing, and substitutes "ß" for "ss" when deemed appropriate to "normal" orthography. It makes many of these changes without informing the reader. See Roland Reuss, "'genug Achtung vor der Schrift'? Zu: Franz Kafka, Schriften Tagebücher, Briefe. Kritische Ausgabe," *Text Kritische Beiträge* 1:107–26. The edition that is at work typographically reproducing Kafka's manuscripts is the *Franz Kafka-Ausgabe (FKA)* of the Stroemfeld/Roter Stern Publishing House, but *The Boy Who Sank Out of Sight* has not yet appeared in this edition. See further my "On Translation Mistakes, with Special Attention to Kafka in Amerika," in *Zwiesprache: Theorie und Geschichte des Übersetzens*, ed. Ulrich Stadler (Stuttgart: Metzler, 1996), 143–57.

15. Franz Kafka, *Beschreibungen eines Kampfes und andere Schriften aus dem Nachlaß*, in *Franz Kafka, Gesammelte Werke in zwölf Bänden, nach der Kritischen Ausgabe (KKA)*, 5:11–13.

16. *Der Prager Kreis* (Stuttgart, Berlin, Cologne, Mainz: W. Kohlhammer, 1966). Mark Anderson has also perceived the usefulness of this essay for his reading of *The Boy Who Sank Out of Sight*, which chiefly concerns the wandering, erratic visuality of Karl Rossmann's experience (Anderson, *Kafka's Clothes*, 120). I shall be concerned, however, with the antithetical experience of *rapture*: Karl fixates on individual images and loses himself, or unconsciously finds himself, in the act of seeing without apperception.

17. In *Gegenwart* [a Berlin weekly], vol. 69, nos. 7 and 8, February 17 and 24, 1906.

18. *Der Prager Kreis*, 93.

19. The Schopenhauerian gesture in Kafka's response is largely unavoidable

since Brod's text already contains this reference. In one place he mentions Schopenhauer by name and in another writes: "The beautiful never falls into the sphere of the will: it is independent of personal interest" (No. 7/103).

20. Ibid., 94.

21. In fact, Brod never literally employs this term, although he certainly writes about "aesthetic apperception." Meanwhile, he does define "apperception" quite adequately. See note 25.

22. In *The Human Motor: Energy, Fatigue, and the Origins of Modernity* (New York: Basic Books, 1990), Anson Rabinbach discusses the late nineteenth-century preoccupation with "the new calculus of energy and fatigue" (9): "For Nietzsche, as for many nineteenth-century thinkers, fatigue was identified with modernity itself." To Nietzsche's—and Huysmans's and Weber's—testimony we can now add Kafka's.

23. In Hermann Broch's trilogy *The Sleepwalkers* the character Bertrand observes, "How completely imprisoned we all are in conventional feeling. But feelings are inert, and that's why they're so cruel. The world is ruled by the inertia of feeling" (53). Again this position might sooner be attached to Kant than to Kafka, for whom the world is ruled by inertia pure and simple.

24. Brod has talked about the "aesthetic *zone* [*Zone*]," the mental space capable of accommodating newness in experience and hence of allowing aesthetic pleasure to occur. Kafka rewrites the word "zone" as "edge [*Kante*]."

25. Here is Brod's fuller definition of the term "apperception," which he abstracts from contemporary, turn-of-the-century psychology: "By 'apperception' psychology understands the reception and appropriation [*Aufname und Aneignung*] of a newly occurring perception [*Vorstellung*] by means of an already existing perception or entire cluster of perceptions. In different psychological systems the terminology varies.—Consider the mind at a certain moment in time. It evidently contains a host of perceptions, memory-images, fantasies, concepts, etc. As each new perception enters the mind, this perception selects from the abundance of existing perceptions one that is related to it and joins itself to it. This assimilation and enrichment of the mind is termed 'apperception.' As Volkmann notes, 'Every newly entering perception disturbs the hovering assimilation [*schwebende Angliederung*] of the older perception. To this extent it disturbs the composure of the spirit; hence the movement contains something of the character of *affect*' [*Grundriß der Psychologie*]." There is as yet nothing in this account, however, about *aesthetic* apperception.

26. Immanuel Kant, *The Critique of Judgement*, trans. James Creed Meredith (Oxford: Clarendon, 1964), 35.

27. "'Thus it is easily [*zwanglos*, unforcedly] explained . . .' That will come as no surprise, for from the beginning everything is already anticipatorily [*vor-*

greifend, proleptically] forced to cling to the apperception, as to a banister." The diction of the subject matter of the proof theorem appears to mingle with that of doing theorems.

" 'From the same theory [is] explained . . .': that is a little trick [*Kunst-stückchen*]. From this sentence—that is, as best as I can get a clear view on it—there follows the sole proof of the theory, which proof, therefore, you had to experience first [*zuerst*] and not as a consequence. 'One instinctively resists . . .': this sentence is a traitor."

28. *Das Schloss*, 280. I discuss this passage in *Franz Kafka: The Necessity of Form* (Ithaca, N.Y.: Cornell University Press, 1988), 154.

29. "He sees everything solidly and ambiguously at the same time." Edwin Muir, "Introductory Note," in Kafka, *America*, vii.

30. My translation of the following passages from *The Boy Who Sank Out of Sight* is occasionally abridged to highlight their saliency.

31. Franz Kafka, *Der Verschollene*, in *Franz Kafka, Gesammelte Werke in zwölf Bänden, Nach der Kritischen Ausgabe* (*KKA*), 60.

32. Ibid., 132.   33. Ibid., 162.

34. Ibid., 201.   35. Ibid., 200.

36. Ibid., 209.

37. Walter Benjamin, "The Work of Art in the Age of Mechanical Repro-duction," *Illuminations*, ed. Hannah Arendt, trans. Harry Zohn (New York: Harcourt, Brace and World, 1968), 242.

38. "The greater the share of the shock factor in particular impressions, the more constantly consciousness has to be alert as a screen against stimuli; the more effectively it does so, the less do these impressions enter experience (*Erfahrung*), tending to remain in the sphere of a certain hour of one's life (*Er-lebnis*)." Walter Benjamin, "On Some Motifs in Baudelaire," *Illuminations*, 165.

39. *Der Verschollene*, 9.

40. Readers of Derrida on Nietzsche take note.

41. Or, perhaps, "them's some apples!"

42. Or, perhaps, "the whole nine yards."

43. *Der Verschollene*, 289–94.

44. Ibid., 94.

45. "I brought Kafka several new books from Neugebauer bookstore to look at. As he leafed through the pages of a volume with drawings by Georg Grosz, he said: . . ." Gustav Janouch, *Gespräche mit Kafka* (Frankfurt: S. Fischer, 1968), 205. The drawing referred to by Janouch allegedly appeared in a book published before 1921. Even with the help of the Grosz scholar Beth Lewis, I have not been able to locate any such drawing. It does resemble in certain ways the draw-ing "Abrechnung folgt," 1922.

46. Janouch, *Gespräche mit Kafka*, 206. The complete quote: "Capitalism is a

system of relationships, which go from inside to out, from outside to in, from above to below, and from below to above. Everything is relative, everything is in chains. Capitalism is a condition both of the world and of the soul." *Conversations with Kafka*, trans. Goronwy Rees (New York: New Directions, 1968), 151–52.

47. This mention of commodities derives from the chapter entitled "The Fetishism of Commodities" in Marx's *Capital*, vol. I.

48. Franz Kafka, *Tagebücher*, Band 1: 1909–1912, in *Franz Kafka, Gesammelte Werke in zwölf Bänden, Nach der Kritischen Ausgabe (KKA)*, 90.

49. *Dearest Father*, trans. Ernst Kaiser and Eithne Wilkins (New York: Schocken, 1949), 40.

50. *The Diaries of Franz Kafka, 1914–1923*, trans. Martin Greenberg (New York: Schocken, 1949), 200–201.

Chapter 7

1. Walther Killy and Hans Szklenar, *Georg Trakl: Dichtungen und Briefe*. Historische-Kritische Ausgabe, 2 vols. I: Gedichte. II: Dokumente und Zeugnisse, Briefe (Salzburg: Muller, 1969).

2. Walther Killy, *Über Georg Trakl* (Gottingen: Vandenhoeck and Ruprecht, 1967), 34. For a summary of the various ways critics have attempted to identify Trakl's "meaningless" diction—calling Trakl's sequences "noncausal but rather local," "evocative," "hermetic," "oscillations between sense and senselessness"—see Ulrike Rainer, "Georg Trakls *Elis*-Gedichte: Das Problem der dichterischen Existenz," *Monatshefte* 72, 4 (1980): 401–15.

3. This problematic is thematized apropos of Hölderlin's poetry in terms of "muteness" and "excess of signification" by Eric Santner, on p. x and throughout his study *Friedrich Hölderlin: Narrative Vigilance and the Poetic Imagination* (New Brunswick: Rutgers University Press, 1986).

4. "Georg Trakl in wechselnder Deutung," *Literatur und Kritik* 93 (1975): 133. Cited in Michael Sharp, "Georg Trakl: Poetry and Psychopathology," in *The Turn of the Century: German Literature and Art, 1890–1915*, ed. Gerald Chapple and Hans H. Schulte (Bonn: Bouvier, 1981), 126.

5. For an excellent skeptical piece on Heidegger's reading of Trakl, see Véronique Fóti, "The Path of the Stranger: On Heidegger's Interpretation of Georg Trakl," in *Review of Existential Psychology and Psychiatry* 17, 2 and 3 (1986): 223–33.

6. Bernhard Böschenstein, "Hölderlins späteste Gedichte," in *Über Hölderlin*, ed. Jochen Schmidt (Frankfurt: Insel, 1970), 174.

7. Siegbert Prawer, "Grammetrical Reflections on Trakl's 'De Profundis,'" *German Life and Letters* 22, 1 (October 1968): 48–59.

8. Maire Kurrik, *Georg Trakl* (New York: Columbia University Press, 1966). Michael Francis Sharp, *The Poet's Madness: A Reading of Georg Trakl* (Ithaca, N.Y.: Cornell University Press, 1981).

9. Sharp, *The Poet's Madness*, 48 and throughout.

10. Kurrik, *Georg Trakl*, 9.

11. Sharp, "Georg Trakl: Poetry and Psychopathology," 126.

12. Michael Hamburger, "'Trakl in English.' Reading and Discussion of Translations of Selected Poems," in *Londoner Trakl-Symposion*, ed. William E. Yuill and Walter Methlagl (Salzburg: Otto Müller Verlag, 1981), 118. With word-for-word literalism the first stanza of *De Profundis* reads: "It is a stubble-field, into which a black rain falls. / It is a brown tree, which stands there, lonely. / It is a hissing wind, which circles round empty huts. / How sad this evening."

13. Prawer, "Grammetrical Reflections," 52.

14. Friedrich Hölderlin, *Sämtliche Werke*, ed. Friedrich Beißner (Stuttgart: Kohlhammer, 1961), 3:150.

15. *Friedrich Hölderlin: "Bevestigter Gesang": Die neu zu entdeckende hymnische Spätdichtung bis 1806*, ed. Dietrich Uffhausen (Stuttgart: Metzler, 1989), 62, 60.

16. Cited in Simon Goldhill, *Reading Greek Tragedy* (Cambridge: Cambridge University Press, 1986), vi.

17. An "aporia" is a passage in speech or writing incorporating or presenting an irresolvable difficulty or a doubt.

18. In *Erinnerung an Georg Trakl*, 11. Cited (in German) in Sharp, "Georg Trakl: Poetry and Psychopathology," 121.

19. Walter Benjamin, *Kleine Prosa, Baudelaire Übertragungen*, in *Gesammelte Schriften*, in Suhrkamp-Taschenbuch Wissenschaft 934, ed. Tilman Rexroth (Frankfurt a.M.: Suhrkamp, 1972), IV:1:101.

20. Hölderlin, *Sämtliche Werke*, 3:15. Friedrich Hölderlin, *Hyperion and Selected Poems*, ed. Eric L. Santner (New York: Continuum, 1990), 1–133.

21. In Thomas Mann's *Doctor Faustus* Nepomuk Schneidewein is Adrian Leverkühn's "Neffe und . . . Augenweide [nephew and feast for his eyes]."

22. I owe the last two examples to a most incisive letter from Professor Sigrid Mayer of the University of Wyoming.

23. Compare the observation made by Walter Kaufmann apropos of a suggestive sentence in Nietzsche's *The Birth of Tragedy*. Nietzsche wrote about the tragic chorus, "The chorus is the 'ideal spectator' insofar as it is the only beholder, the beholder of the visionary world of the scene [Der Chor ist der 'idealische Zuschauer,' insofern es der einzige *Schauer* ist, der Schauer der Visionswelt der Szene]." (The German can be found in Friedrich Nietzsche, *Werke in drei Bänden*, ed. Karl Schlechta [Munich: Carl Hanser Verlag, 1954],

1:50.) Kaufmann adds, "The word *Schauer* could also mean shudder, the shudder of holy awe; and while this is certainly not the primary meaning intended here, it somehow enters into the coloring of the sentence." *The Birth of Tragedy,* in *Basic Writings of Nietzsche,* trans. and ed. Walter Kaufmann (New York: The Modern Library, 1968), 62.

24. Fóti, "The Path of the Stranger," 228.

25. The assonantal side of Trakl's language encourages slippage, dissolves firm distinctions. Winfried Kudszus, in a meditation on Trakl, is drawn by Trakl to re-pose Rilke's famous question: "*Wer war* Trakl?" and founders knowingly on the assonance of his own question: "The difference between the word related to identity and the one referring to time is minimal. . . . Who will want to insist on categorical difference, on separations made once and for all, on divisions between time and identity?" Winfried Kudszus, *Poetic Process* (Lincoln: University of Nebraska Press, 1995), 2.

26. In a gripping passage from the *Denkwürdigkeiten eines Nervenkranken* composed by the German jurist Daniel Paul Schreber, an older contemporary of Trakl and himself a paranoid schizophrenic of genius, he describes the speech of the nervous birds he hallucinates: "The miraculously created birds do not understand the *meaning* of the words they speak; but apparently they have a natural sensitivity for the *similarity of sounds.* Therefore if, while reeling off the automatic phrases, they perceive *either* in the vibrations of my own nerves (my thoughts) *or* in speech of people around me, words which *sound* the same or similar to their own phrases, they apparently experience surprise and in a way fall for the similarity of sound; in other words the surprise makes them forget the rest of their mechanical phrases, and they suddenly pass over into *genuine* feeling" (*Memoirs of My Nervous Illness,* trans. Ida Macalpine and Richard A. Hunter [Cambridge, Mass.: Harvard University Press, 1988], 168–69). The strong surprise these birds feel at perceiving assonance stresses the necessary qualification on the ecstasy of semantic dissonance I've posited, the fact that it proceeds in a field of homophonous order and articulation, of phonetic assonance, which itself excites strong feeling, so that this shattering dissonance must be described as the complex, negative pleasure of undoing pleasure. For a rich analysis of the Schreber phenomenon, see Eric Santner, *My Own Private Germany: Daniel Paul Schreber's Secret History of Modernity* (Princeton: Princeton University Press, 1996).

Chapter 8

1. The German text of "Dichtermuth" and "Blödigkeit" follow, from *Friedrich Hölderlin: "Bevestigter Gesang": Die neu zu entdeckende hymnische Spätdichtung bis 1806,* ed. Dietrich Uffhausen (Stuttgart: Metzler, 1989), 56–57.

DICHTERMUTH

Sind denn dir nicht verwandt alle Lebendigen?
　　Nährt zum Dienste denn nicht selber die Parze dich?
　　　　Drum! so wandle nur wehrlos
　　　　　　Fort durch's Leben, und sorge nicht!

Was geschiehet, es sei alles gesegnet dir,
　　Sei zur Freude gewandt! oder was könnte denn
　　　　Dich belaidigen, Herz! was
　　　　　　Da begegnen, wohin du sollst?

Denn seitdem der Gesang sterblichen Lippen sich
　　Friedenathmend entwand, frommend in Laid und Glük
　　　　Unsre Weise der Menschen
　　　　　　Herz erfreute, so waren auch

Wir, die Sänger des Volks, gerne bei Lebenden,
　　Wo sich vieles gesellt, freudig und jedem hold,
　　　　Jedem offen; so ist ja
　　　　　　Unser [Vater] Ahne der Sonnengott,

Der den fröhlichen Tag Armen und Reichen gönnt,
　　Der in flüchtiger Zeit uns, die Vergänglichen,
　　　　Aufgerichtet an goldnen
　　　　　　Gängelbänden, wie Kinder, hält.

Ihn erwartet, auch ihn nimmt, wo die Stunde kömmt,
　　Seine purpurne Fluth; sieh! und das edle Licht
　　　　Gehet, kundig des Wandels,
　　　　　　Gleichgesinnet hinab den Pfad.

So vergehe denn auch, wenn es die Zeit einst ist
　　Und dem Geiste sein Recht nirgend gebricht, so sterb'
　　　　Einst im Ernste des Lebens
　　　　　　Unsre Freude, doch schönen Tod!

BLÖDIGKEIT

Sind denn dir nicht bekannt viele Lebendigen?
　　Geht auf Wahrem dein Fuß nicht, wie auf Teppichen?
　　　　Drum, mein Genius! tritt nur
　　　　　　Baar in's Leben, und sorge nicht!

Was geschiehet, es sey alles gelegen dir!
　　Sey zur Freude gereimt, oder was könnte denn
　　　　Dich belaidigen, Herz, was
　　　　　　Da begegnen, wohin du sollst?

Denn, seit Himmlischen gleich Menschen, ein einsam Wild,
Und die Himmlischen selbst führet, der Einkehr zu
Der Gesang und der Fürsten
Chor, nach Arten, so waren auch
Wir, die Zungen des Volks, gerne bei Lebenden,
Wo sich vieles gesellt, freudig und jedem gleich,
Jedem offen, so ist ja
Unser Vater, des Himmels Gott,
Der den denkenden Tag Armen und Reichen gönnt,
Der, zur Wende der Zeit, uns die Entschlafenden
Aufgerichtet an goldnen
Gängelbanden, wie Kinder, hält.
Gut auch sind und geschikt einem zu etwas wir,
Wenn wir kommen, mit Kunst, und von den Himmlischen
Einen bringen. Doch selber
Bringen schikliche Hände wir.

2. Walter Benjamin, "Zwei Gedichte von Friedrich Hölderlin. 'Dichtermut'—'Blödigkeit,'" *Gesammelte Schriften*, ed. Rolf Tiedemann and Hermann Schweppenhaüser (Frankfurt a.m.: Suhrkamp, 1972), 2(1):105–26. "Two Poems by Friedrich Hölderlin: 'The Poet's Courage' and 'Timidity,'" trans. Stanley Corngold, *Selected Writings*, ed. Michael Jennings (Cambridge, Mass.: Harvard University Press, 1996), 1:18–36.

3. The word is odd for having other, exceedingly negative connotations. Adelung's dictionary defines "Blödigkeit" as "weakness [*Schwäche*]," as in "weakness in understanding [*Blödigkeit des Verstandes*]"; "fearfulness [*Furchtsamkeit*]" or "timidity [*Zaghaftigkeit*]," as in the presence of danger, though this meaning is archaic; and, finally, "shyness [*Schüchternheit*]," as in inopportune bashfulness in social intercourse. It is presumably the last sense that Hölderlin has mainly in mind. See Johann Christoph Adelung, *Grammatisch-kritisches Wörterbuch der Hochdeutschen Mundart* (Leipzig: Breitkopf, 1793), 1082.

4. Michael Jennings, "Benjamin as a Reader of Hölderlin: The Origins of Benjamin's Theory of Literary Criticism," *German Quarterly* 56, 4 (Nov. 1983): 554–62; and, more recently, Rainer Nägele, "Benjamin's Ground" and David E. Wellbery, "Benjamin's Theory of the Lyric," in *Benjamin's Ground*, ed. Rainer Nägele (Detroit: Wayne State University Press, 1988); and Rudolf Speth, *Wahrheit & Ästhetik: Untersuchungen zum Frühwerk Walter Benjamins* (Würzburg: Königshausen and Neumann, 1991).

5. "Goethes Wahlverwandtschaften," *Gesammelte Schriften* 1(1):123–201. "Goethe's Elective Affinities," trans. Stanley Corngold, *Selected Writings*, 1:297–360.

6. *Pindarübertragungen von Hölderlin. Prolegomena zu einer Erstausgabe* (Jena: E. Diederichs, 1911). In the matter of the indebtedness of Benjamin's essay to the views of the George Circle (to Friedrich Gundolf, among others), the most significant influence is Hellingrath's dissertation. Speth, in *Wahrheit und Ästhetik*, is highly informative on these and other of Benjamin's intellectual sources.

7. Friedrich Norbert von Hellingrath, *Hölderlin-Vermächtnis*, ed. Ludwig von Pigenot (Munich: F. Bruckmann, 1936), 65.

8. Gershom Scholem, *Walter Benjamin—die Geschichte einer Freundschaft* (Frankfurt a.M.: Suhrkamp, 1975), 26.

9. This avoidance of personal agency could evoke the Benjamin of 1932, who remarked: "If I write a better German than most writers of my generation, I owe it in good part to a single rule, which runs: Never use the word 'I,' except in letters. The exceptions to this commandment I have allowed myself can be counted on the fingers of one hand." The Hölderlin essay does not contain a single one of these exceptions.

10. Benjamin, *Gesammelte Schriften*, 2:921.

11. Benjamin also wanted to dedicate his *Berliner Chronik*, written in the 1930's, to Fritz Heinle.

12. Benjamin, *Selected Writings*, 23. Page numbers in parentheses in the body of this essay henceforth refer, first, to pages in volume one of the above-named edition. For the reader's convenience, I also add page numbers (with asterisks) corresponding to page numbers from Benjamin, *Gesammelte Schriften* 2(1). Benjamin's essay on *Elective Affinities*, in which he refashions materials excavated from the unpublished Hölderlin essay—notions of poetic truth, of myth and the mythic—also contains the obligatory reference to Pindar: "Yet as valuable as concrete realities might be for the interpretation of a work, it hardly needs to be said that the productions of a Goethe cannot be viewed as those of a Pindar" (*Selected Writings*, 298). This mention is hard to motivate except as an allusion to the earlier essay.

13. Walter Benjamin, *Briefe* (Frankfurt a.M.: Suhrkamp, 1966), 133.

14. Ibid., 513.

15. "What Benjamin first and Heidegger thereafter called 'das Gedichtete.'" Theodor Adorno, "Parataxis: Hölderlin's Late Lyric Style," *Notes to Literature*, trans. Shierry Meyer (New York: Columbia University Press, 1991). Theodor Adorno, "Parataxis. Zur späten Lyrik Hölderlins," in *Hölderlin-Aufsätze*, ed. Jochen Schmidt (Frankfurt: Insel, 1970), 341. In his study of Benjamin's essay, Rainer Nägele explores the figure of the "ground" as the essential dimension of Benjamin's revision of the poetic object, proposing for "das Gedichtete" the neologism "poematized" in order to stress the strangeness of the concept. "Benjamin's Ground," in *Benjamin's Ground*, ed. Nägele, 19–37. I am not sure,

however, that the term needs to be overmarked to such a degree of strangeness; "poetized" (as a noun) is odd in English but linked to a lively precedent in Emerson, who used the locution participially, in 1837: "Instead of the sublime and beautiful," he writes, "the near, the low, the common was explored and poetized." *The American Scholar*, in *Nature, Addresses, and Lectures* (Boston: Houghton-Mifflin, 1895), 110.

16. Michael Jennings, *Dialectical Images: Walter Benjamin's Theory of Literary Criticism* (Ithaca, N.Y.: Cornell, 1987), 192.

17. For remarks on form and content, see *Einbahnstraße*, in Walter Benjamin, *Kleine Prosa, Baudelaire Übertragungen,* in *Gesammelte Schriften*, Suhrkamp-Taschenbuch Wissenschaft 934, ed. Tilman Rexroth (Frankfurt a.M.: Suhrkamp, 1972), IV:1:107.

18. See Nägele, "Benjamin's Ground," 25.

19. David Wellbery discusses this nexus of considerations in his essay, "Benjamin's Theory of the Lyric," in *Benjamin's Ground*, ed. Nägele, 42.

20. Adorno, "Parataxis," 342. Adorno's helpful remark projects a linkage of the category to that of "the obscure" in Benjamin's later essay on Goethe's novel *Elective Affinities* ("Goethes Wahlverwandtschaften"). There the obscure is also the condition for the sheltering-manifesting of beauty.

21. "Das Gefühl durchdringt die Poesie, dass sie die authentische Interpretation des Lebens selber zu geben habe." Wilhelm Dilthey, *Gesammelte Schriften*, ed. Georg Misch (Göttingen: Vandenhoeck and Ruprecht, 1923), 5:37.

22. Ibid., 7:195. At the same time, Dilthey's formulation of the category of *Erlebnis* leaves it moot whether it does indeed imply *at any point* the copresence of a subjective consciousness that could then be excised—whether, namely, it should be thought of as a mediating term (as I employ it here) or as an immediate term, implying a fusion of life and subjective agency that precedes the dissociation of subject and object. See my *The Fate of the Self: German Writers and French Theory* (Durham, N.C.: Duke University Press, 1994), 66–72.

23. "Geistesgegenwart haben heißt: Im Augenblick der Gefahr sich gehen lassen." *Gesammelte Schriften*, ed. Tilman Rexroth, VI:207.

24. The cogency and relevance of this notion come to the fore, according to Edward Said, in the work, for one, of the musicologist Jean-Jacques Nattiez. "What Nattiez suggests is that to be unfaithful to Wagner is to be faithful to him: 'Every producer, every conductor, proposes a *possible* Wagner.'" Wagner's "poetry"—that is, each operatic performance—is rightly realized as one possible "solution" of his task, of an operatic *Gedichtetes*. "The Importance of Being Unfaithful to Wagner," *London Review of Books* (February 11, 1993): 11.

25. Anachronistically, because the category is Heidegger's to describe his *Elucidations* (*Erläuterungen*) of Hölderlin's poetry some twenty years later (*Erläuterungen zu Hölderlins Dichtung* [Frankfurt a.M.: V. Klostermann, 1951]). For

an incisive analysis of the shortcomings of Heidegger's texts on Hölderlin's poetry, see Klaus Weimar and Christoph Jermann, "'Zwiesprache' oder Literaturwissenschaft?: Zur Revision eines faulen Friedens," *Neue Hefte für Philosophie* 23 (1984): 113–57.

26. Wellbery stresses this moment as marking a decisive turn from Dilthey's aesthetic philosophy of life ("Benjamin's Theory of the Lyric," 40). Hölderlin's task, following Benjamin, is not any manner of expression of life but of its transformation. On the other hand, this is not to rule out the partial consistency of Benjamin's argument with that of Dilthey, whose poetics is marked by a tension between two senses of *Ausdruck*: immediate expression and expression as the significant constitution (hence transformation) of the inchoate.

27. This thesis on Heidegger's *Erläuterungen* is put forward in Paul de Man, *Blindness and Insight*, rev. 2nd ed. (Minneapolis: University of Minnesota Press, 1983), 254. It is an extreme thesis.

28. One neo-Kantian strain is also evident in Benjamin's scientistic rhetoric: "law of identity," "functional unity," "series," etc.

29. Ian Watt offers this "working definition" of myth: "a traditional story that is exceptionally widely known throughout the culture, that is credited with a historical or quasi-historical belief, and that embodies or symbolizes some of the most basic values of a society." *Myths of Modern Individualism: Faust, Don Quixote, Don Juan, Robinson Crusoe* (Cambridge: Cambridge University Press, 1996), xii.

30. Friedrich Hölderlin, *Sämtliche Werke*, ed. Friedrich Beißner (Stuttgart: Kohlhammer, 1943–72), 4:281. Discussed in Jennings, *Dialectical Images*, 193.

31. See Speth, *Wahrheit und Ästhetik*, who speaks of the radical transformation in Benjamin's evaluation of myth. In the Hölderlin essay "it is an archaic projection of the might of an all-powerful reality upon a heaven peopled with gods" (95); by the time of the *Elective Affinities* essay of 1924, it is entirely negative.

32. Compare, again, such a formation as "*Weiberängstlichkeit*" in Franz Kafka, *Das Schloß*, ed. Malcolm Pasley (Frankfurt a.M.: Fischer, 1982), 294.

33. Bart Philipsen, "Herz aus Glas—Hölderlin, Rousseau und das 'blöde' Subjekt der Moderne," in *Bild-Sprache: Texte zwischen Dichten und Denken*, ed. L. Lamberechts and J. Nowé (Leuven: Universitaire Pers, 1990), 177–94.

34. Ibid., 192.

35. Hamburger, *Friedrich Hölderlin, Poems and Fragments*, 660.

36. Adorno's essay on "Parataxis" is an eminent resource. In *Über Walter Benjamin*, Adorno wrote: "In all phases [of his development], Benjamin linked [*zusammengedacht*] the downfall of the subject with the salvation of man." *Über Walter Benjamin* (Frankfurt a.M.: Suhrkamp, 1970), 14.

37. Of course, Kant's allowance of so-called "ancillary [*anhängende*]" cognitive and moral values in aesthetic experience complicates matters.

38. Martin Heidegger, "Letter on Humanism," in *Martin Heidegger, Basic Writings*, ed. David Farrell Krell (New York: Harper and Row, 1977), 219. Weimar and Jermann find Heidegger's concept of the *Kehre* mendacious—not at all an innocent category.

39. De Man, *Blindness and Insight*, 50.

40. Let us be clear about this: This gesture shuns the entire problematic of how a consciousness could be a middle and not an abyss. It courts what I termed earlier, in distinguishing between Hölderlin and Nietzsche, "the ontological circle: the aporia that arises when a self, by the lights of its own individual activity, attempts to posit and define being" (see Chapter 3). In Benjamin's example, the poet's heart would have to be a transparent vehicle of a sacred being. Benjamin makes of the poet's activity, as Michael Jennings puts it, "not something that eventuates an intermittent sense of the transcendental but rather the actual residence of a form of truth in the world." Jennings, "Benjamin as a Reader of Hölderlin," *German Quarterly* 56, 4 (Nov. 1983): 552. This totalizing gesture is specifically excluded from Benjamin's essay on Goethe's novel *Wahlverwandtschaften* (*Elective Affinities*). In "Parataxis" Adorno indirectly registers the predicament for a consciousness in identifying the poet's lassitude with something less than truth or divinity—with the "oriental principle" (377) and then, even more astonishingly, with *paratactic* language as such (364).

41. Benjamin's rendering of an "affect"—courage—as a mode of the being of the subject outside and beyond itself anticipates Heidegger's thinking of affect. See, for example, his analysis of the affect of will to power in Martin Heidegger, *Gesamtausgabe*, II. Abteilung, *Vorlesungen 1923–1976, Nietzsche: Der Wille zur Macht als Kunst* (Frankfurt: Klostermann, 1985), 62.

42. And also enabled, however cryptically, by the politics of "princes."

43. Speth, *Wahrheit und Ästhetik*, 48.

44. *The Birth of Tragedy*, in *Basic Writings of Nietzsche*, trans. and ed. Walter Kaufmann (New York: The Modern Library, 1968), 128, 60.

45. Apropos of the beneficent death of the poet in "Timidity," Jennings notes the centrality of the example of Empedocles (from Hölderlin's dramatic fragment *Empedocles*); in both works "the poet's death frees his song from the bounds of his subjectivity and thus objectifies and universalizes it" ("Benjamin as a Reader of Hölderlin, 554). The relevance of the comparison is confirmed by Bernhard Böschenstein: "To the degree that Empedocles casts off features of individuality, he becomes the unifying point of historical developments, he becomes the middle of time." "Das neuzeitliche Ich in Hölderlins Tod des Empedokles," in *Das neuzeitliche Ich in der Literatur des 18. und 20. Jahrhunderts: zur Dialektik der Moderne: ein internationales Symposion*, ed. U. Fülleborn and M. Engel (Munich: Fink, 1988), 163.

46. Consult Rousseau's "Fifth Promenade" (in *Les Rêveries du promeneur solitaire*) and Chapter 12 of *Les Confessions*. In his essay, Bart Philipsen at first distin-

guishes the state of mind of "Blödigkeit" as less mystified than states of romantic enthusiasm aiming at social transformation; but this privilege accruing from a self-consciously performed demystification cannot be maintained. Philipsen then proceeds to deconstruct the claims for this transparency, reckoning it one more mystification among others (one wonders how Philipsen judges his "own" demystification of the privilege of Rousseau's demystification). The valuable distinctions that Philipsen makes along the way do not require that one draw the same conclusions from them, and I am using them differently in a different context.

47. De Man, *Romanticism and Contemporary Criticism*, ed. E. S. Burt, Kevin Newmark, and Andrzej Warminski (Baltimore: Johns Hopkins University Press, 1993), 50–73.

48. Consult Andrzej Warminski, *Readings in Interpretation: Hölderlin, Hegel, and Heidegger* (Minneapolis: University of Minnesota Press, 1987), 11–22.

49. "Goethes Wahlverwandtschaften," in *Gesammelte Schriften* I(1):140; *Selected Writings*, 1:309.

50. This is Speth's formulation, in *Wahrheit und Ästhetik*, 49.

51. Friedrich Hölderlin, *Sämtliche Werke*, ed. Friedrich Beißner (Stuttgart: Kohlhammer, 1943–72), 4:243.

INDEX

In this index an "f" after a number indicates a separate reference on the next page, and an "ff" indicates separate references on the next two pages. A continuous discussion over two or more pages is indicated by a span of page numbers. *Passim* is used for a cluster of references in close but not consecutive sequence.

Library of Congress Cataloging-in-Publication Data

Corngold, Stanley.
   Complex pleasure : forms of feeling in German
literature / Stanley Corngold.
      p.   cm.
   Includes bibliographical references and index.
   ISBN 0-8047-2939-5 (cl.)
   ISBN 0-8047-2940-9 (pbk.)
   1. German literature—History and criticism.
   2. Literature—Aesthetics.   3. Literature—
Appreciation.   4. Emotions in literature.   I. Title.
   PT75.C67   1998
   830.9—dc21   97-27866
                                          CIP

♾ This book is printed on acid-free, recycled paper.

Original printing 1998
Last figure below indicates year of this printing:
07   06   05   04   03   02   01   00   99   98